THE FACES OF SCIENCE FICTION

Photographs by Patti Perret

Introduction by Gene Wolfe

Project Coordinator: Mark Bingham

BLUEJAY BOOKS INC.

Manufactured in the United States of America

First Bluejay printing: October 1984

Designed by Rhea Braunstein

Library of Congress Cataloging in Publication Data

THE FACES OF SCIENCE FICTION

In loving memory of my brother Jay, whose compassion and convictions shaped the way I am today.

To Mark Bingham, for his companionship and his collaboration. 23,000 miles in the car together—this must be love.

Acknowledgements

To my publisher, Jim Frenkel: thanks for being so helpful and cooperative throughout this project, for allowing me to make the book I wanted to make and continually supporting me with sound advice.

"A writer's stock in trade is his/her time."
To all the writers for being so generous with their stock in trade, a generosity that made this book possible.

To Betsy Wollheim: thanks for exposing me to science fiction, for first starting me on this project, and for your invaluable second opinion throughout the making of this book.

Thanks to the following people for so many different reasons: Chuck Kelton, Gene Wolfe, Alice Sheldon, Joan Vinge, Don and Elsie Wollheim, Joe and Gay Haldeman, Forry Ackerman, Joann Hill, Frank Balazs, Clifford and Alma Perret, Martine P. Glas, Carmen Perret, Peter Stampfel, Linda Perret, Mark Hood, Bill and Fern Smith, Jean Doumanian, Henry Holmes Smith, and Kathy Kennedy.

CONTENTS

PREFACE

When I began work on this book I wasn't a fan or even much of a reader of science fiction. My exposure to science fiction was mostly through films. Like most people, I called science fiction "sci-fi", (something I soon learned not to do in front of science fiction writers, "sf" being the *proper* term.) Now, eighteen months and twenty-three thousand car miles later, I know a little more about science fiction and a lot more about those who write it.

How did this book come about? Let's go back in time—it's Autumn in New York, 1982. I was sitting around with a group of friends after seeing a movie (Road Warrior) discussing what all free-lancers talk about sooner or later: What next? This was a big question for me because I was about to leave New York after living there for four years and move back to New Orleans—going back to my roots, but uprooting myself to do so. After working primarily on TV and movie productions I felt the need to produce a cohesive body of work independently. I had been working for Betsy Wollheim for several weeks, printing her photographs. Relaxing that night, I realized the obvious—a book of portraits of science fiction writers! Betsy was excited by the idea and offered to help me make connections within the field.

Betsy's initial help came in the form of a list of "the 150 most important living SF writers" and a copy of the Science Fiction Writers of America directory. I took these items back to New Orleans, perusing them for a few weeks before taking action. Meanwhile, two heavy boxes of sf books appeared on my doorstep, also courtesy of Betsy. To learn about sf, I simply began to read it, discovering that sf was Big Fun as well as an education.

I began writing letters to those writers Betsy suggested I photograph. I called two New Orleans writers, Jo Clayton and George Alec Effinger. They were happy to do it. However, soon I received replies to my letters, *all* of them saying, "Thanks, but no thanks." Undaunted, I revamped the letter, adding selected "career highlights". The new letter, coupled with calls from Betsy, achieved results. I flew to New York to shoot Isaac Asimov, Fred Pohl, Chip Delany, Tom Disch and, most significantly, Joan Vinge. It was while shooting Joan that I met Jim Frenkel. Jim took immediate interest in the idea. Six months later he decided to go ahead with it. (During this interlude, the list of writers was edited to its present form, first by Don Wollheim and then by Jim.)

After signing the contract, I went to work photographing the bulk of the writers. This required much planning and correspondence, followed by months of travel. My husband Mark took care of the details, freeing me to concentrate on photography.

There's no one way to approach a project like this. Should the photographer do thorough research, learning details of each writer's life and work, or just go in cold and shoot? I sometimes had only an hour to be in and out of a writer's house. More frequently I was allowed the time I requested—three hours. I felt it would be more helpful in understanding sf writers, to read the writers' work—rather than biographies or interviews. Of course, once the project was rolling, writers would give me the lowdown on some of the more notorious scribes. These character sketches were often helpful sneak previews, but just as often gave me a false impression since many writers only know one another from conventions where people are known to behave differently than in their homes.

Each writer has contributed a personal statement to accompany their photograph. I'm not about to delve into the various concerns covered in the statements, but one theme, that of sf writers and sf in general being a "family" seems to have come up quite often. Not everyone in this "family" seems to think alike or write alike but even the most reclusive seemed at least partially in tune with and interested in the SF community. The thing that struck me most strongly about these people was that no matter how different they were, they were not people merely involved in a common literary conceit—but people with a strong philosophical dedication to what they were writing. I'm very grateful to all the writers I photographed, not only for being part of this book, but for perhaps my best reward of all—I now read science fiction.

PATTI PERRET, July 20, 1984

FOREWORD

My father died four years ago last May. A succession of health problems took him from prosperity to divorce, loss of property and eventually, the life of a derelict. I often lost track of him during those last years of his life. One spring day he went out and bought a shotgun, for the purpose of ending it once and for all. He got too drunk. He missed, damaging a lung and shoulder, but no more. This stunt landed him in a V. A. hospital where he underwent psychiatric observation and worked with a physical therapist to regain use of his arm. While in the hospital he met a woman thirty years his junior. They fell in love. Upon release, they pooled their disability money and moved in together. Her mother came to live with them. Both women were quite large. My father called them, lovingly, the "whales". They would all drink together. One night they went out to an arcade and had computer tee-shirts made of the faces of mother and daughter together. My father took these shirts to a printer and created his own, one of a kind, Save The Whales tee-shirt.

One day I got a call. My father was in the hospital again. His organs were failing. He could go any time. My sister and I took the train from the city up to the hospital in Connecticut. My father was bright yellow. I thought about science fiction. Where was I? Who was this yellow person resembling my father? I sang in his ear for hours. The doctor told me that hearing was the last thing to go. I sang his favorite songs—he loved Johnny Mathis. I sang "Somewhere Over The Rainbow," "In My Solitude" and even "Louie Louie." Finally it was over. My sister and I went back to the city. I wrote a song on the train. My father was cremated and scattered over his favorite trout stream.

The next day I rented a van and went back to Connecticut to pick up his papers and other belongings. He was a psychologist and had all kinds of tests. I went to the apartment he had shared with the two women. They didn't believe he was dead. Since they weren't family per se, the hospital didn't inform them of his death. The two women had called my father Doc. They kept saying "Oh Doc, he'll be all right. He always gets better." These two women had no idea of my father's actual background. He had reinvented his life for their benefit. I was not the son he had described. All through the packing and moving these two women told me wonderful things about my father, as if he'd be coming home any minute. They would end each line of praise with WE HAVE FUN. They must have said WE HAVE FUN about fifty times. Upon leaving the apartment I went into a state of numb depression which lasted for weeks. I kept hearing WE HAVE FUN, WE HAVE FUN.

My life reminds me of science fiction. Today is, however, the last day of my year-long fling with science fiction. I worked with Patti on this book. Robert Bloch described my function as, "the schlepper." But I had fun. My favorite duty was reading the work of all the writers Patti photographed. I don't keep up with SF trivia—the only time I've read *Locus* was sitting on the can in some writer's bathroom. I'm mainly interested in the writing, though I did enjoy meeting the writers themselves. They were an exemplary group of human beings—with a few exceptions. Artists who work hard are dear to my heart. These writers not only work hard, but they seem to play hard as well. I didn't find these people to be odd, strange, kooky, schizophrenic or in any deviant way undesirable. A bunch of regular guys and gals, to be quite honest.

Some of the visits began as photo shoots and ended up as memorable events. Staying up late listening to Dean Ing talk about racing cars, designing space craft, fishing and war; spending hours going through Greg Bear's soundtrack collection; obtaining temporary Nirvana in Joe Haldeman's kitchen through his great cooking as well as sizeable consumption of a liqueur called Rumona; making two visits to Forry Ackerman's (notice that he sports an I Love SF button in his photo); spending a lazy late afternoon drinking wine with Kate Wilhelm and Damon Knight; going to Algis Budrys's favorite restaurant where everyone knew him and yelled at each other across the room; talking music with Charles Sheffield; talking cosmos over eggs with Ted Sturgeon; finding that Dr. Pournelle did not bite and that his assistant, John Carr, looked like one of the Grateful Dead and not a drill sergeant. Keith Laumer was nothing short of inspirational. Sure he tried to hit Patti with his cane, but after I fixed his tv he warmed up with a number of great stories. Mr. Laumer made me very aware of my good fortune: I have my health and enough sanity to get by in this world. Robert Bloch had the best off the cuff one liners of anyone in the field; through F. M. Busby I learned of the wonders of Augsburger beer. Patti and I have become friends and pen pals with Allie Sheldon. Whoops, the deadline is about 30 minutes away. To all those writers who provided us with beautiful lasting moments and were not mentioned here, sorry, you know about deadlines.

I love reading the statements. Last night I put them in order and read through. I liked how some writers were serious, others went for self aggrandizing, others for whimsy. Looking at the photographs I recalled how each writer reacted to being photographed. For some it was business as usual. Ray Bradbury had been shot so many times that he could even keep writing during the shoot without seeming rude or disinterested. For some it was a big career moment, for others just a pain. Some writers were openly scornful of the book, justifying their participation as part of that necessary evil: publicity. One writer said the book was blackmail. He didn't want to be photographed but felt not being in the book would be slighting his importance in the field.

Here comes the deadline. Got to get on that subway—head up to Bluejay. Don't forget, WE HAVE FUN.

MARK BINGHAM, July 20, 1984

INTRODUCTION

In writing this introduction to Patti Perret's THE FACES OF SCIENCE FICTION, I'm achieving a lifelong goal, and gloriously.

You see, I'm notoriously bad at introductions. It was I who, while writing a first-contact story, introduced a green spider-thing from Algol under the name of Rawn Ray-Gun; and when I introduce new acquaintances to my daughters, I invariably call Melpomene "Thalia," and Thalia "Melpomene" (those aren't their real names, but then I always forget their real names.)

Now thanks to the book you're holding, I can abandon the sad errors of the past for a look at the wonders of the present. (And Yes, this would make a wonderful present for anyone you know who likes stories of robots, rocket ships or both.) There have been books before that purported to give you pictures of your favorite science fiction authors, but all of them I have seen provided only postage-stamp size snapshots, bereft of any pretension to character and artistic insight. These books were, in short, rather like the yearbook of some dim and dismal high school offering only remedial reading for adults. Except that they were inferior to that yearbook in omitting all the neat stuff like: "Don't ask 4E what he and Jo did after the prom" and "Real Wookies wear Dozois T–shirts."

Quite frankly, if Patti Perret had done that kind of a book, I would not have written this introduction. Instead, she has given me the longed-for opportunity to fulfill my ambition of getting an introduction right for once. She has met with the leading American writers of science fiction in their homes; she has examined their work and looked at their work spaces; and then (and only then) she has photographed them with the effortless mastery of a portrait photographer at the top of her profession. Here are Poul Anderson, Piers Anthony, and Isaac Asimov as they *are*, recognizable if you have met them only casually, marvelously recognizable if you have the privilege of their friendship.

Here is Marta Randall, science fiction's glamorous gremlin, who once pinched Wilson Tucker, Bob Tucker, and Hoy Ping Pong in a single derriere live and on stage, and who sometimes shakes publishers like apple trees. Meet Joan Vinge, warm and bright as a bonfire on a crisp October evening; and Algis Budrys in all his pride, wisdom, and humility. May I have the pleasure of presenting Ray Bradbury? I never knew he shared my passion for Li'l Abner until I saw him here.

Surely such pictures would be enough to make any book worthwhile, but there's much, much more. All these writers have provided samples of their writing to accompany Patti Perret's classic photographs. John Kessel (for an instance I can't resist quoting) tells us that, "Science Fiction is a lot like Buffalo," and goes on to prove it. Fritz Leiber, amateur astronomer and master storysmith, explains that, "A good story travels farther if not faster than light." While Judy May opines, "Puccini could have set it to music."

Earnestly, honestly, and without reservation, I recommend "Niven's Laws" to you; there are eleven (why should Larry stop at ten commandments?), and they are the distilled experience of a writer who refuses to fool himself. Frederik Pohl speaks for all of us when he writes, "But if there is hope for humanity, I think it lies among those who have contributed to or learned from science fiction." And by *us,* I mean you, as well as all the people to whom I'm introducing you; for as Charles Sheffield has found, "There is no insider group in sf."

So come on in and sit down. Share the sofa with Kate Wilhelm, of the misty hair and supernatural smile; with the elfin Ursula K. Le Guin, a fascinating writer whose hobby is Japanese cat arranging. Steal a kiss from Damon Knight, *capo* of the Milford Mafia. Shake the hands of laid-back Ed Bryant, George "Railroad" Martin, and the Great Gordie Dickson; of Somtow Sucharitkul, who's collaborating on a science-fiction opera with me, and joltin' Jerry Pournelle, whom I'd sooner have on my side than Attila the Hun. Swap some war stories with Joe Haldeman, the best writer to come out of Viet Nam; say howdy to Buck and Juanita Coulson, reg'lar down-home Hoosier folks who jist happen to own about thirty thousand books; help Mike Bishop and Ben Bova toast Tom Disch.

Damn it, I never was any good with introductions, but you don't need them anyway. Just come on in and meet the gang, reader! Write your name inside the cover and join us.

—Gene Wolfe

ALFRED BESTER

I've been a writer and editor all my professional life, and sf is only one of the many media in which I've worked. But I love it most because it's the last frontier of complete creative freedom, prose *vers libre* as it were, in which the artist is allowed any and all wild experiments with people and places.

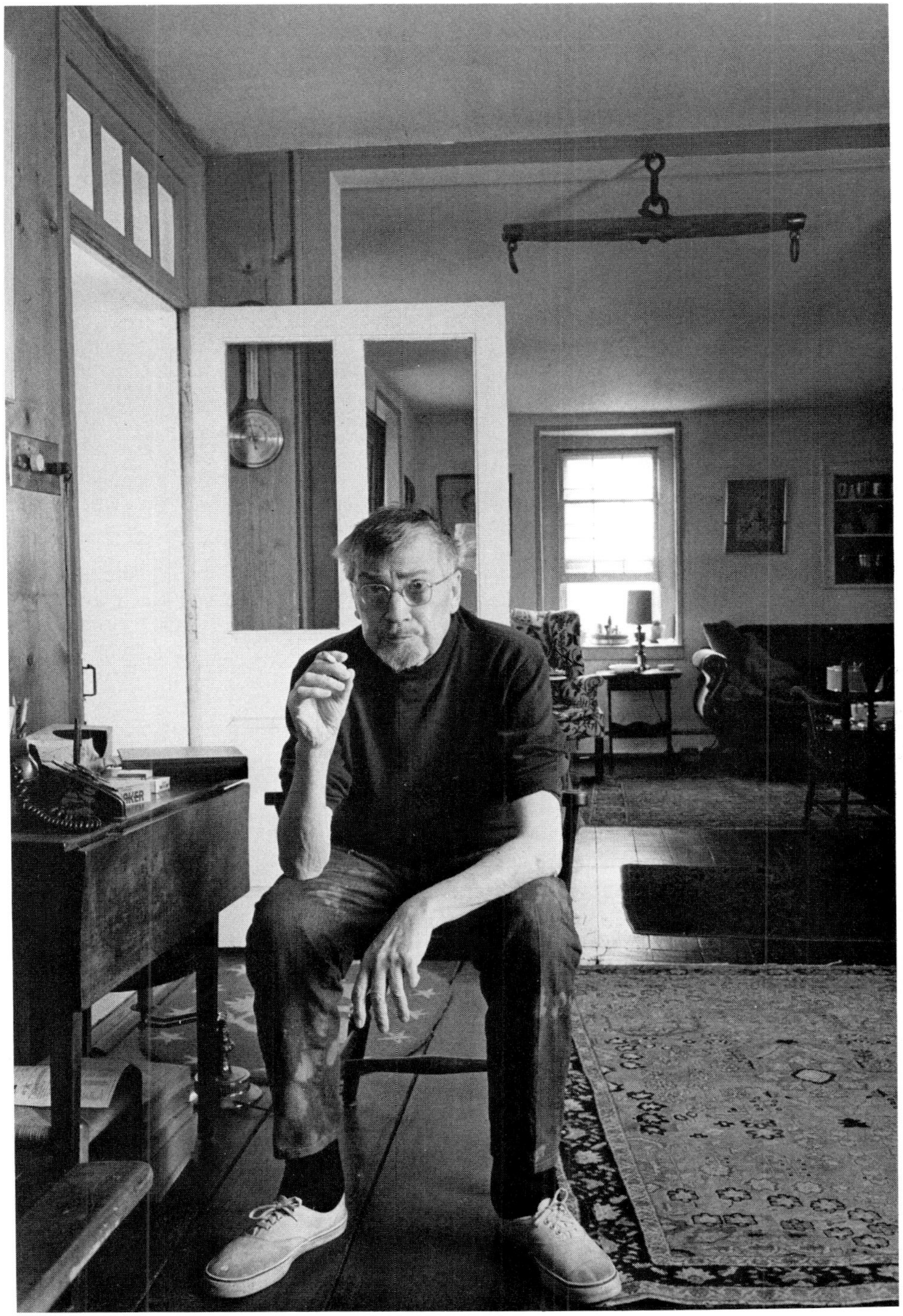

URSULA K. LE GUIN

A ROUND, BUFF, SPECKLED POEM

If she flies on quail's wings,
sure she won't fly far.
Eagle Men do big things,
make wars, fly to stars.
She's here. There they are:
I, I, up in the sky,
never nothing but I, I, I.
Eye in the telescope
looks back, can't see hope.
Steel Eagles lay steel eggs,
hatch what chick?
Death fast! Death quick!
Quail Woman and Quail Man
keep their covey as they can.
Quail walks on short legs,
Quail flies on short wings,
Quail does long things.

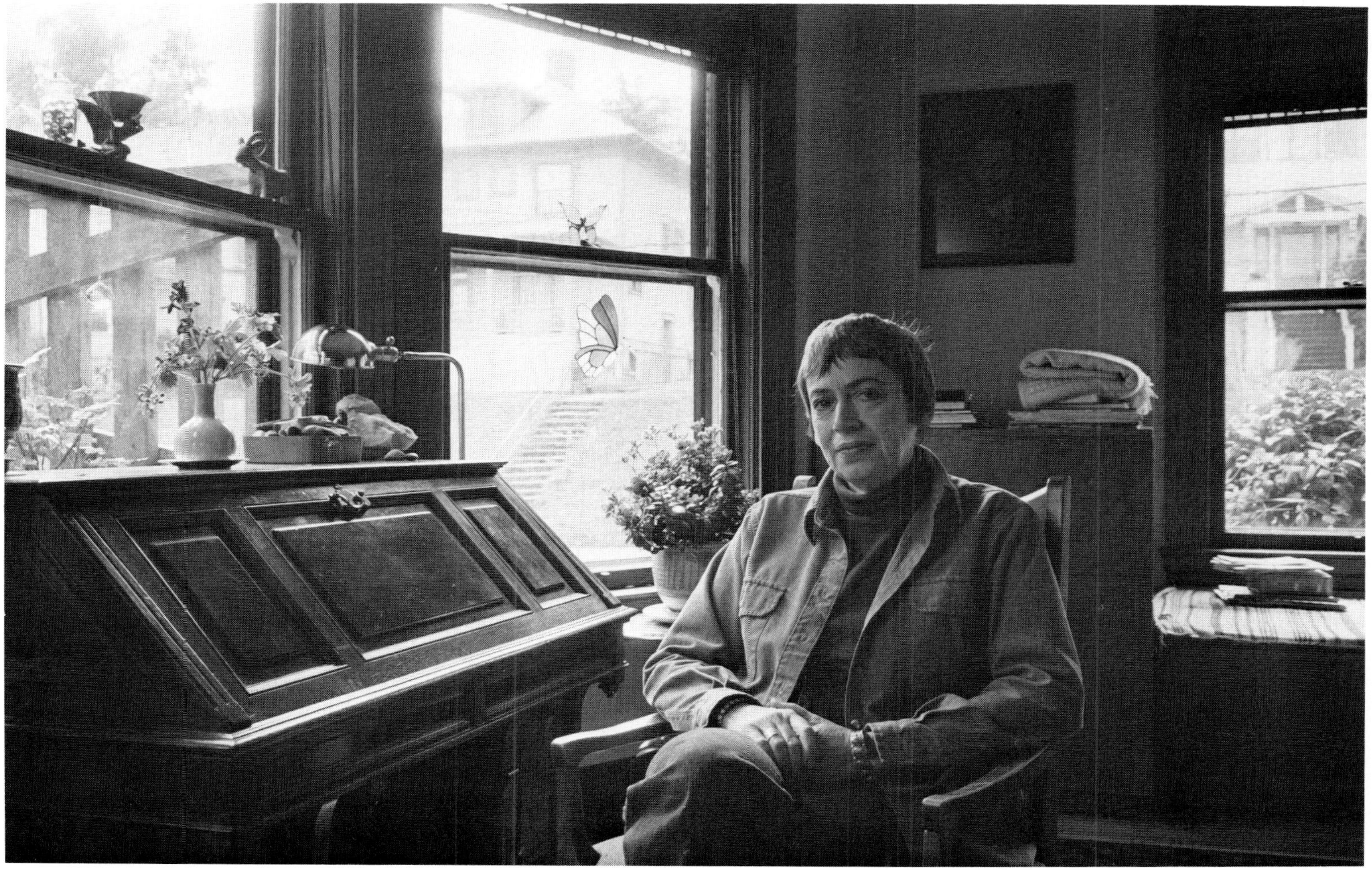

HAL CLEMENT

SERIOUS HOBBY

It's a little hard to decide whether I face science fiction with all the solemnity of a priest before the altar, or regard it as life's principal amusement. Certainly I take my science seriously—I believe quite firmly that without it most of humanity will starve, and most of the rest die fighting over the scraps, in the fairly near future; and for me, science fiction and science came together from the beginning.

I still remember the Buck Rogers frame, which I have since identified as being in late February of 1930, in which I heard of Mars and distances of millions of miles. I asked my father what this was all about. He didn't know either, but trundled me down to the local public library, from which I returned with a book on astronomy under one seven-year-old arm and a Jules Verne novel under the other. Serious science and recreational reading have stayed together in my life ever since, and there is no disputing that I greatly prefer stories in which careful attention is paid to the science.

On the other hand, I am a good enough scientist to know that neither I as an individual nor humanity as a species can ever be certainly right about anything, and I have not lost the ability—at least, not for too long at a time—to laugh at myself. I know better than to suppose that any ideas I gestate, no matter how good they may seem at the time, are the final answer to human problems. I think, on the whole, the fun side of sf wins out.

In any case, if I do come up with humanity's salvation, I'll probably be underground before anyone knows about it. So why worry?

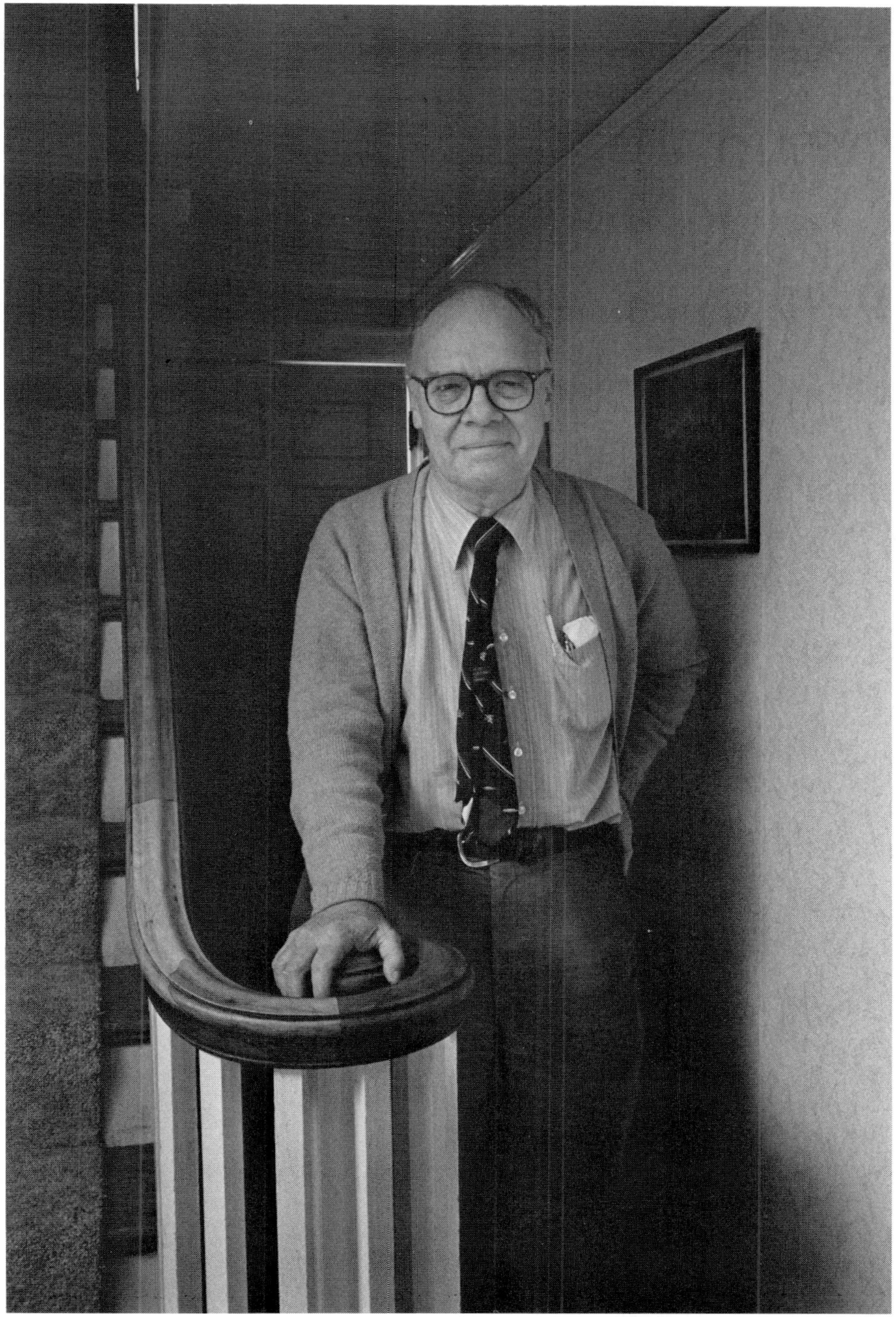

NORMAN SPINRAD

Unique among writers, with few exceptions like Norman Mailer and Gore Vidal, sf writers have higher face recognition value than any other writers, due to their public appearances at sf conventions. Now it would seem that we will have even wider face recognition value, with the publication of this book. For better or for worse.

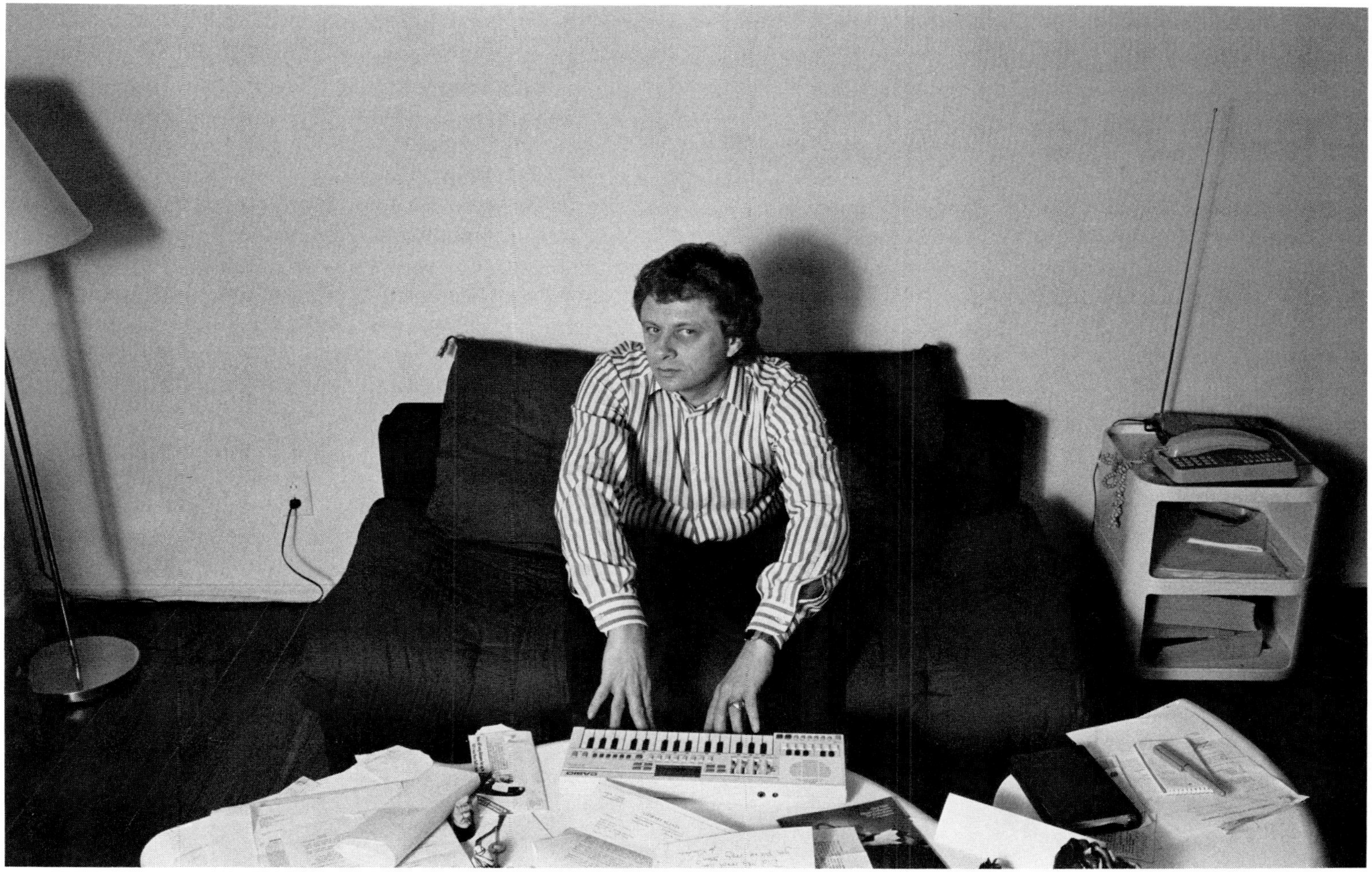

JACK WILLIAMSON

Science fiction was an odd little world when I discovered it in the old *Amazing Stories,* back in 1926. We called it "scientifiction," a term that always had to be explained. We, those early readers and soon-to-be writers, were most of us misfits, out of step where we were and dazzled by its visions of more exciting worlds and times. Science fiction let us live them, turned real in our young imaginations.

Not that science fiction has to be prophetic. More of it was always pure escape, but most of us need occasional escape. Nor has science fiction been my only world. Another is Portales, New Mexico, where I have a fine life with Blanche, the girl I knew and admired in our country school long ago, even before Hugo Gernsback named science fiction.

Yet I've spent a lot of my life in science fiction. A larger world now, it no longer needs explaining. It still exists in its own special dimension, inhabited by some of the brightest and most exciting friends I have. I'm fond of them and happy to be with so many of them in this book.

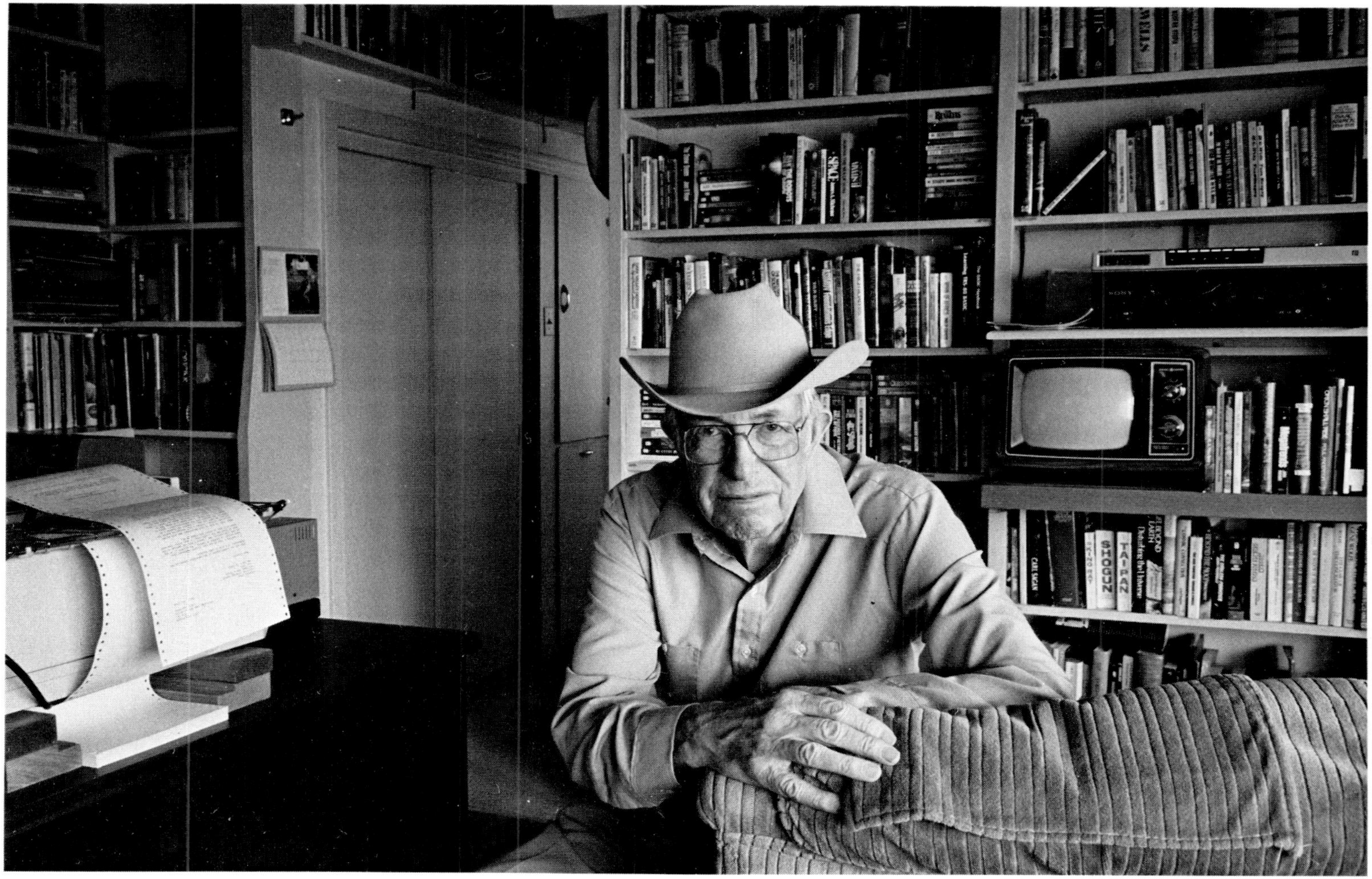
SHOGUN
TAIPAN
CARL SAGAN

JOE HALDEMAN

Compared to "normal" writers, science fiction writers are a remarkably sane and friendly bunch. This was brought home to me strongly a few years ago when five of us converged on a large department store in the Midwest for a joint autograph party.

The woman charged with organizing the affair was terrified. She'd never been able to bring together even two writers without egos clashing unpleasantly; the one time she'd had three together had been a disaster. Now five were going to meet her at a fancy restaurant—five with ages from the twenties to the sixties, styles from conventional space opera to avante-garde gonzoism, conservative and liberal, male and female, black and white—she was looking forward to at least indigestion and possibly to broken crockery and eviction.

But we greeted each other like long-separated relatives, had a riotous good time over dinner, then picked up a bottle and went back to the hotel to trade gossip until the small hours. She was amazed. She'd expected to be presiding over a snarling confrontation, and instead was a guest at a reunion.

It is like family. I look forward to seeing our album.

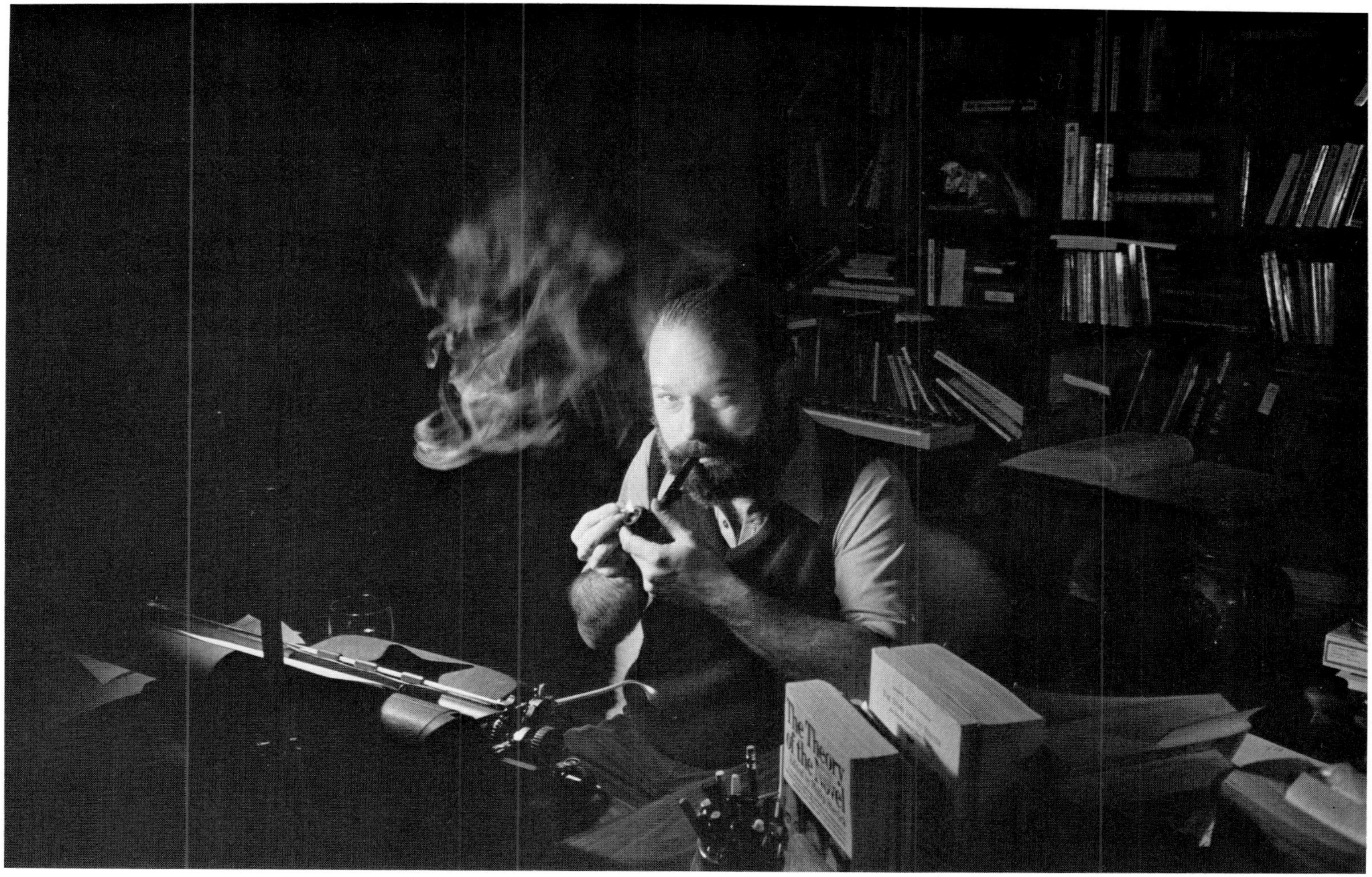
The Theory

ROGER ZELAZNY

Science fiction is a special way of regarding the world. Science fiction writers treat with people, things and events in terms of possible consequences. In the Middle Ages we might have been theologians, and we probably would have been burned as heretics. This is because, after a time, it is hard not to look at everything this way—at the thing itself and at the long (or short) shadow it casts before it across a twisted landscape. A slightly stark image, I note, and things sometimes do fall out that way. But the practice is fun, and getting paid for it makes it a profession. I profess science fiction, and I'm probably a lot happier than I would have been in the Middle Ages even if I didn't get caught in the wrong speculation. We have nicer bathrooms. I wonder whether anyone foresaw them, back then?

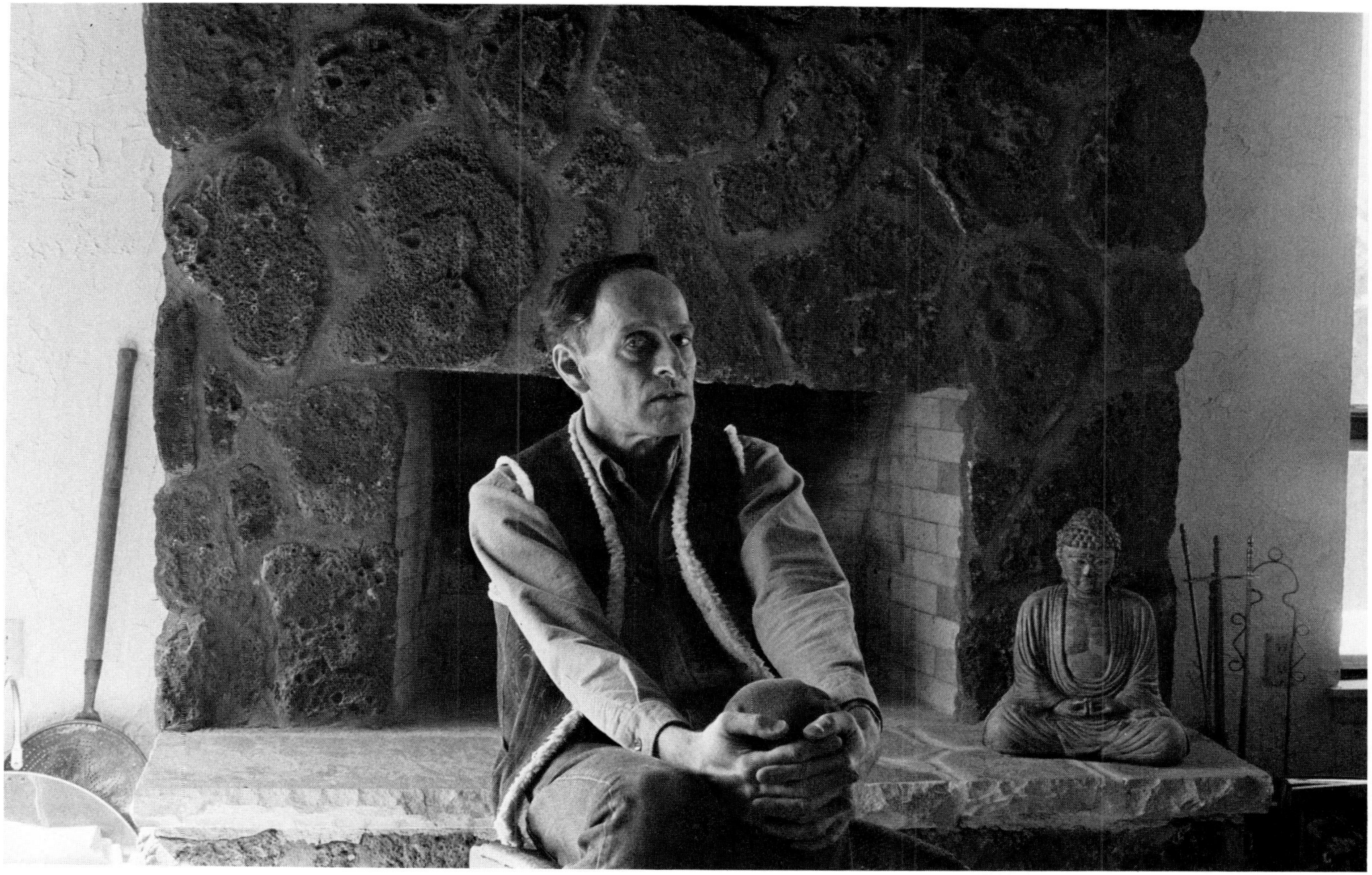

PIERS ANTHONY

The plant labors all the year, green and growing and undistinguished. At last, in its season, it blooms, and all the folk remark on the beauty of the flower. Yet that bloom is only the product of the plant. It is wrong to see the flower as the only important thing, for it is the plant that makes it—yet it is the aspect of the plant designed to receive attention, and should be judged as such.

Similarly the writer labors to produce his narrative, and if it is wrong to treat that narrative as if it had no genesis, still it is the aspect the writer chooses to be represented by. Judge the writer by his narrative rather than by his picture—but do not scorn the picture any more than the green foliage of the plant, for these may be alternate avenues to comprehension of the whole.

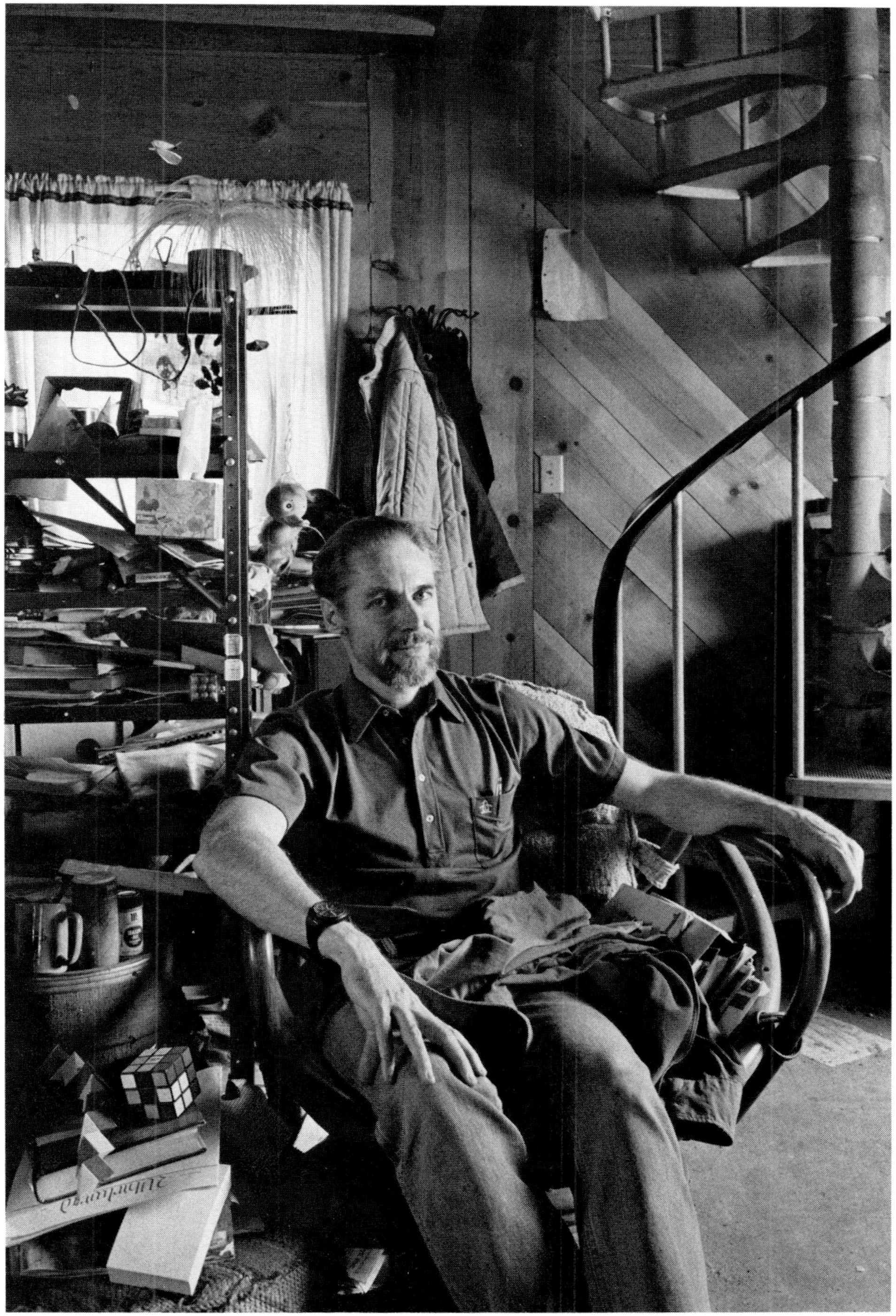

MIKE RESNICK

Who in the world wants to look at pictures of writers?

What's to see?

It seems to me that you'd be better off looking at the inside of a writer's head than the outside, because that's his essence: it's where he lives. His workbench is his imagination, and his tools are his loves and his hates, his hopes and his fears. Show him a seed and he'll dream a flower, show him a child and he'll dream a king; show him a flaw and he'll dream perfection; and, because he can be a pretty tricky guy, show him perfection and he'll dream a flaw. And sometimes, when he's really on his game and the old curve ball is breaking just right, he'll put all the facts aside and just dream the truth.

All these things he can do, and it makes the inside of his head a pretty interesting place: the more you look, the more you'll find.

But making the outside interesting? That's another union.

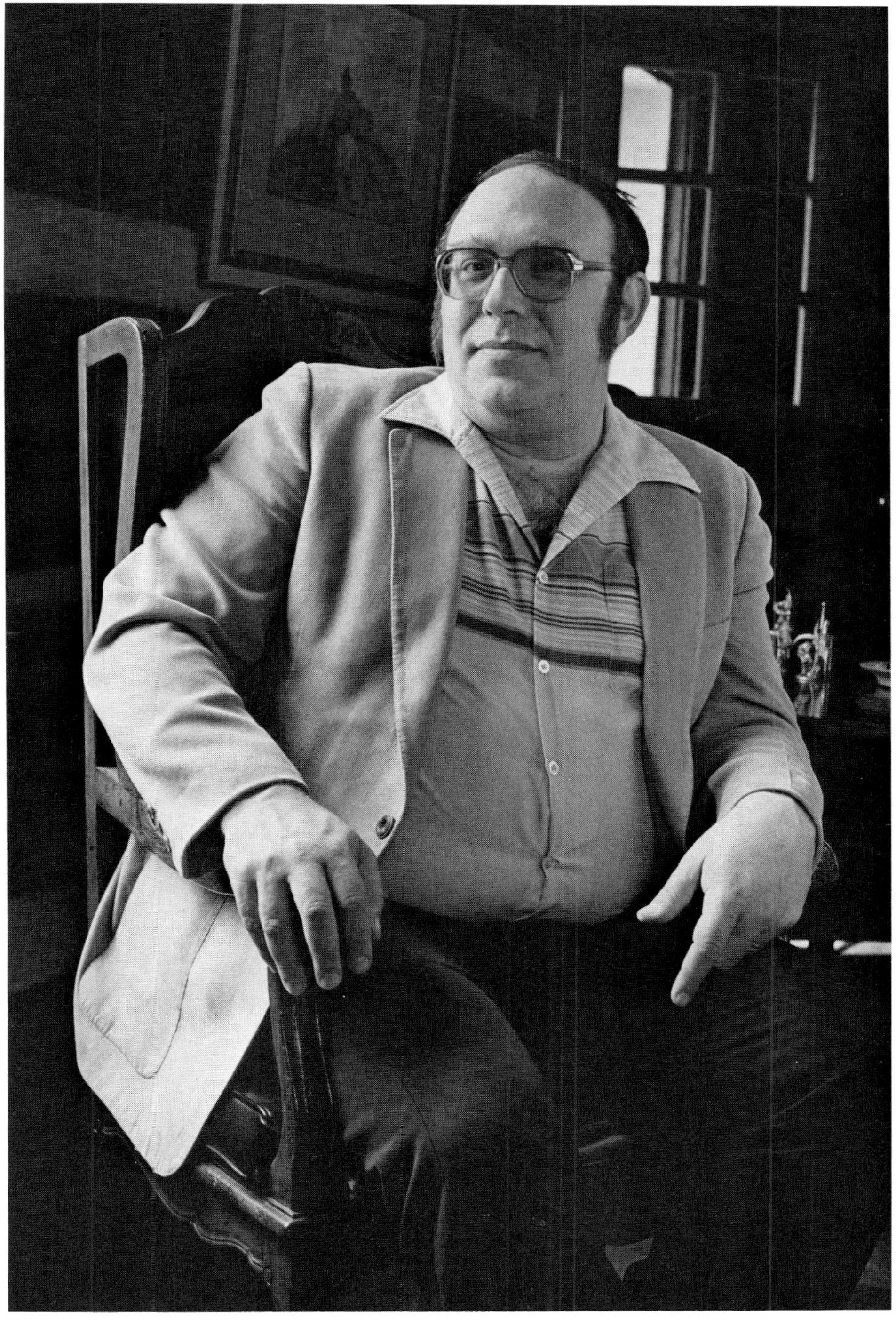

FORREST J. ACKERMAN

Sometimes I think Earth has got to be the insane asylum of the universe. . . . and I'm here by computer error. At sixty-eight, I hope I've gained *some* wisdom in the past fourteen lustrums and it's obligatory to speak plain and true about the conclusions I've come to; of what I have been educated to believe by such mentors as Wells, Stapledon, Heinlein, van Vogt, Clarke, Pohl, (S. Fowler) Wright, Orwell, Taine, Temple, Gernsback, Campbell and other seminal influences in scientifiction. I regret the lack of any female writers but only Radclyffe Hall opened my eyes *outside* sci-fi*.

I was a secular humanist before I knew the term. I have not believed in God since childhood's end. I believe a belief in *any* diety is adolescent, shameful and dangerous. How would *you* feel, surrounded by billions of human beings taking Santa Claus, the Easter bunny, the tooth fairy and the stork seriously and capable of shaming, maiming or murdering in their name? I am *embarrassed* to live in a world retaining *any* faith in church, prayer or a celestial creator. I do not believe in Heaven, Hell or a Hereafter; in angels, demons, ghosts, goblins, the Devil, vampires, ghouls, zombies, witches, warlocks, UFOs or other delusions and in very few mundane individuals—politicians, lawyers, judges, priests, militarists, censors and just plain people. I respect the individual's right to abortion, suicide and euthanasia. I support birth control. I wish to Good that society were rid of smoking, drinking and drugs.

My hope for humanity—and I think sensible science fiction has a beneficial influence in this direction—is that one day everyone born will be whole in body and brain, will live a long life free from physical and emotional pain, will participate in a fulfilling way in their contribution to existence, will enjoy true love and friendship, will pity us 20th century barbarians who lived and died in an atrocious, anachronistic atmosphere of arson, rape, robbery, kidnapping, child abuse, insanity, murder, terrorism, war, smog, pollution, starvation and the other negative "norms" of our current civil(?)ization. I have devoted my life to amassing over a quarter million pieces of sf and fantasy as a present to posterity and I hope to be remembered as an altruist who would have been an acceptable citizen in Utopia.

*I created the term thirty years ago and am proud of its universal acceptance except for a die-hard minority of vociferous critics quixotically determined to denigrate or destroy it: clearly a lost cause.

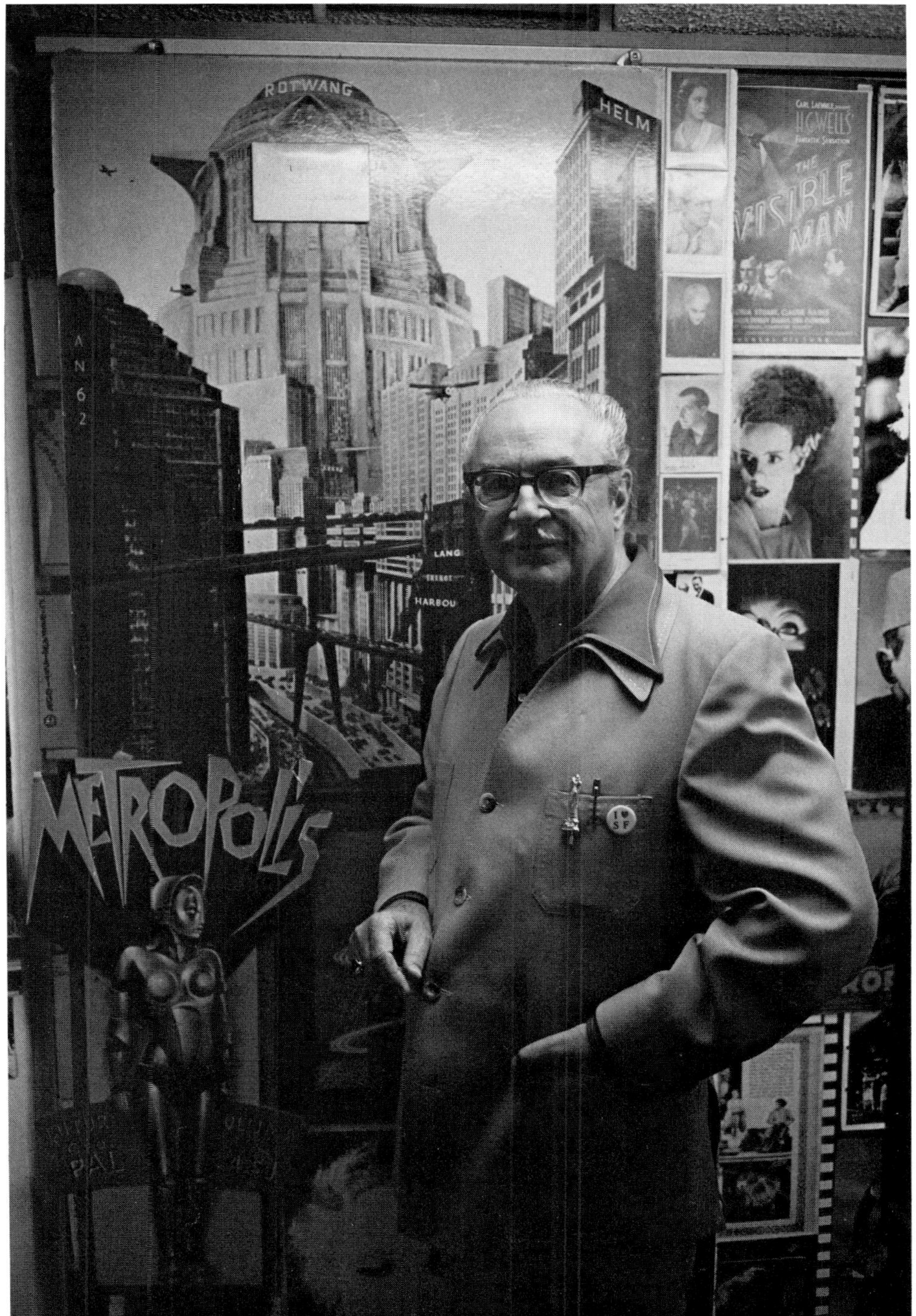
ROTWANG
HELM
LANG
METROPOLIS
H.G.WELLS
MAN

CLIFFORD D. SIMAK

For fifty years, as a newspaperman, I sought to write the truth. In the beginning I tended to believe there could only be one truth—if all the facts were pulled together, all opinions weighed, then the truth would stand revealed. As time went on I came to know there was no single truth, but many truths. Truth was not all black and white; there were many shades of truth. Finally knowing this, I continued, as newsmen still do today, to strike as close to truth as one man might be able.

In science fiction, once I had gone through my apprentice years of writing, I realized that fiction writers, in common with newsmen, also search for truth, working even more avidly for truth, and, perhaps, for greater truths. I tried to glimpse the truth—or the many truths—in the human condition, the human heart and mind and, as an extension, in the hearts and minds of aliens and robots. At times I told myself that in life and intelligence, not only human, but all life and intelligence, lies the greatest truth of all, the final truth of all.

I would suspect that most science fiction writers, aware of it or not, are seekers after truth. And that in truth (or as close as we can come to it) exists the hope of, not only mankind, but the universe.

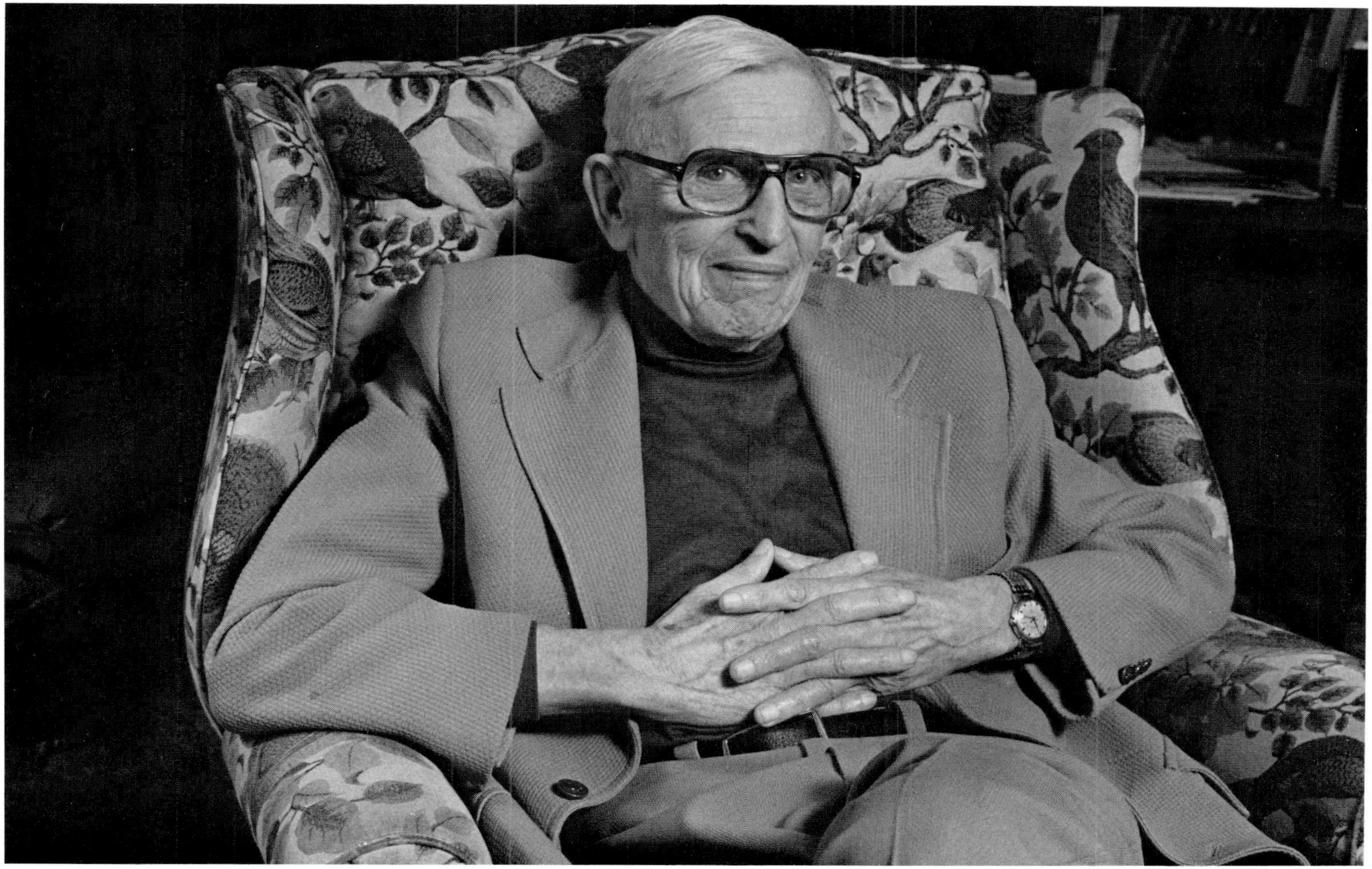

JO CLAYTON

First draft
earnest and passionate
lecturing the world
railing against
    injustice   willed ignorance   greed
    all things unfair
    this ism and that
    the thick-headed perversity of war

and when my wisdom presses my shoulders round
(having grown so ponderous and huge)

remembering farm days on the San Andreas Fault
(farm sand bumpa bump under bare feet   there is
nothing certain in this world)

or the bland blue gaze of cats
(who know a thing or two about pretentiousness)

smile
sigh
cross it all out

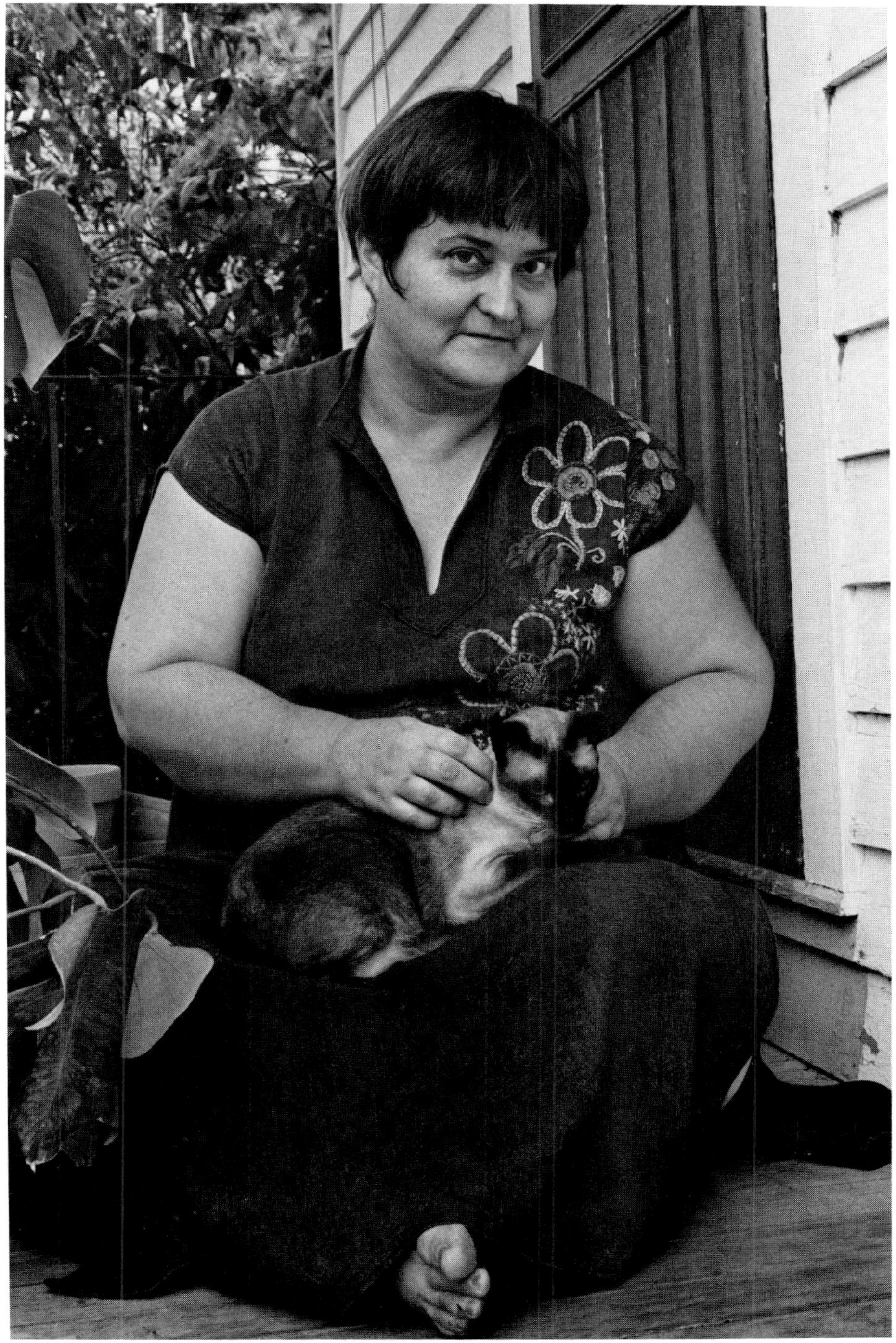

FRANK BELKNAP LONG

Science fiction and fantasy writers possess, I've always felt, a very special kind of discontent with things as they are. They look either to the future or the past with a burning desire to enrich the present with splendid visions of what the past has been *at its very best,* with its mythical, Arthurian-legend glories, or to a future that modern science will immeasurably enrich if it is guided by humanistic impulses of a high order. Some writers, in both of these closely related genres are far traveled and extremely active; others are predominately of a contemplative nature, who place a high value on creative leisure and quieter kinds of achievement. It is this second approach, or lifestyle, that I have, by temperment, most greatly favored, although circumstances have, on occasion, forced me to abandon it. Through it all I have probably remained an incurable romanticist.

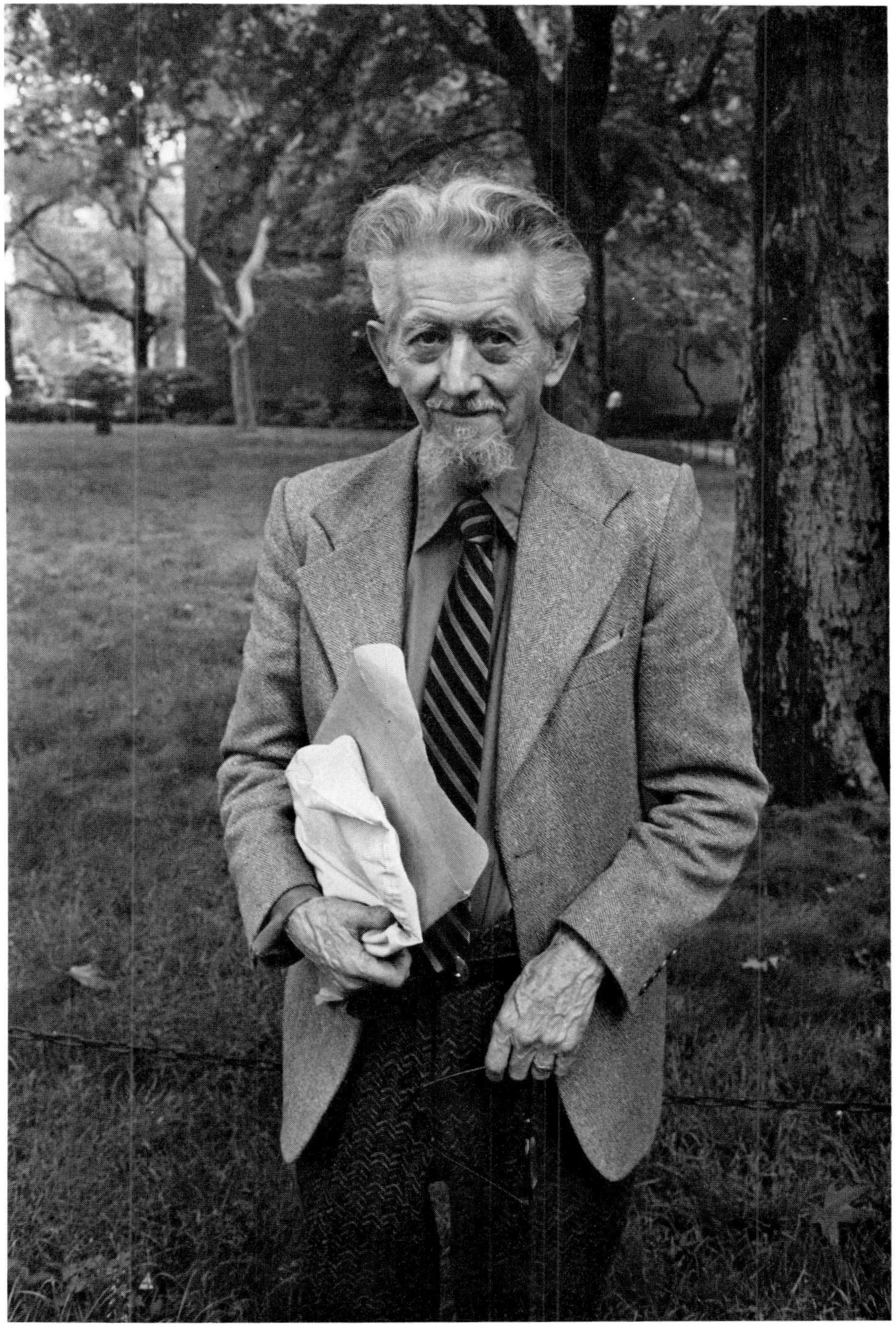

SOMTOW SUCHARITKUL

I am a creature of two worlds: not just East and West, but also of words and music; in some circles I am better known as a composer than as a science fiction writer. Being an artist in the West (or even a plain human being) is exactly like being a baby in a supermarket. You are being pushed up and down the aisles in a sequential manner; but the shopping cart being what it is, you can only face backward. You cannot perceive the overall structure of the supermarket, but as you see more and more of it, always looking backward, you begin to grow. In Asia we see things quite differently. You must imagine a kind of winged baby hovering above the supermarket and perceiving the whole thing at once. Thus art is not a developmental process in time, but something all there, all at once; in Western art a painting or a photograph such as the one you're looking at now may have this non-developmental quality, but in Asian art even the works of literature and music may partake of it.

This conflict is probably at the heart of who I am and how my writing should be read. Which am I to be: the hovering baby who never grows, or the developing baby who never flies?

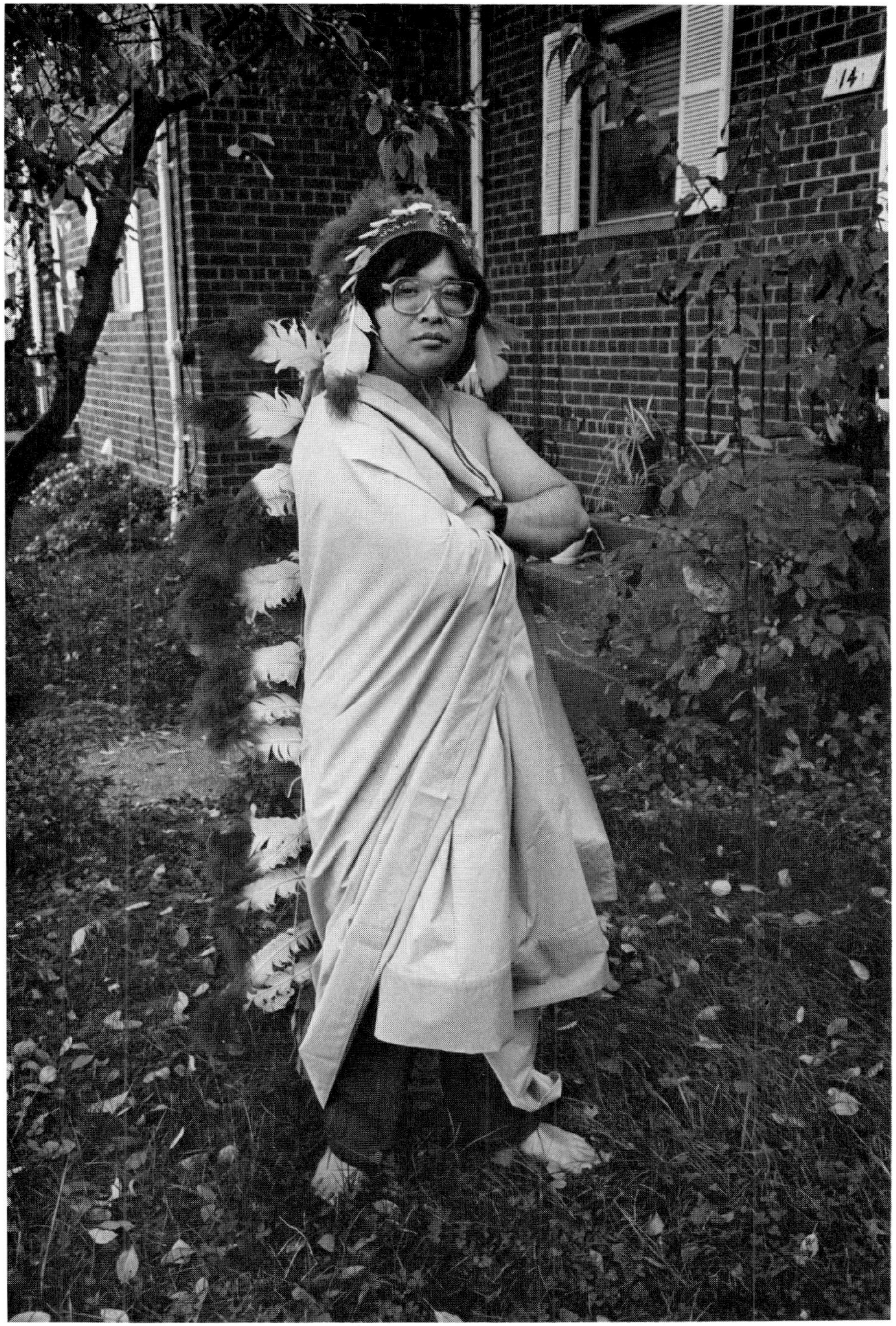
14

DAVID DRAKE

I was born in 1945; sold my first story in 1965; became a full-time writer in 1981; and was quite ridiculously embarrassed at having my photograph taken for this volume.

I suppose the reasons for my embarrassment come down to control; most things seem to come down to control with me. A novel puts me on display in a far more intimate fashion than a picture possibly could—but still, I have theoretical control over everything in a work of fiction. I cannot change the fact that on the day this picture was taken I was five-foot eleven, weighed a hundred and fifty pounds stripped, and had the facial features you see. Nothing wrong with any of those things. They're just beyond my control. . . .

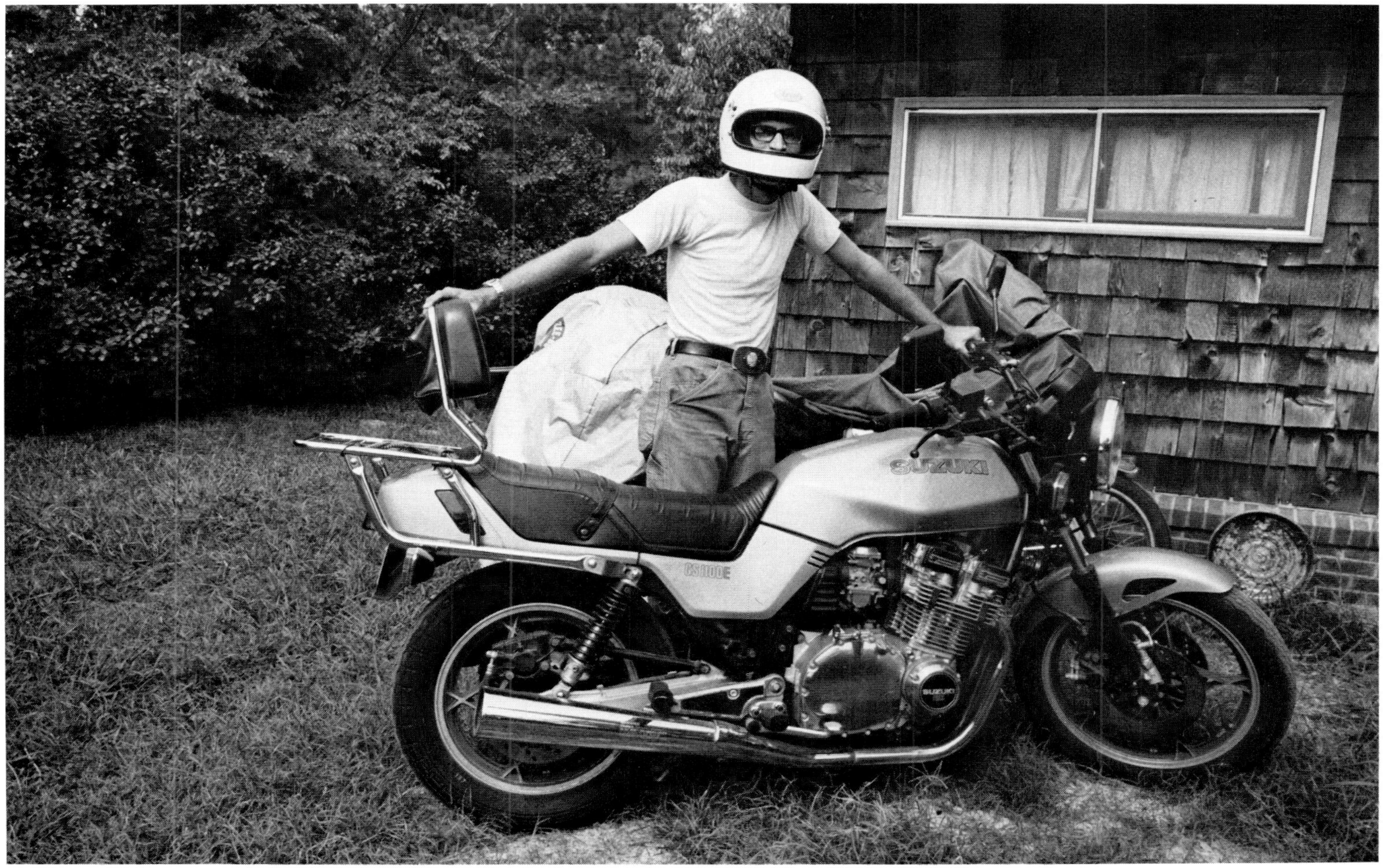
SUZUKI
GS1100E

ALGIS BUDRYS

On the face of it, no one should care what a writer looks like. But I always have, and so do most other people, I've noticed. Up to now, this phenomenon has always baffled me.

But sitting here, paging through some of the photos already taken for this book, seeing my friends, I've suddenly figured it out. The reason I need to see pictures of writers is that I need evidence they actually exist. I need photos; not drawings, not paintings; I need actual physical effects of indurate light on incorruptible chemicals. And more than that, I need to see the detail in that evidence; the texture of the skin touched by what of life it has encountered, the eyes set in a certain manner, the head held in ways that close listening has taught it. I need to see where the spinner sits, what setting this creator has found, and that has found this creator.

Otherwise, I would believe as I used to believe—that stories were the reports of real things. The idea of an actual person inventing this reality was utterly foreign to all experience. Things were, and one learned of them; the world was open of itself, unfolding itself spontaneously and generously to its children. Everything was real, various, beautiful, and generous.

Well, we learn better, don't we? And so evidence of the existence of spinners becomes desirable; perhaps at times more desirable than anything. We tend to think then, I believe, that only they stand between us and something that is not beautiful. We invest them with hope.

But the fact of the matter is that the world is more various than one feels it is, for it made them. Perhaps because it knows how it would look without them, but I prefer to think simply because it can't help itself.

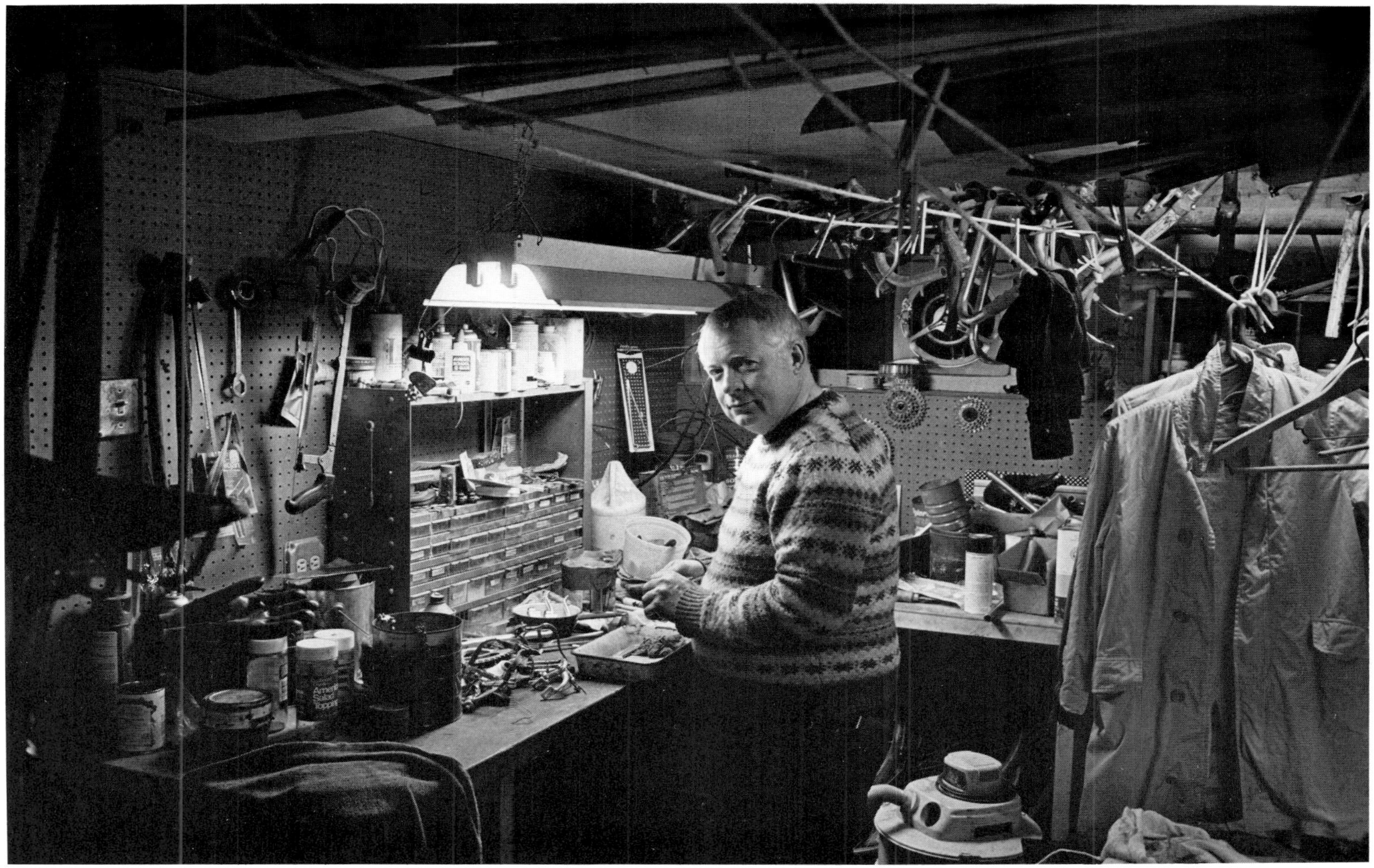

RAY BRADBURY

I am one of those fortunate people who were born to be joyful writers and discovered the fact early on. It began to surface when I was eight and fell deeply in love with Amazing Stories and Wonder Stories. It really burst apart in me when I was twelve and started writing sequels to Edgar Rice Burroughs Martian novels. I have written every single day of my life since then, with no dry spells and no stopping for anything. I am not so much a science fiction writer (which many deny) as I am an Idea Beast. Any idea that nags or bites or waves at me I respond to with a yell and a dash for the typewriter. Large or small, any fancy, notion, concept or revelation is welcome. The History of Ideas as a pageant of dreams fashioning themselves into three dimensional machines, is certainly my quiet madness. Mysteries in abundance surround us. Trying to solve some of them to survive, is the business of all of us writers and the people who jog along ahead of us, the scientists. I have at least ten thousand more days in me, which means a few million more words to go. I can hardly wait to get to them.

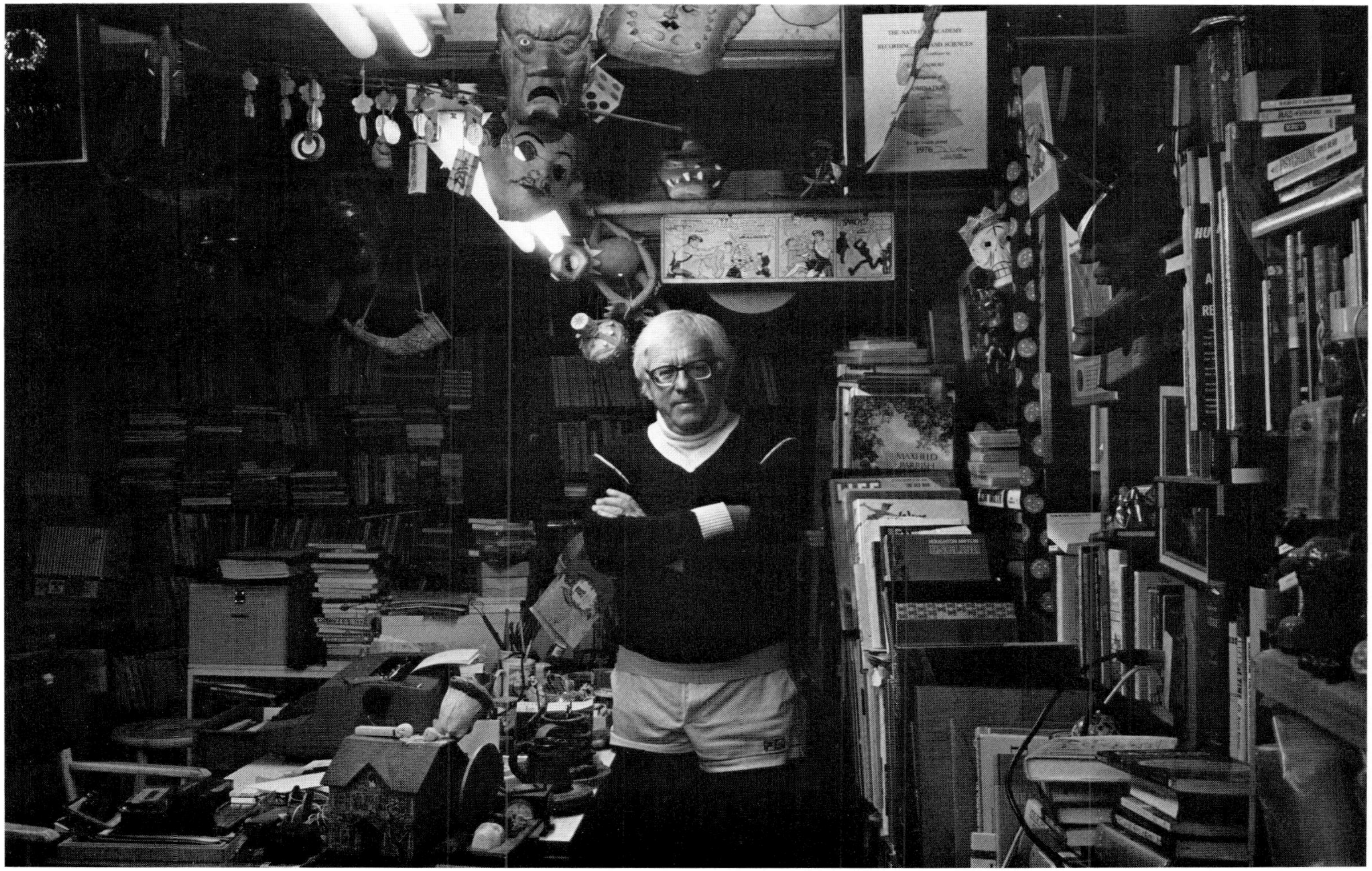

C. L. MOORE

I was born in a cabbage patch.

I find the odor of gasoline glamorous.

I have now told you the important facts of my life but it would seem unappreciative to contribute merely a blank page to this book so I shall go on and tell you a few other things about myself. Well, actually about my writing.

I have been time-oriented since the beginning. The Alendar stepped right out of the calendar; Ednes was excerpted from W*ednes*day: Julhi sprang "fourth" from the month of similar name; and Cenbe had its origin in De*cembe*r. Yarol had a different origin: He was of—literally—Royal birth, being an anagram of the typewriter I was using to write "Shambleau".

Shambleau and Jirel bear a close relationship to each other, and both, I believe, unconsciously reflect the woman I wish I could have been. I owe a great deal of my literary outpourings to Himself, My Unconscious.

If there is anything else you want to know about me, please address it to the Dead Letter Office, because I really hate writing about myself.

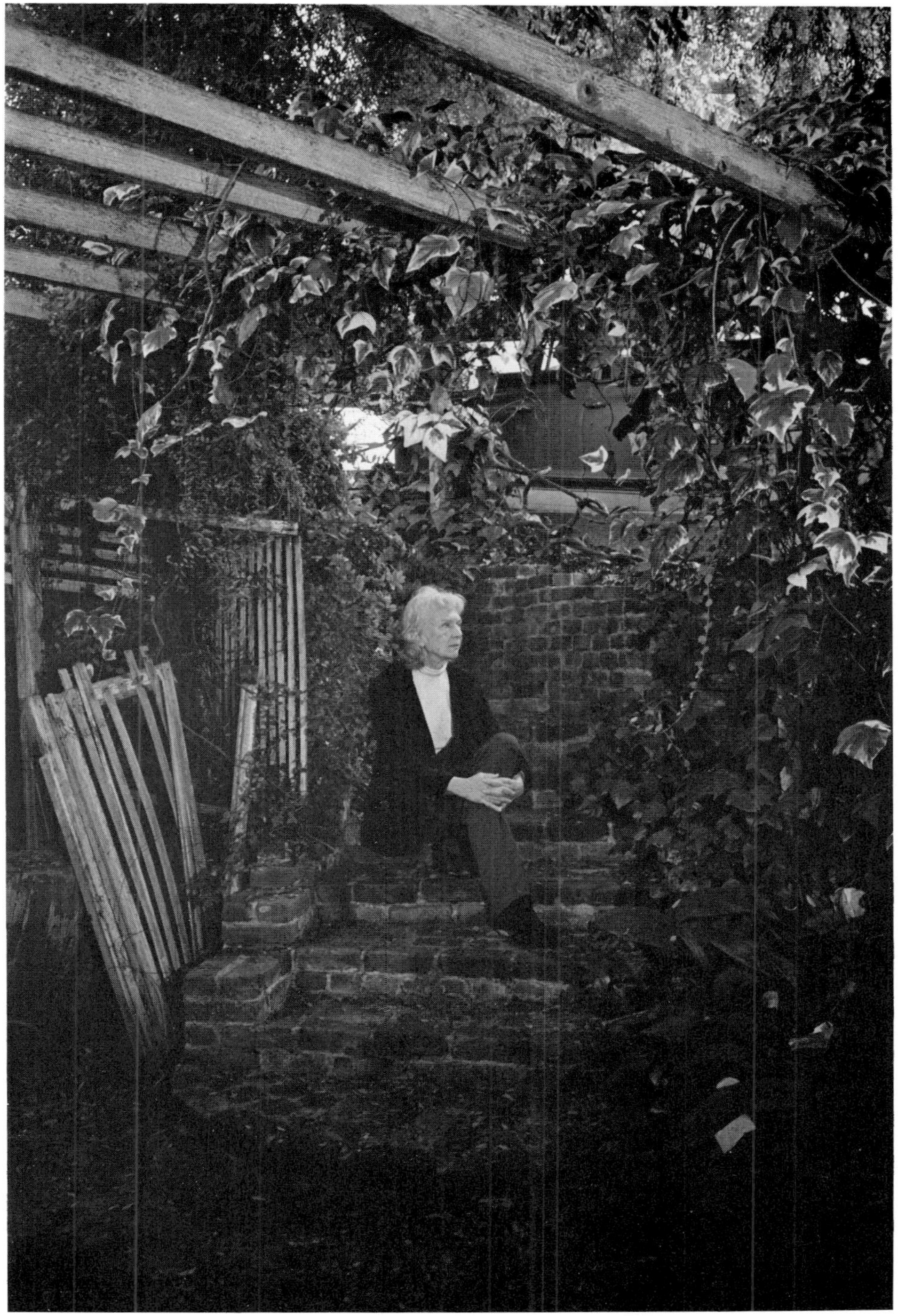

Without doubt, Science and Technology have the power which Magic and Sorcery tried and failed to reach, to magnify the individual and his/her reach enormously. Therefore, as with its predecessor, Magic, it would seem that the most pressing need for Science would be the identification and cultivation of individuals who would possess the quality, the excellence, and the strength of character to employ such powerful devices and techniques. We are speaking here about Ethics, but that is only the barest sort of beginning; and we are also talking about systems which are more comprehensive, not less, as has been the case so far.

We all fall into the error of reaching for those things whose ends can be seen most clearly—and then wondering why their promise evaporates even as we grasp it most tightly to us. But the real things which define our lives are invariably those things whose ends we cannot see.

When I look out into my back yard and see the mourning dove perched on the sunlit rim of the old hand-me-down wheelbarrow, delicate pink feet on rusty, muddy metal; when I see the flowing shadows and golden footprints of the sun in the oriental garden; *then* I know with a certainty no science can dispel that there will never be enough time—I will not finish it.

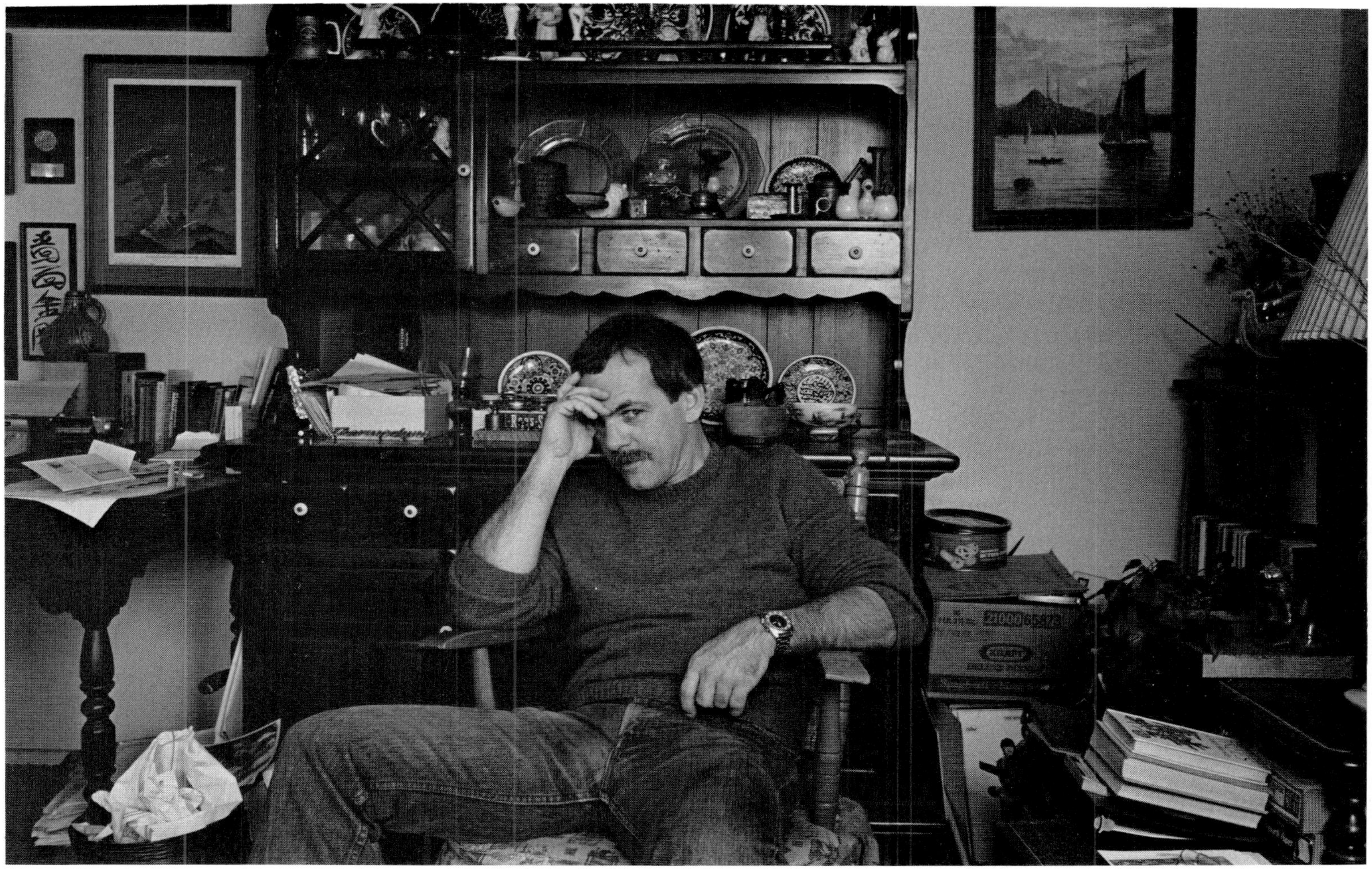
KRAFT

FRED SABERHAGEN

It seems to me on most hours of most days that the best job in the world is mine. I'm sure at all hours that I share my profession with some of the world's most intensely alive people, even though some of them speak with a profound pessimism. They are also some of the world's most interesting people, so I look forward to having my own copy of this book when it's completed.

Looking forward is of course a large part of our job, and of human life itself, if that life is lived with any intensity at all. In our time we live amid exploding knowledge and opportunity for our race. We live, as all our ancestors have lived, amid dangers, but now the physical threats are coming more and more under our control. And it has never been beyond our power to control the spiritual ones.

The late twentieth century seems to me one of the best moments in human history in which to be intensely alive.

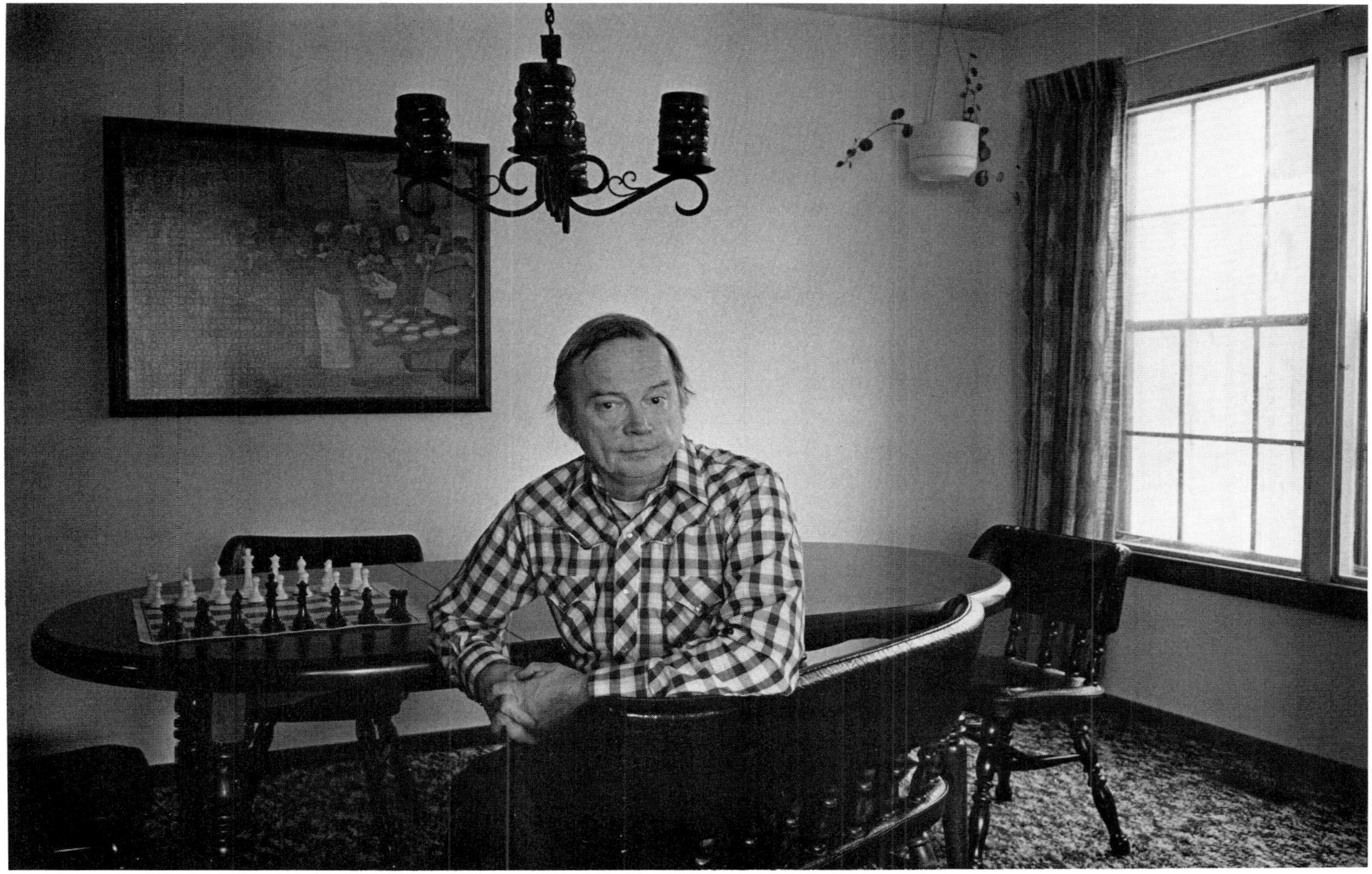

JOHN KESSEL

I grew up in Buffalo, New York.

Buffalo is one of those cities that's hard to love, and yet I find myself defending it against those who know it only as the snow capital of the world. It's a grimy industrial city that has seen better days: the lake is polluted, the economy is reeling, the climate gets horrible press, and the sports teams seem to rise to respectability only to lose when the chips are down. The women and men who live there are thought of as a little backward: why else would they live in Buffalo? Buffaloians are naturally sensitive about all this abuse and can get very defensive, which doesn't help matters any—they'll refuse to admit there's *anything* wrong with their home town.

Science fiction is a lot like Buffalo. I grew up there, too. I wouldn't want to live either place exclusively for the rest of my life, and I'll be the first to criticize neighborhood eyesores and the bad habits of the citizens, but nothing infuriates me more than to hear the genre (or the city) put down by someone who's never lived there, who drives through on the interstate or the list of Hugo winners and thinks he's seen the best the place has to offer.

So where do I live? Raleigh, North Carolina.

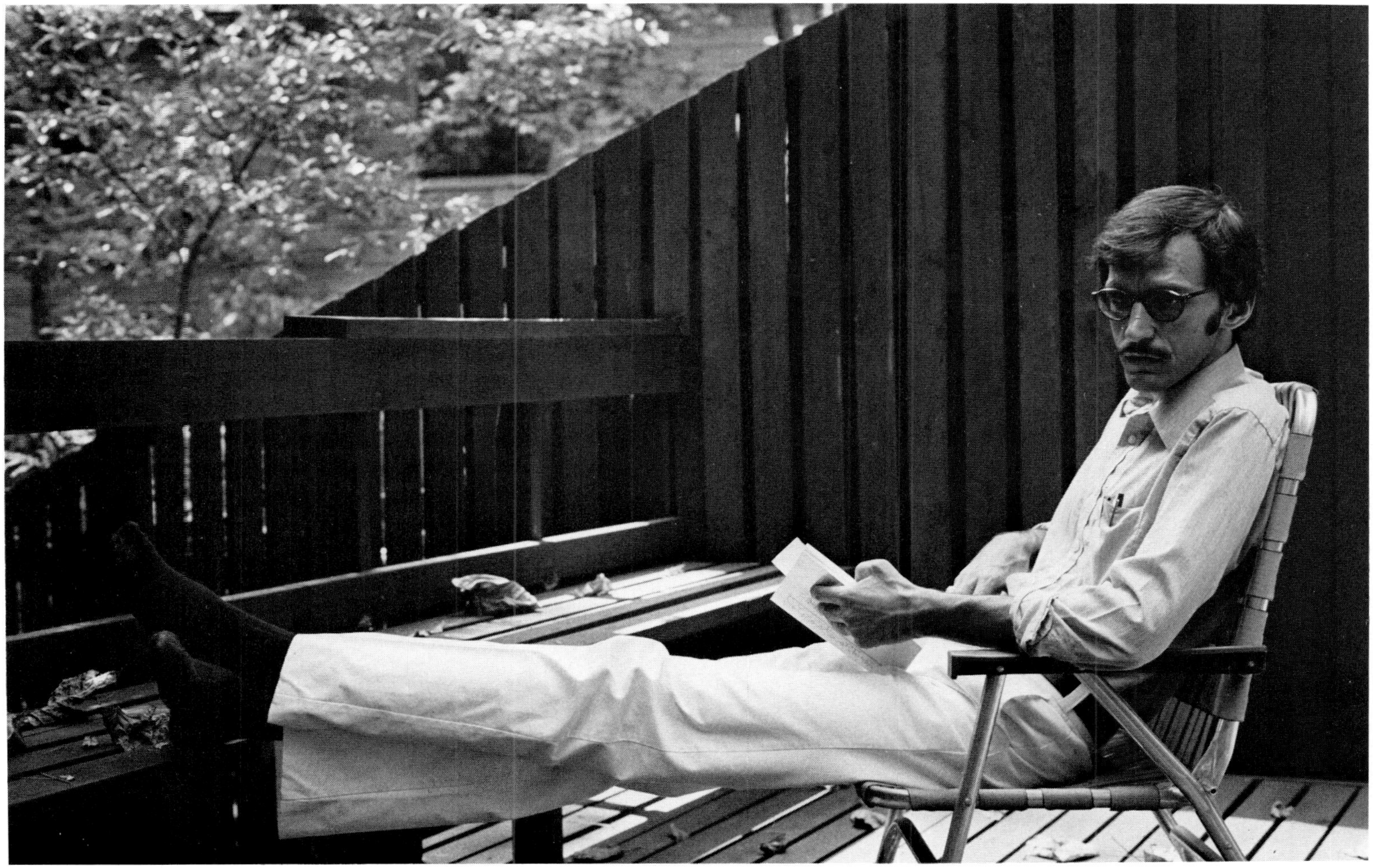

DAVID BRIN

The life of an SF author can be interesting, even fun. (Especially when one earns enough to keep slathering Denebian Debt-Wolves away from the airlock.) When success comes, one can taste popularity and yet remain, when one chooses, a private person.

Still, I often think I might rather have been a successful scientist or engineer.

Alas, my tenth muse slept a lot, back at old Caltech. In physics lecture they would present something new and wonderful about the Heart of Nature—perhaps a beautiful and mind-boggling mathematical wonder—and it would come to me like a foreign language that I had learned at great labor, whose poetry seemed momentarily within grasp, then gone again. The figures dancing in my head were too often words and images, not integers.

Of course writers entertain, inform, relate. At our best we enlighten and inspire. Some even believe that the library of SF "scenarios"—stories about the way mistakes might be made—will be invaluable during those frantic first days when we finally contact "Others" out there. Indeed, if the Powers are wise, SF authors will serve on the Reception Committee.

We ARE an imaginative crew.

Still, I try to keep a hand in science, if for no other reason than it refreshes my writing. Anyway, teaching is fun.

I suppose I'll always feel humble in the presence of a True Physicist, one whose eye glitters with direct vision of the very Edge . . . seeing the Singularity and Medusa's head . . . and neither blinks nor turns to stone.

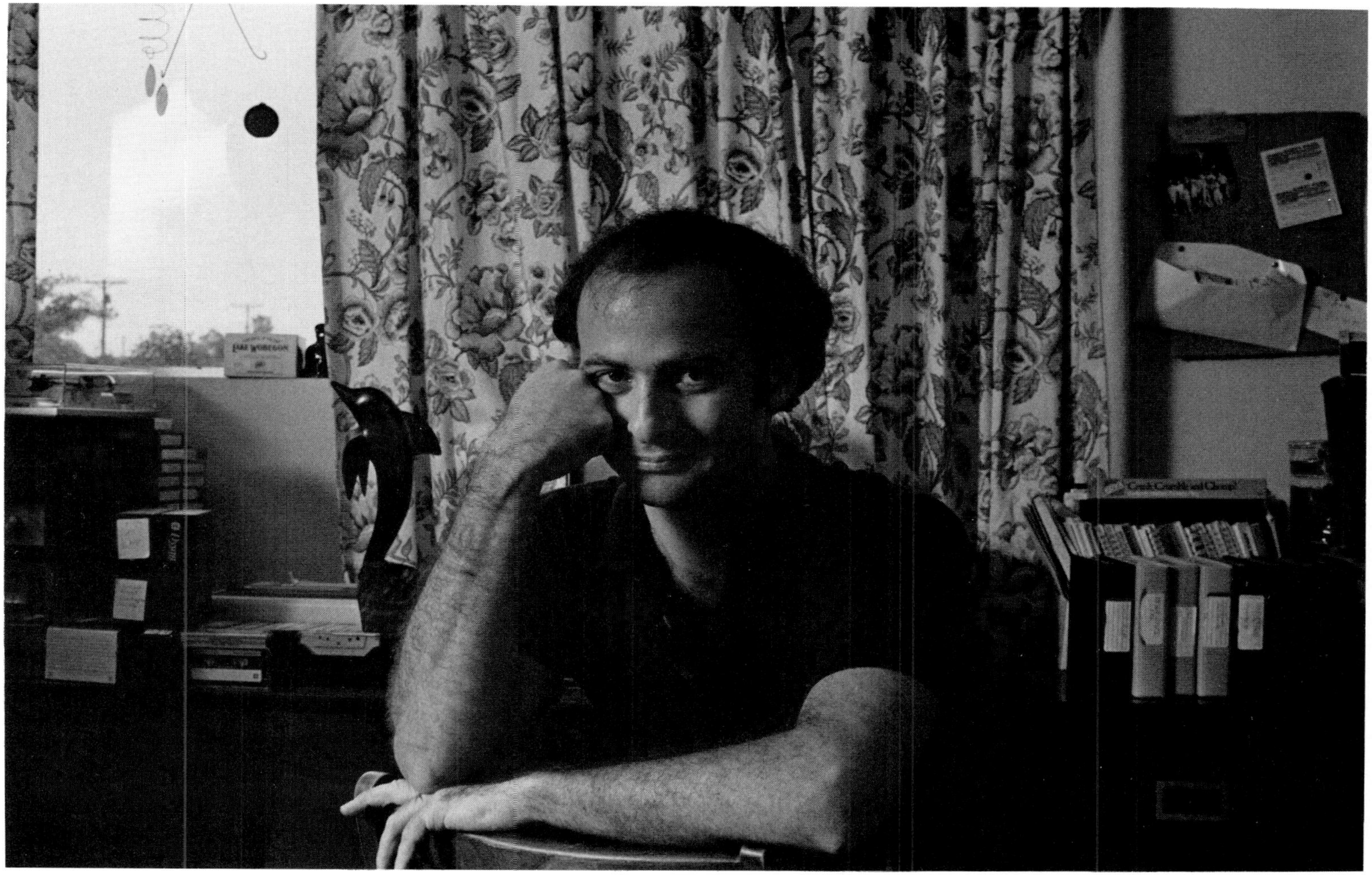

THEODORE STURGEON

Patti Perret is not only a remarkable photographer; but the only human being who has ever told me, repeatedly, to shut my mouth, and made me smile every time.

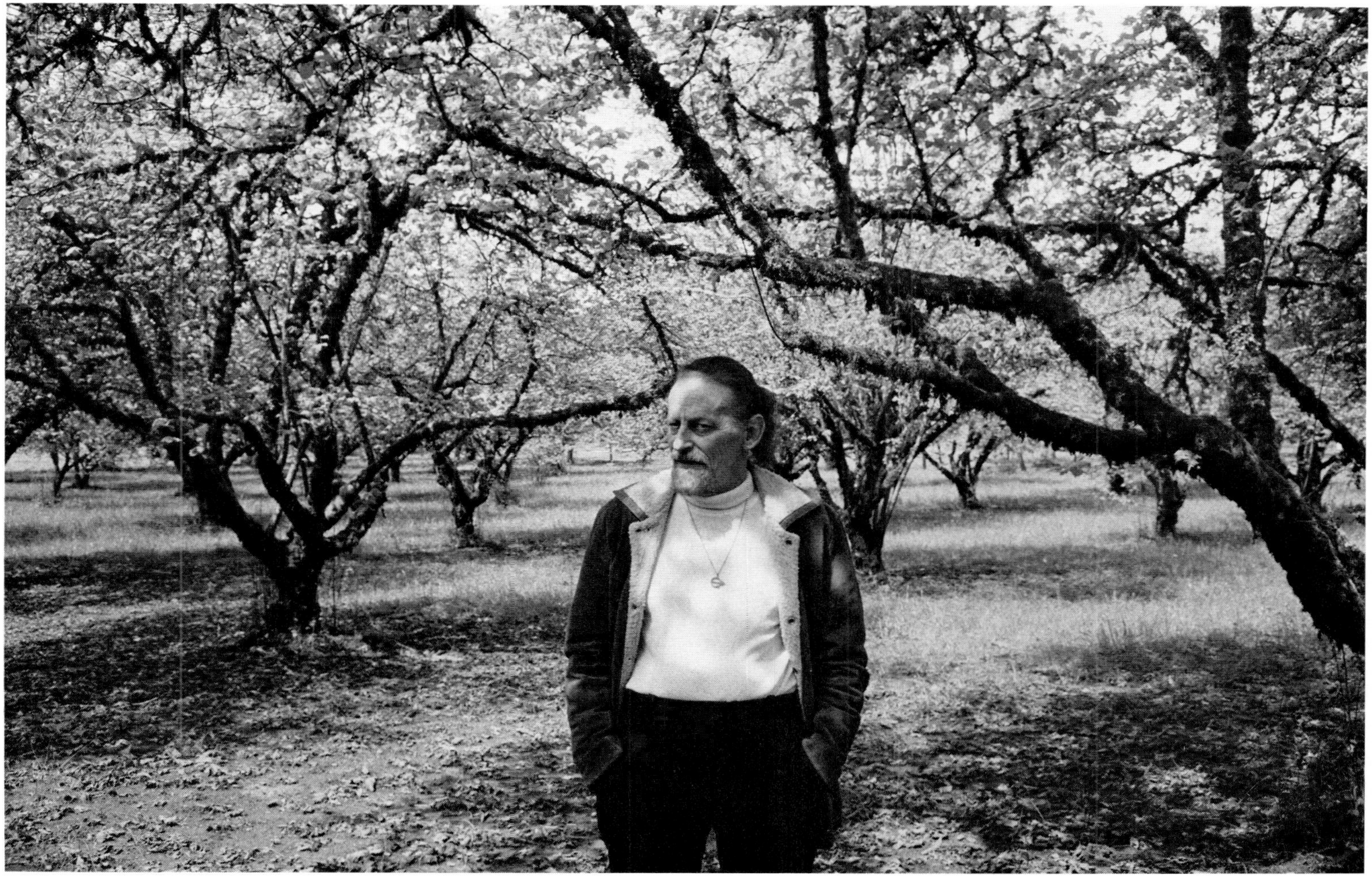

CHARLES SHEFFIELD

When you have been sitting in the audience for most of your life, it comes as a surprise to find yourself suddenly on-stage. And it leaves you unsure how to act.

I grew up in Hull, a town in the north of England. For my first eighteen years, until I went away to college, I was the only person that I knew who read science fiction. Stupid as it sounds, it never occurred to me that the appearance of sf magazines in a little back-street shop in the middle of town meant that *somebody* had to be reading them apart from me. I never met those others, because the shop mainly sold pornography. The customers (me included) would slink in when no one else was on the street, then buy and hurry away with their prizes. This led me to think that sf must be disreputable, wicked, and not socially acceptable. I was right. Sf is not inside the accepted social order, and that is probably its most important attribute. It is modern literature's most powerful tool for describing today's society, and like satire in earlier centuries it is naturally outside the pale.

It is also the outsider's preferred form of reading. So as someone who always felt like an outsider, it was natural that I would go on reading and enjoying sf for my first forty years, without ever considering the possibility of writing it. And when I finally did start to write, I *still* felt like an outsider—even with respect to sf itself. It's part of a general paranoia: there had to be things going on that I was not part of and did not understand.

In the fall of 1983 I realized—with a good deal of surprise—that there is no insider group in sf; suddenly I found that I had met most of the people whose writings I had been enjoying for so long, and they were not a mystery group at all. They were, in fact, a very nice and closely-knit community, independent-minded but supportive of each other. And I feel very pleased and proud to be sitting here, rubbing shoulders with Theodore Sturgeon and Isaac Asimov and the rest.

I have only one major worry. When I was young my whole attitude to the world was shaped by Jack Williamson, Clifford Simak, Arthur Clarke, and Robert Heinlein; the writings of Fred Pohl, Isaac Asimov, Poul Anderson, Alfred Bester, Frank Herbert, and Hal Clement largely made me what I am today. It worries me that someone may now be absorbing my odd world view and making it part of their own. That much responsibility is disturbing.

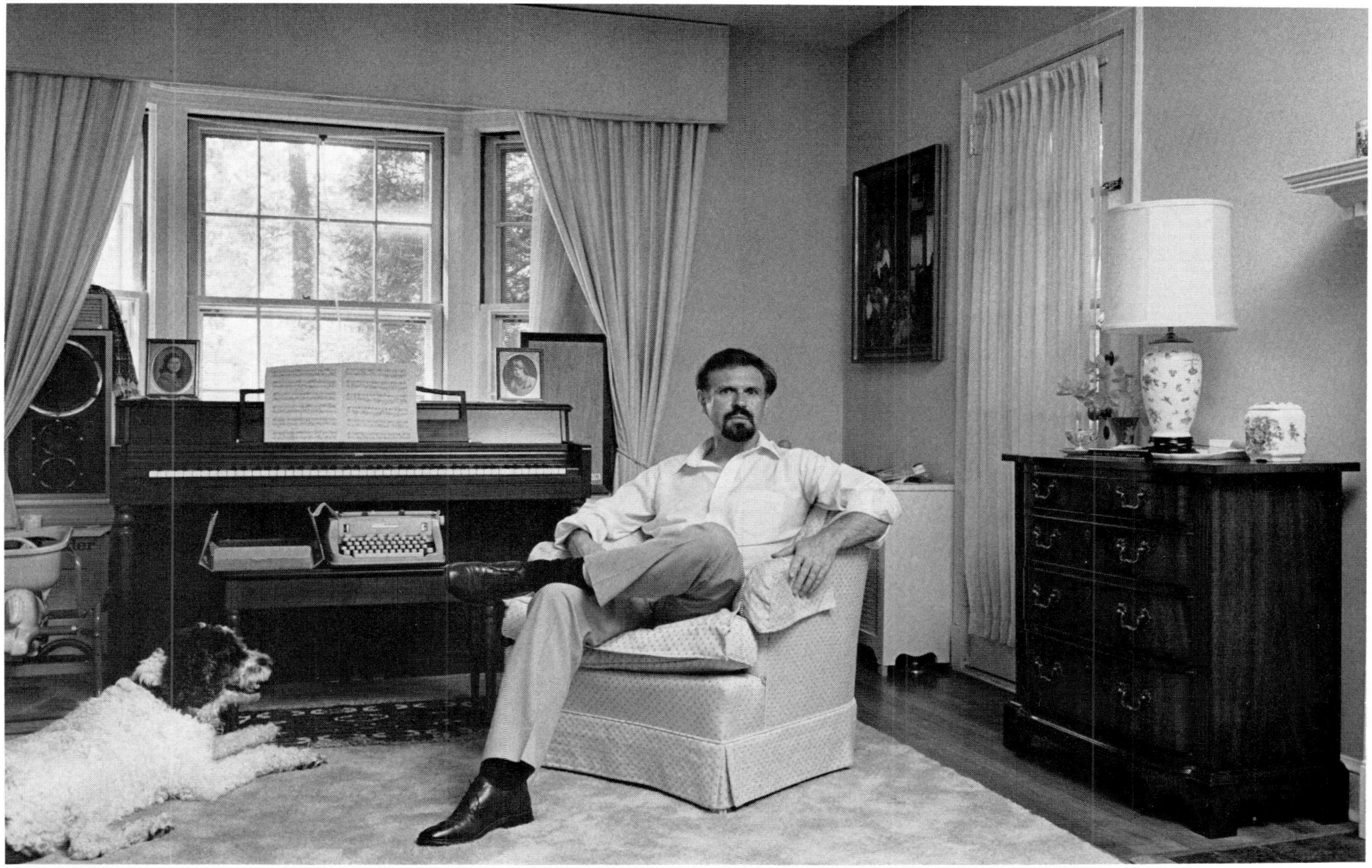

ISAAC ASIMOV

I haven't a modest bone in my body—at least when it comes to science fiction. I'm proud of what I've *produced,* but not of *me.* My *stories,* and those of several hundred other writers are the face of science fiction.

To put it as briefly as I can, I'm against personality cults even when I'm the beneficiary.

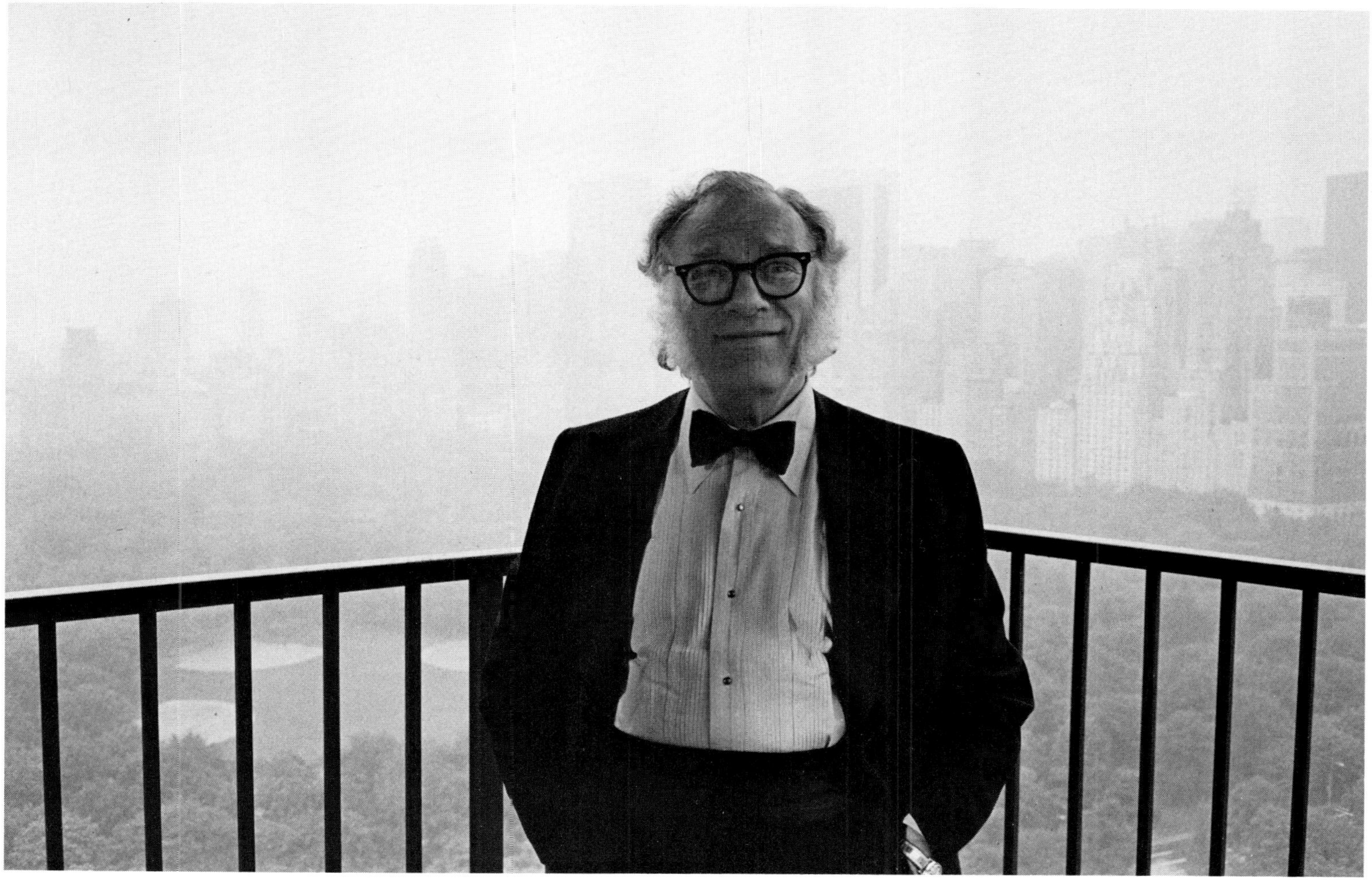

FRITZ LEIBER

I occupy one of the half billion or so stations in the speech web of story-telling, gossip-trading, observations-sharing English-speaking minds. And am in touch, via translations, with maybe a half billion more (no hindi, chinese, swahili as yet).

And potentially (Who knows what the future holds, what the secrets are?) keyed into the incalculably vaster web of all speaking, imagining, curious minds, wherever they may house.

It's my job to keep my station in good working order, busily receiving and sending, with a particular emphasis on fiction and science, and with my antennae burnished and honed to catch, embellish, reweave, and re-transmit hints of the strange, the mysterious, the wondrous.

Now that I'm getting older I note I'm developing a weakness for fact, especially personal, as against fiction. (Truth I don't meddle with, it's far beyond me. I leave it to the superminds.) I cater to this deplorable weakness of mine by writing regular columns, "Moons & Stars & Stuff" for *Locus* and "On Fantasy" for *Fantasy Review*. But I know none of my messages travel far without generous lacings of fiction to give them wings. A good story travels farther if not faster than light and the opposite of death is not so much life as imagination.

Another new difficulty. Some people, including myself, seem to age faster than the characters I've based on them in my stories. Some even have the nerve to die. New characters take time to season. Of course there are elixirs of youth, but they're almost too easy. In my last swordly adventure of Fafhrd and the Gray Mouser I put special curses of old age on them, compulsions to stargaze and collect trivia, so they could share my septuagenerian sufferings and those of a close friend of mine—and escape back to middle age! Then there's reincarnation, the transmigration of souls, even more desperate remedies. I'm thinking of signing a pact with the Devil.

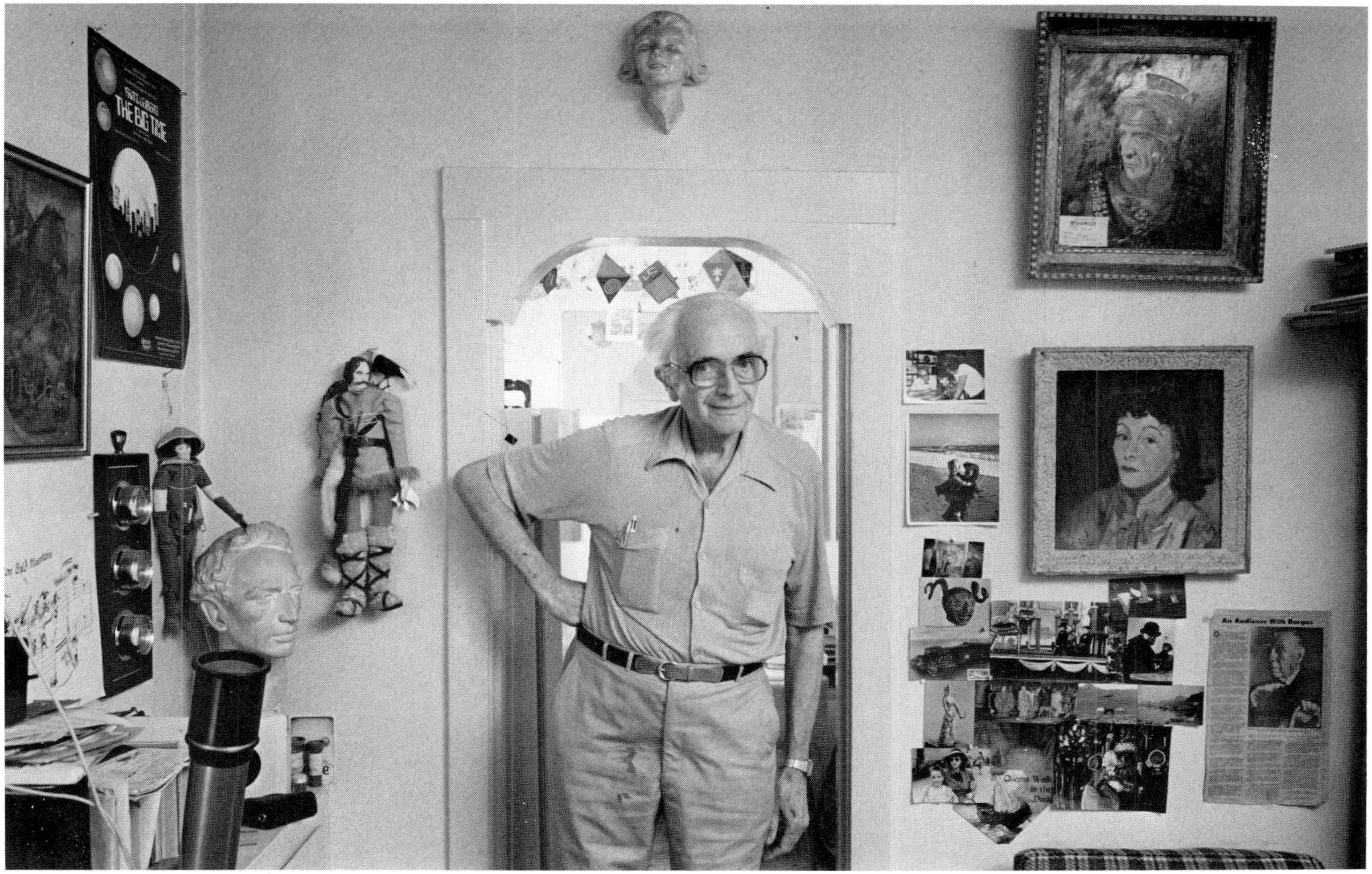
THE BIG TREE
An Audience With Borges

DAMON KNIGHT

"A long time ago I used to think that when we make art, we're celebrating the natural world, praising it, and that's what it's all about. What I think now is that we're here because we can make a kind of beauty the universe can't make by itself. The natural world can make a crystal, or an ocelot; or a poplar tree with the wind blowing through it, but it can't make a painting, or music, or stories."

—GENE ANDERSON, in *The Man in the Tree*

KATE WILHELM

. . . I always feel as if I've been gone longer than I have. It's been three weeks this time, and now the corn is high over my head, eight feet tall, nine feet . . . One of the cats is under the corn—Pumpkin. She greets me with her hoarse Siamese-like noises, but she does not stir. It is very hot today, cool there in the deep shade. An emerald-green frog is on top of the beans in my colander. When I add more beans, it hops out, vanishes under a canopy of bean leaves. Earlier I spotted a salamander in the potatoes where the earth stays cool and moist under a deep mulch of straw. Thoughts of the new novel chase each other through my mind. A scene that isn't right yet . . . I try it from a new perspective, another viewpoint, let it play itself out in the mental theatre where all scenes are enacted over and over. Every year the ground is richer, in better condition than before; it gives me little presents now. A volunteer tomato plant is heavy with paste tomatoes. I wasn't sure what kind they would be when I first saw it, hoed around it, and let it be. In the middle of the beans there is a stray potato plant, thriving among the foreigners. Red skin? Kennebec? Netted gem? I won't know until I dig it out next month—another surprise. I don't know the names of the characters in the new novel yet. They talk to each other, but seldom to me, unless I trick them into it, put them in a scene where it is necessary to reveal their names. I don't use those scenes. How many such scenes, other scenes, have I played out, lived through, discarded? Living through the scene from *his* viewpoint has cleared up a problem with it, I think. Once more, from *her* viewpoint this time. If I don't try to see it too hard, I can perceive a golden shower of pollen falling straight down in the windless day, the promise of seed fulfilled. I have my scene; it is time to go back inside, think dinner thoughts, freeze beans . . . It is good to be working. I tuck the new scene back among the others, content with it, and leave the garden to the salamanders, the jewel-like frogs, a sapphire dragon fly, and the golden pollen fall.

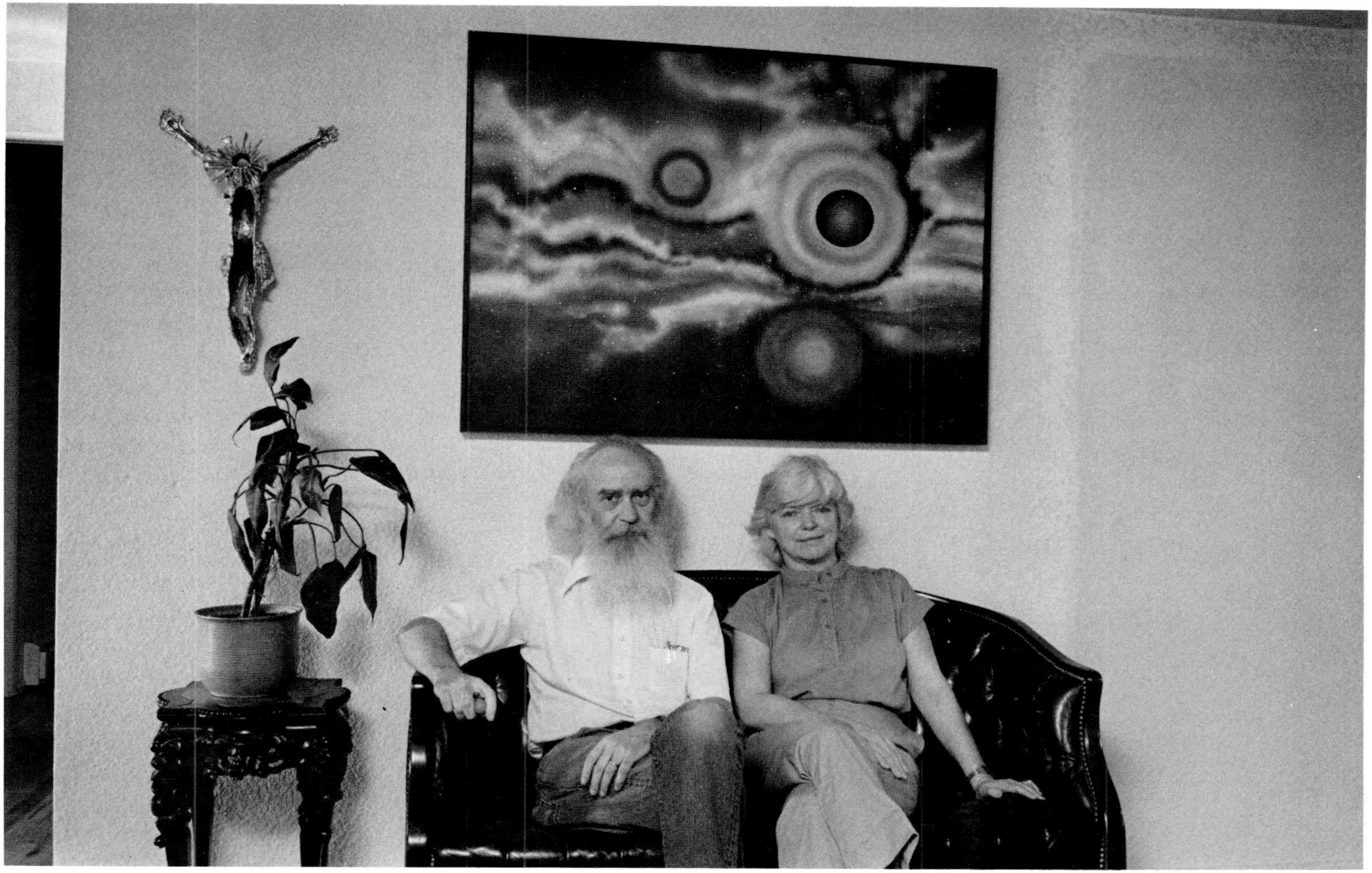

ROBERT AND JUANITA COULSON

Science fiction is marvelously entertaining if you don't take it too seriously. Avoid readers who expect the genre to produce the Great American Novel, or who think it already has. Especially avoid authors who think they've written it. With this kept firmly in mind, there's a wonderful time to be had with the books, magazines, fanzines, filksongs and conventions in the science fiction field. We've been enjoying ourselves in the ranks for over thirty years now, and expect to continue for a good many years more.

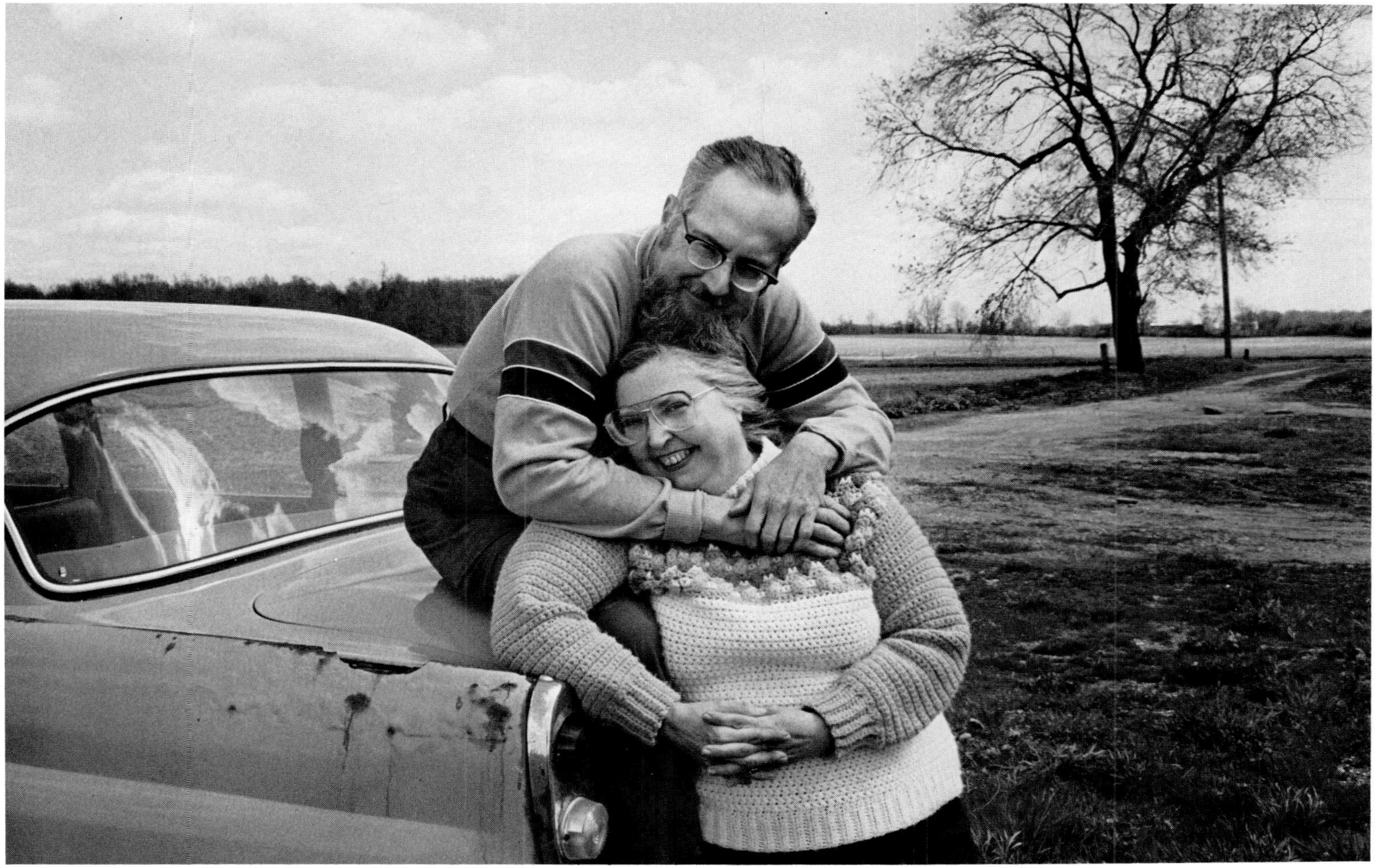

MARION ZIMMER BRADLEY

Ever since I discovered the existence of science fiction in 1946 (I had been addicted to fantasy since I learned to read) I have devoted my life to writing both of them. And during the last forty-odd years, teachers and well-meaning friends have tried to convince me that I had the talent to write "something better" and that I should abandon fantasy and science fiction for something more important.

I've spent a lot of that time making excuses for myself, saying I was using fantasy and science fiction to support myself and learn my craft on the way to something better (in their words). But now I am fifty-three years old and for better or worse, what I am is a science fiction writer, and I will never stoop again to explain or excuse it. I'm proud of what I am. I now don't think there *is* anything better.

Consider. Science fiction encourages us to explore the future—not the rosy future predicted to those who want to sell us technology, nor the bleak future predicted by professional Cassandras who don't trust the human spirit, but *all* the futures, good and bad, that the human mind can envision. Even if none of these futures ever came true, the very fact that we are encouraged to think about them makes humanity a more *thinking* race. That's got to be a good thing. There is never anything to fear more than stupidity, apathy; just *not thinking* is the greatest of human shortcomings and the only sin we can commit against the Holy Spirit.

Fantasy, on the other hand, deals not in futures and might-be, but in the eternal now, the endless Truth of humanity. Fantasy forces us to confront our own archetypes, the inner transformed truths of our own hearts, minds and spirits. What we write about, what we discover in the reading of fantasy, is our inner truth, cut free from the here and now, transformed because isolated and pure from our current cultural shibboleths.

Is there anyone alive who *honestly* believes that it's better to write about politics, corruption on the street, adultery in the suburbs, romantic pap or steamy sex? All these things are of the moment. Already the great realists—Dickens, Hemingway,—are as dated as yesterday's newspaper.

But we're still reading the *Odyssey*.

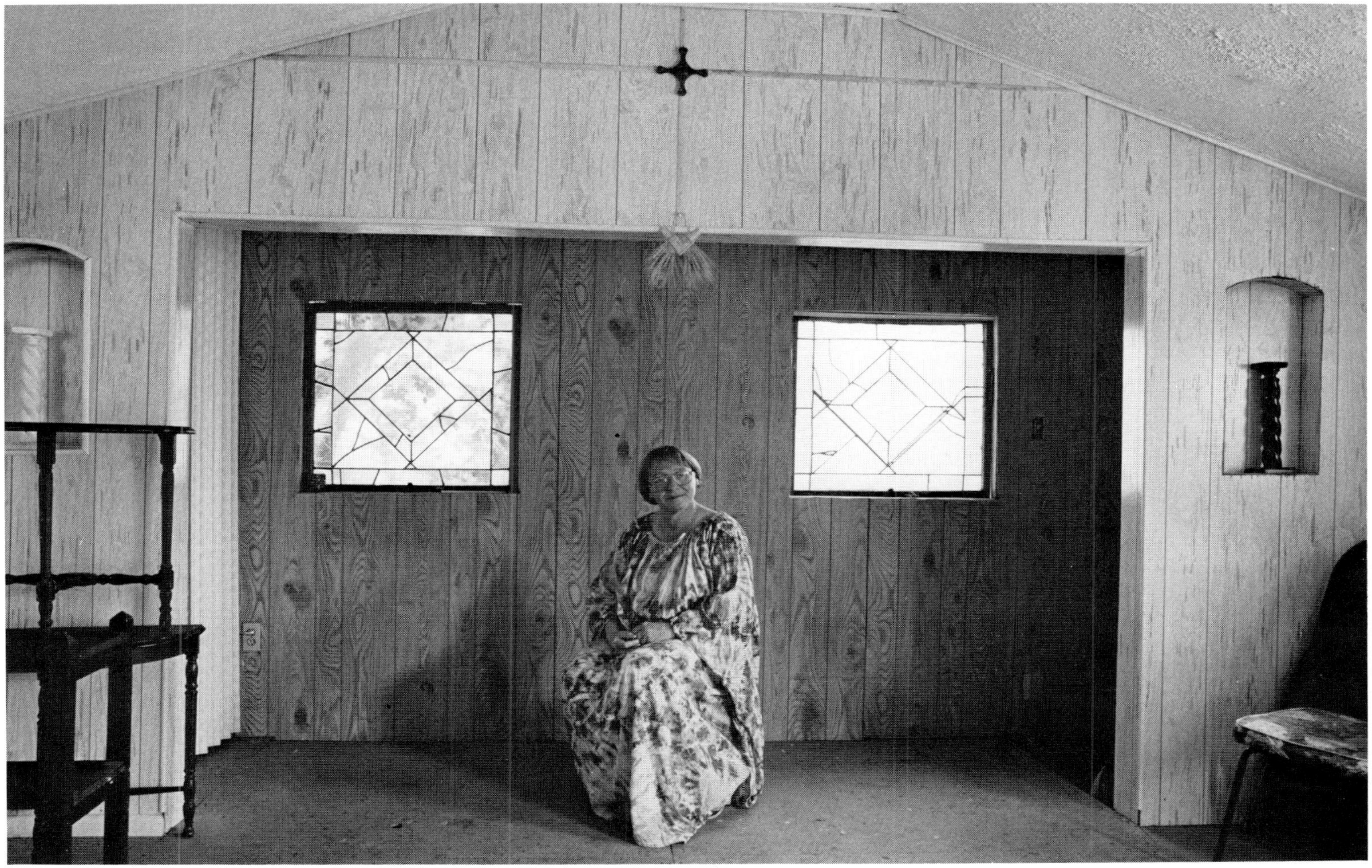

JAMES P. HOGAN

Of all the methods that people have devised throughout history for arriving at beliefs, Science is unique in the way it continually questions itself. It recognizes that whatever is fact will remain so with total disregard for the intensity of human desires for things to be otherwise, or for how many others might be persuaded to share one's convictions. Much of the effort of Science is devoted to exposing deception, particularly self-deception—otherwise ultimately, your plane won't fly. By searching out its errors and self-correcting, Science grows stronger.

And being a writer is essentially similar. Work that is good, bad, or indifferent remains so regardless of the most passionate compulsion on the part of anyone to wish the contrary. Deception results ultimately only in books that won't fly. As in Science, the art lies more in asking "What's wrong with it?" than in getting too excited about what seems to be right—and then being honest with one's self about the answers.

Wouldn't it be nice if the same were true of the beliefs promoted in things like Politics, Religion, and Economics?

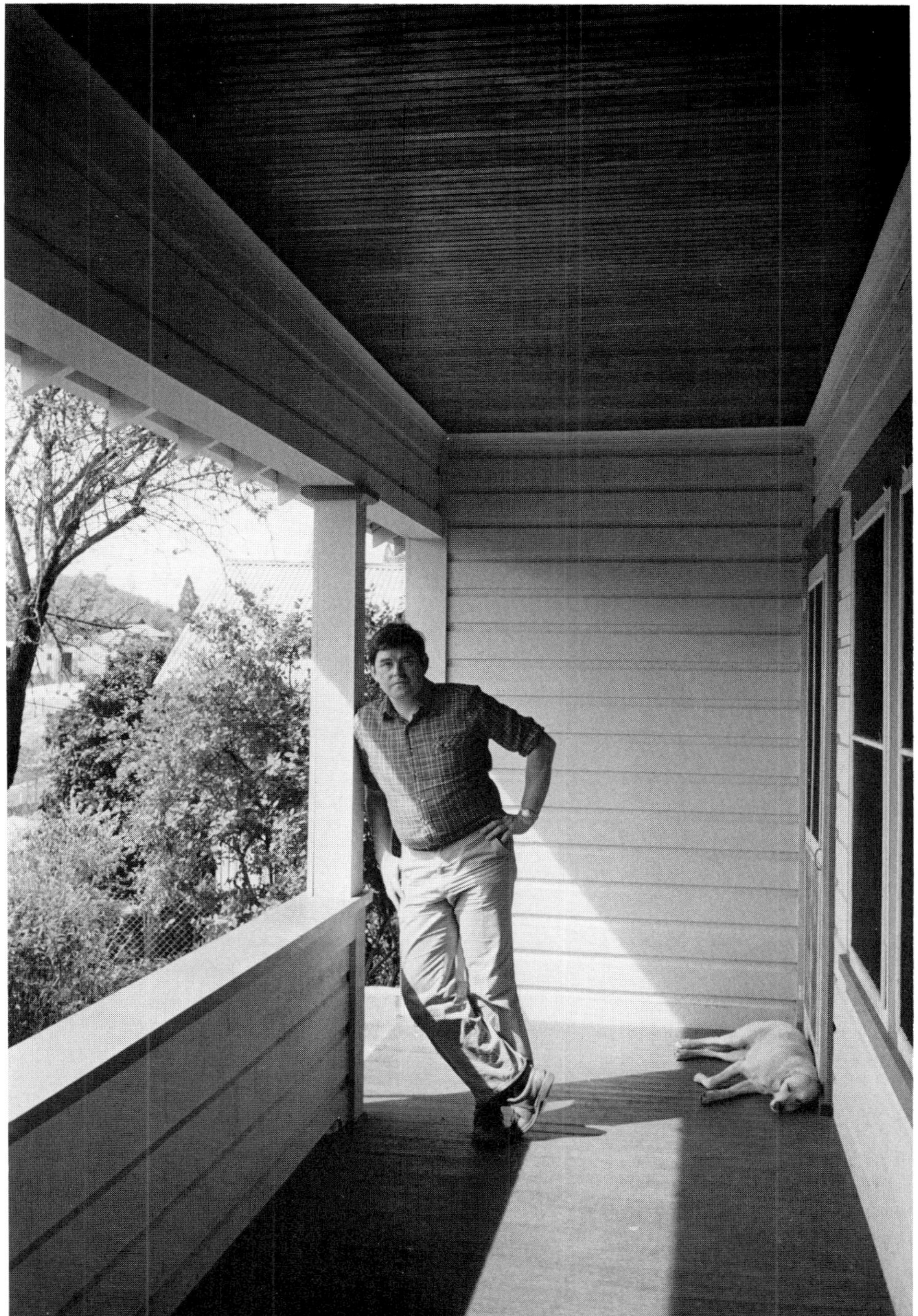

FRANK HERBERT

This will be, in part, a comment on literary criticism.

Fellow writers tell me the most common question asked of them is: "Where do you get your ideas?" A questioner confronted one friend with the demand: "Where did you get *that* idea? Out of your *head?*"

It's a great mystery most people recognize.

One friend responds by saying he gets his ideas in a plain brown wrapper from New York. I usually say I'm a conduit and they come from some other place.

All of which leads to the statement of my belief that the ability to write is a gift and you share it for the benefit of as wide a circle as you can find.

There! I've answered the question to the best of my ability.

Some sneer at this idea and I sympathize with the fear that motivates their response. This attitude of sharing makes you vulnerable. It is so often misunderstood. You might think it's pure ego. After all, there must be something approaching hubris in the belief that you can take a blank sheet of paper and put something on it people will want to read. Yet many of us do it.

I think this is the choice of the artist that all criticism is forced to challenge. And rightly so. But there is some truth in the statement that those who cannot create take up criticism. Then what is proper criticism and where do you find it?

The answer strikes me as rather simple: Time. There is the only valid critic. Does the artist's work stand the test of Time? None of our contemporaries can possibly know for sure. The artist can only hope and the critic parades beliefs, favorable or unfavorable.

The thing being analyzed comes "from some other place" and has to stand the test of its times.

"Dune" was rejected by twenty-two editors and was panned by all of the major critics. Still, it was a best seller and sold thirteen million copies. Does this mean it will stand the test of Time? Of course not. The things "from some other place" are on their own when you release them. That's the way it is with all life.

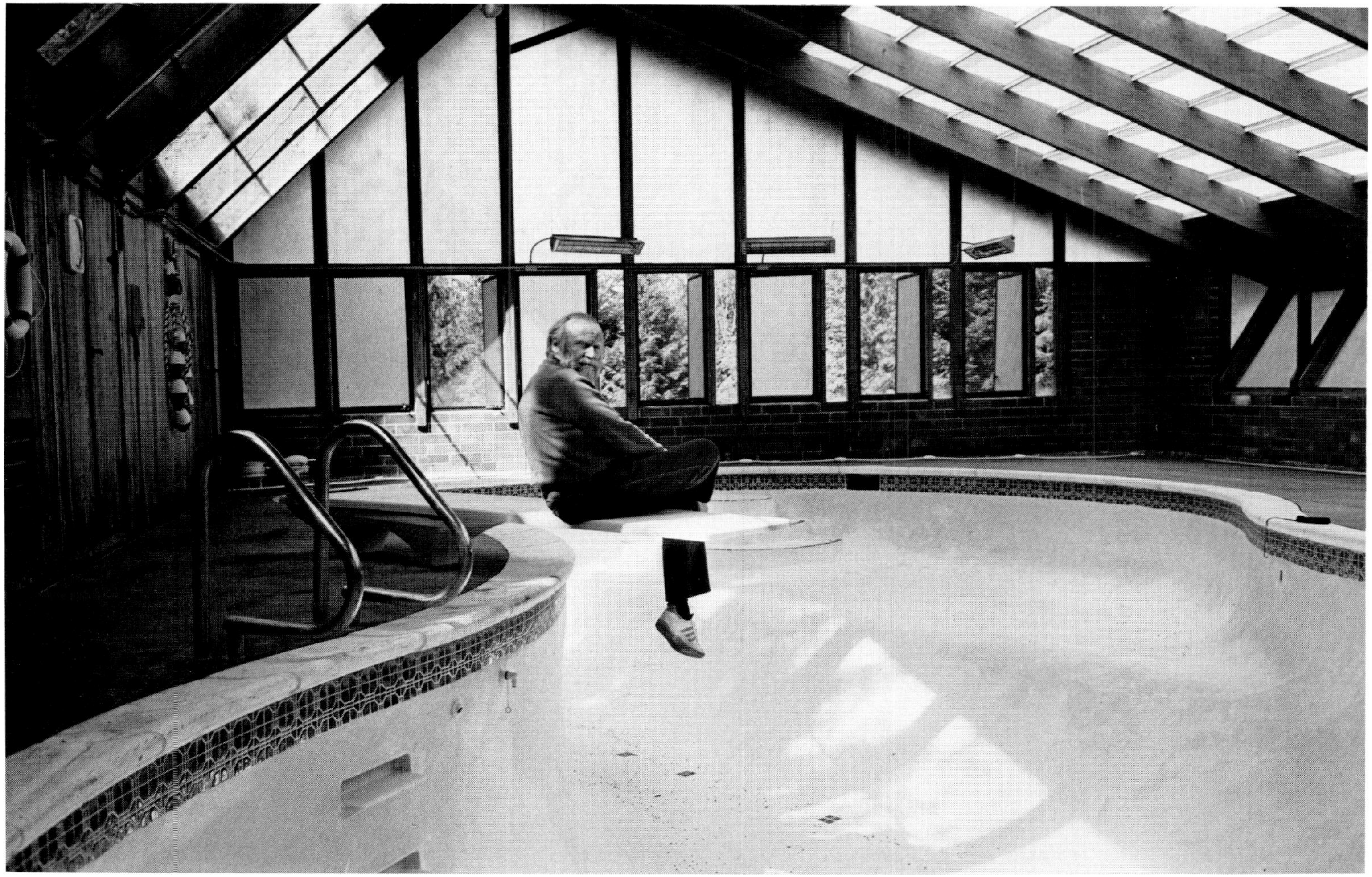

PHILIP JOSÉ FARMER

Though I've seen only a few photographs of the faces (and the bodies) of those in this unique work, I know many of them in the flesh. Not more than two or three look like the stereotyped image of a fantasy or science-fiction writer. These could be photographs of truck drivers, cowboys, winos, astronauts, sea captains, waitresses, lumberjacks, psychiatrists, drill sergeants, rabbis, fencing instructors, terrorists, chemists, drug dealers, stamp collectors, storm window salespersons, incipient St. Joans of the Arc, gurus, GM executives, or what-have-you.

There's very little in these faces and bodies to show that they have struggled with the cosmos, not to mention publishers. Like Jacob with the angel, they have wrestled with the high, and, like St. George with The Dragon, with the low. They are foragers of the universe and veterans of the Eschatological War. Yet very few of the wounds show, and their breasts display no medals. Who could tell that they are all cunctipotent euhemerizers?

It's too bad that the photographer had no camera to catch the auras emanating from the heads herein. Then we could, while seeing the many differences, also see a remarkable likeness. Then we could say, "There is a man or a woman who has explored the seven circles of heaven and the seven circles of hell."

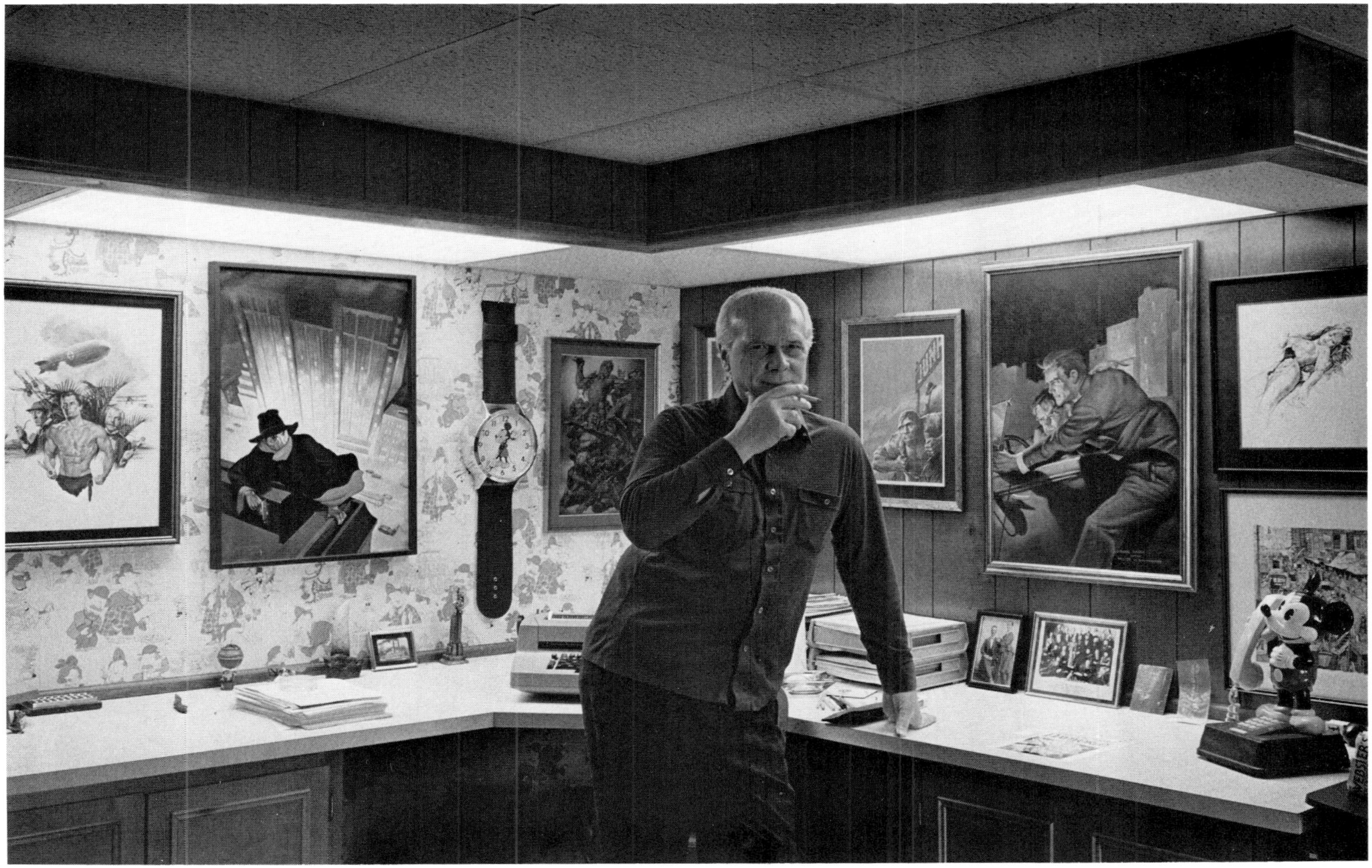

C. J. CHERRYH

I'm a technologist. My scholastic study was classics/archaeology, which is a study of how humanity got from picking up a rock to wondering (eventually) how to find a more efficient rock. Humanity tried to find a more efficient way to produce food and other ordinary and extraordinary things; and as often as ancient humanity got bored with mundanity, the band gathered round the fire and told tales about someone finding a more efficient rock/firemaker/sword/ship—whatever. Which inspired someone to dissatisfaction with the rock/firemaker/sword/canoe at hand. And that someone went out and made a better one.

One thing you learn in archaeology is that there weren't any good old days . . . compared to now. With local blips and dips and peaks in the chart of human affairs, the steady trend has been uphill and better. I'd rather live today than thirty years ago or three hundred or three thousand. And I'd rather live in the future than now. I want to get to space. Maybe somebody will take my books where I can't go—that being the nature of books. Somebody took Homer, who wrote one of the first voyage stories—to a new world beyond a sea he never saw; and hereafter they'll carry him to Mars and further across a sea he never imagined. It's my ambition first to write a book that will push someone to go where I'll never get the chance to—and second to write a book someone will carry along on a voyage I'd like to have made.

Of course—if someone gives me a shuttle ticket . . .

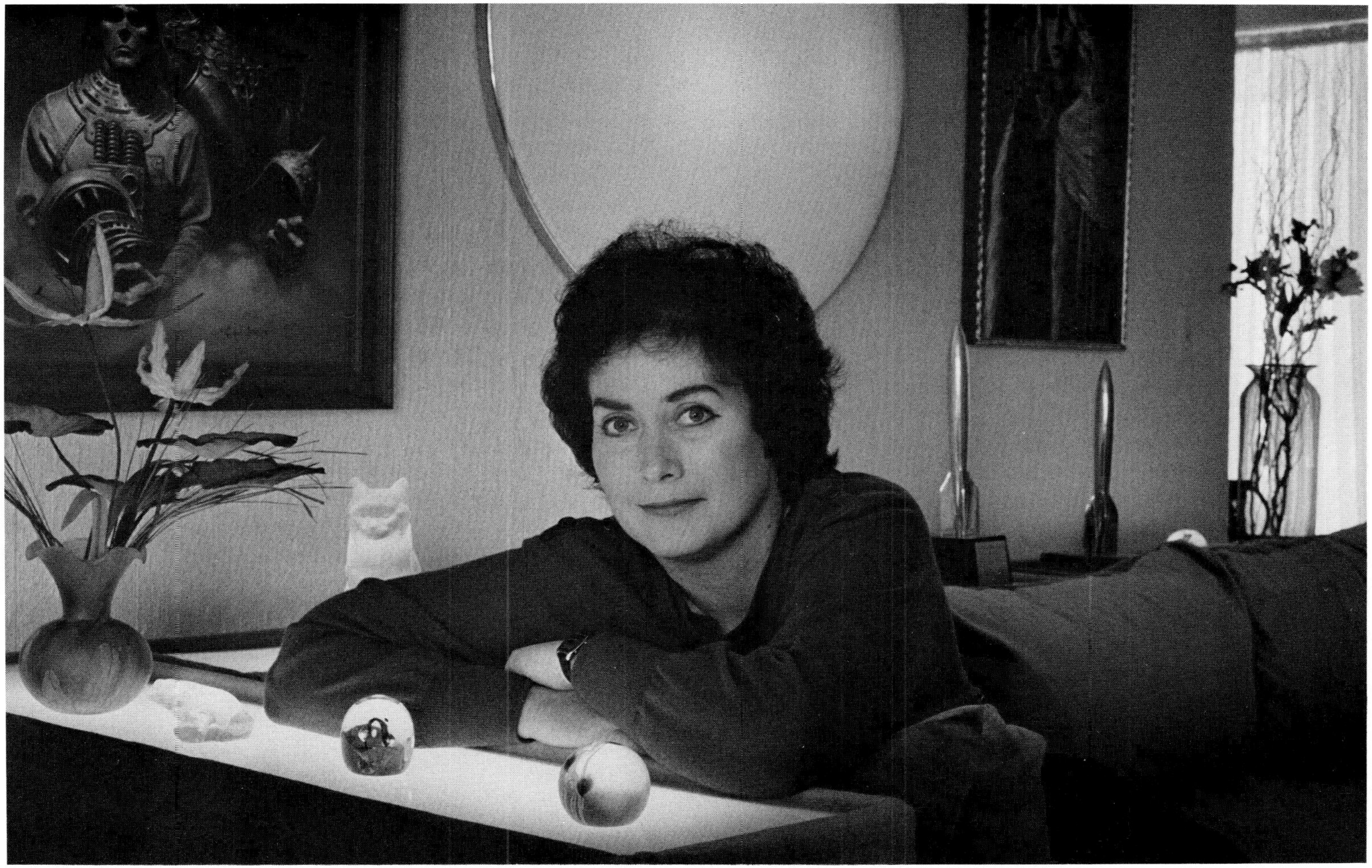

R. A. LAFFERTY

R. A. Lafferty, Born November 7, 1914, Died January 1, 2001

I was born in Iowa and came to Oklahoma when I was four years old. I'm still here.

As a boy I tried unsuccessfully to play the piano and to paint. "Third wish left," I said. "I'll save it for a while."

I'm ten years too late with everything. I was twenty-eight when I first crossed the ocean, first went to war, first discovered the South Pacific. For best effect, all of these enjoyments should have been experienced earlier.

I am introverted, clumsy, left-handed, Catholic, conservative, registered "Independent".

Twenty years ago I gave my first biographical squib: "I am, not necessarily in that order, fifty years old, a bachelor, an electrical engineer, a fat man." Twenty years later I'm still the same age and a bachelor, but now I'm a retired electrical engineer and a semi-retired fat man.

When I was forty-five years old I tried to be a writer and my third wish was realized. I was moderately successful. It didn't put me on easy street but it put me on easy alley.

I became the best short story writer in the world. I've been telling people that for twenty years, but some of them don't believe me. They should remember of whom it was first said, "If they do not believe this, neither will they believe one risen from the dead."

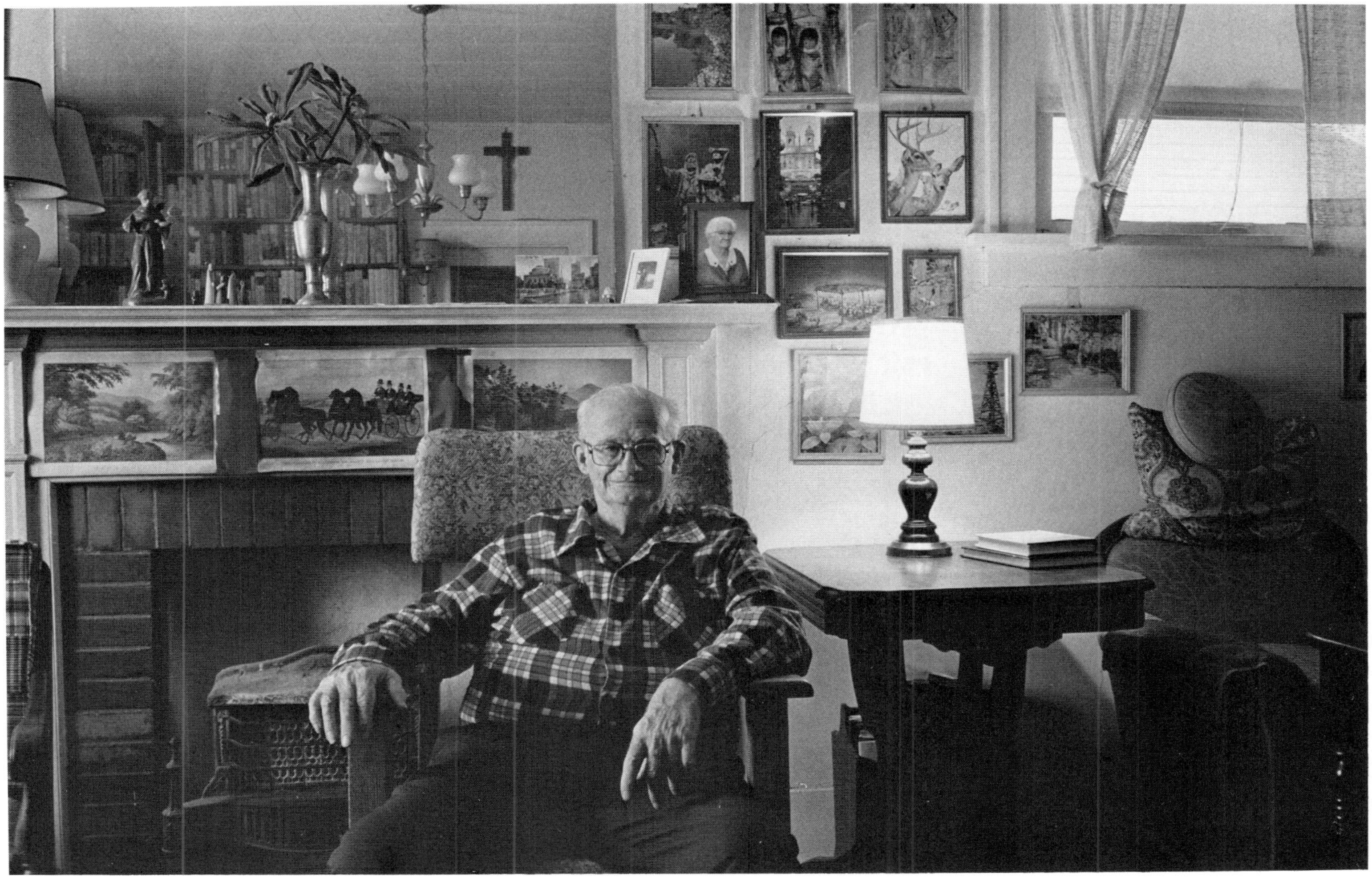

GREG BEAR

I'm having the time of my life. I've wanted to be (and have been) a writer since I was eight years old, perhaps even before that. It's hard to imagine what I'd be if I wasn't a writer—an artist, perhaps, since that's always been my second avocation. Indeed, a few people still think of me primarily as an artist, because it was easier in my early years to show paintings than to force bulky manuscripts on people. Now, publishers condense my manuscripts into portable, convenient packages, and there are those who are unaware I've ever done art.

I'm an information omnivore. I love books passionately. I also love movies; one of my early career choices was to be a special effects artist working in puppet animation. (A friend from those youthful years recently won an Oscar for just such work—and the pride and thrill I feel for him is partly vicarious.) I find it easy to shuttle back and forth between the visual media and literary subjects. And I refuse to abandon the enthusiasms of my youth; I have a packrat household as well as a cluttered brain.

I am proud to count as my influences both E. E. Smith and James Joyce; Arthur C. Clarke and John Steinbeck; Olaf Stapledon and Robert Graves; Robert Heinlein and Joseph Conrad; Ray Bradbury and Leo Tolstoy; James Blish (my God, how that man's ideas haunt me!) and Charles Dickens. And a hundred others, just as full of dichotomies . . . and many of them now, to my delight, friends and colleagues.

The writing is not easy. It's frequently hard and painful work. And I can think of no greater joy.

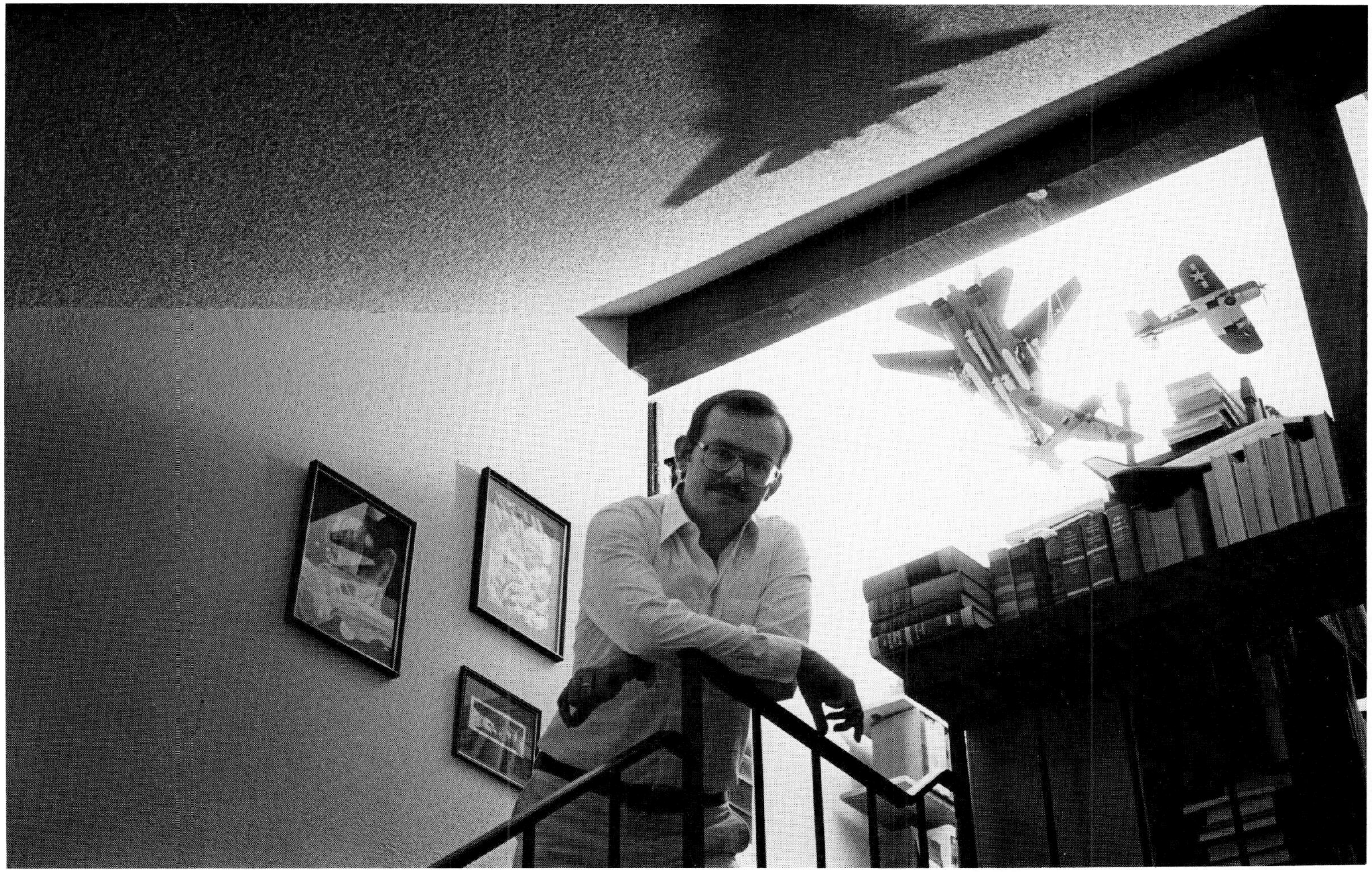

DAVID GERROLD

I get some of my best ideas by thinking up terrible things to do to the people I know. I've lost count of the number of ways I've killed my dog. (My favorite is the time I fed him alive to a giant man-eating caterpillar.) It's a great way to work off my hostilities and it makes for a high level of drama and excitement—both in my fiction and my life.

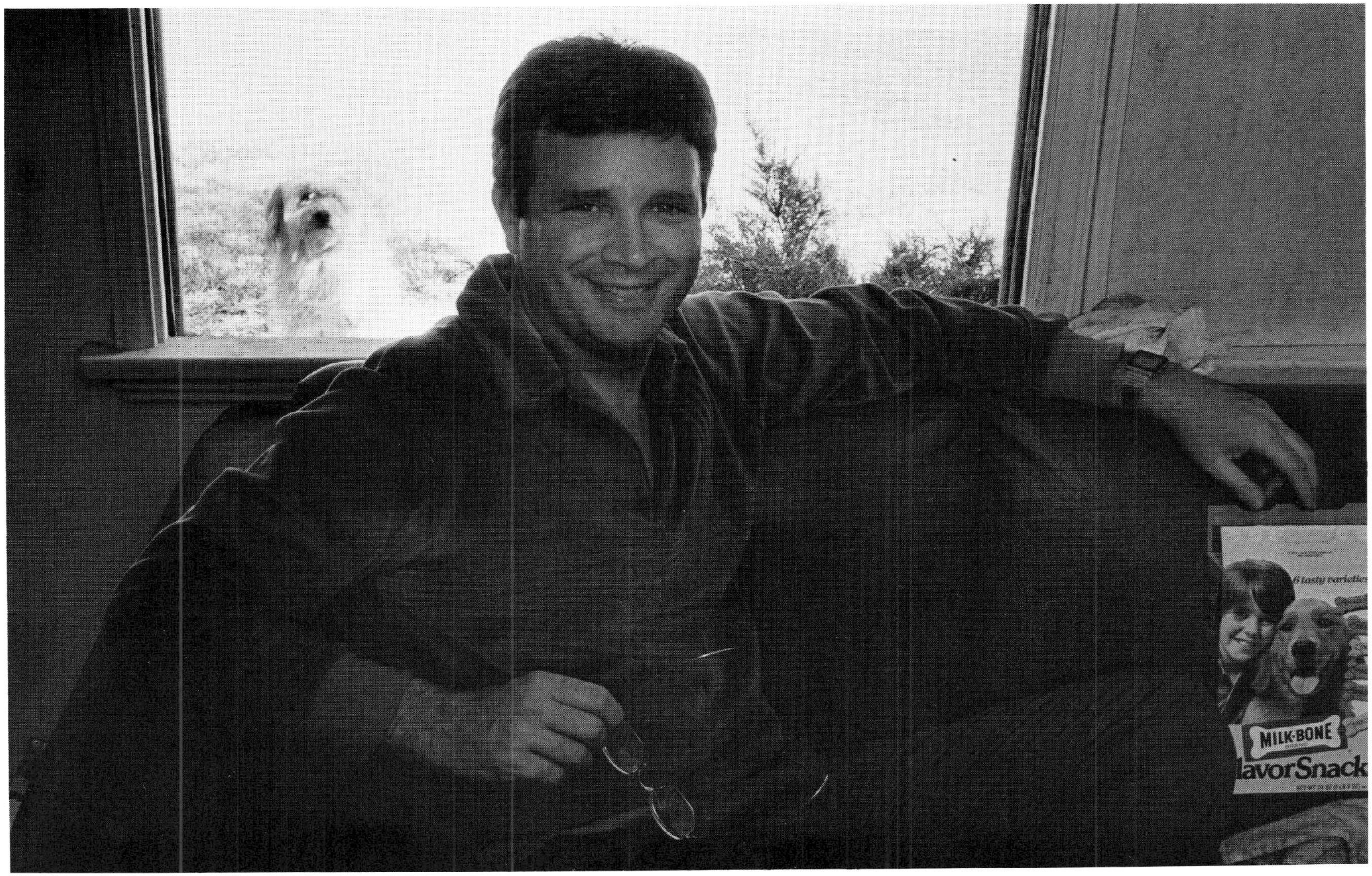
6 tasty varieties
MILK-BONE

GEORGE R. R. MARTIN

It seems funny, but after more than a dozen years of publishing stories in science fiction magazines, winning and losing science fiction awards, and attending science fiction conventions, suddenly I have people wondering if I'm leaving the field.

Well, it's true that *The Armageddon Rag* was a horror-fantasy-mystery about rock music and the 60s, and that *Fevre Dream* was about vampires on steamboats, and that neither wore the sf label. So maybe I have to plead guilty to being a writer first and an sf writer second. Still, if they want me to get out of this field, they'll have to drag me out bodily, kicking and screaming.

We're talking about love, after all, and this relationship goes back a long ways. To Robert A. Heinlein and *Have Space Suit, Will Travel,* the first novel I ever read. To Andre Norton and Eric Frank Russell and H. P. Lovecraft and all the other writers I grew up on, to the comic books and Ace Doubles that I mainlined. To all the bright dreams of childhood.

Sf gave me a career, a passion, a pasttime, a lifetime's worth of friends and lovers, a thousand treasured memories and uncounted imaginary adventures. It enriched my life and shaped it, and probably shaped my face too. I don't know if I'm an sf writer these days; I think the work is more important than the label in any event.

But I'm an sf *person,* and always will be.

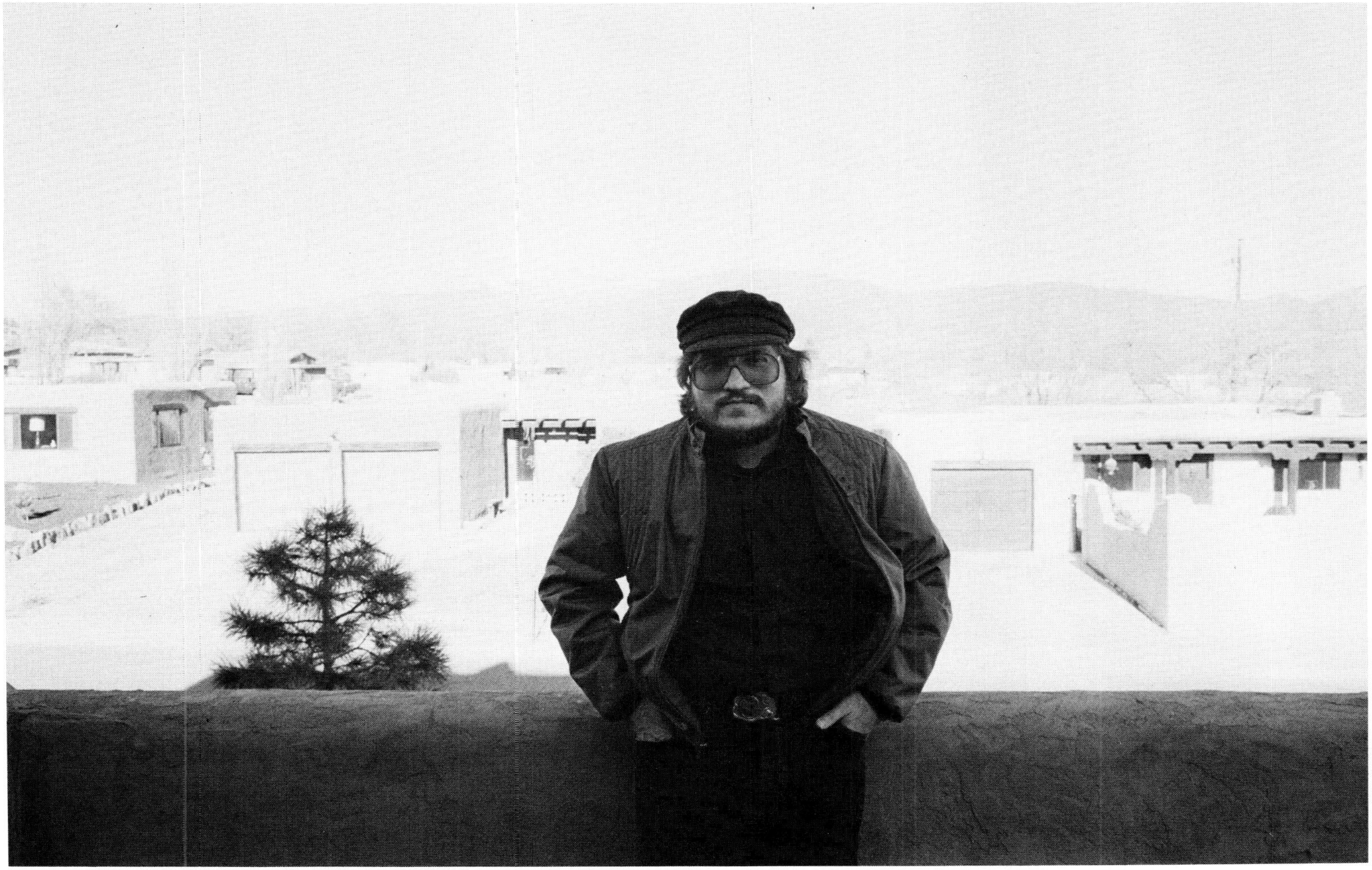

OCTAVIA E. BUTLER

I like being surrounded by books. I've made an effort to be for most of my life. When I was little I used to go to the library to do a lot of my reading and later my writing. Now I have a house filled with books.

My love of writing is an outgrowth of my love of reading. Both helped me to escape boredom, to perform thought experiments, and to deal with the daily news. I can create a world that makes more sense than this one. Or at worst, I can have a good time trying, and, in the process, give others a good read.

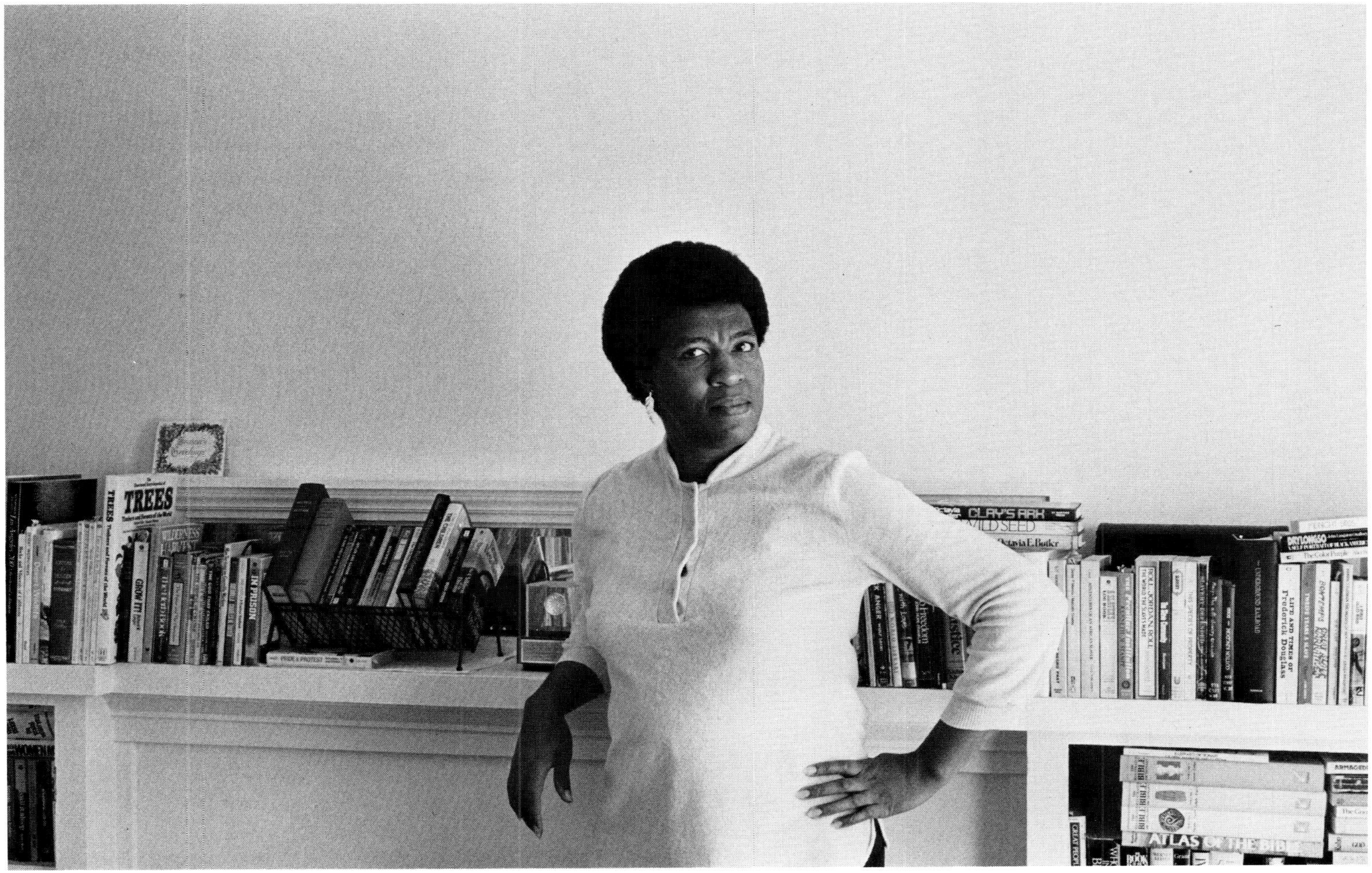
TREES
CLAY'S ARK
WILD SEED
IN PRISON
GROW IT!
LIFE AND TIMES OF Frederick Douglass
ATLAS OF THE BIBLE

JOHN VARLEY

John Varley sat down at his typewriter to write a personal statement for *The Faces Of Science Fiction.* But he decided not to.

The End.

This is the shortest fiction I ever wrote.

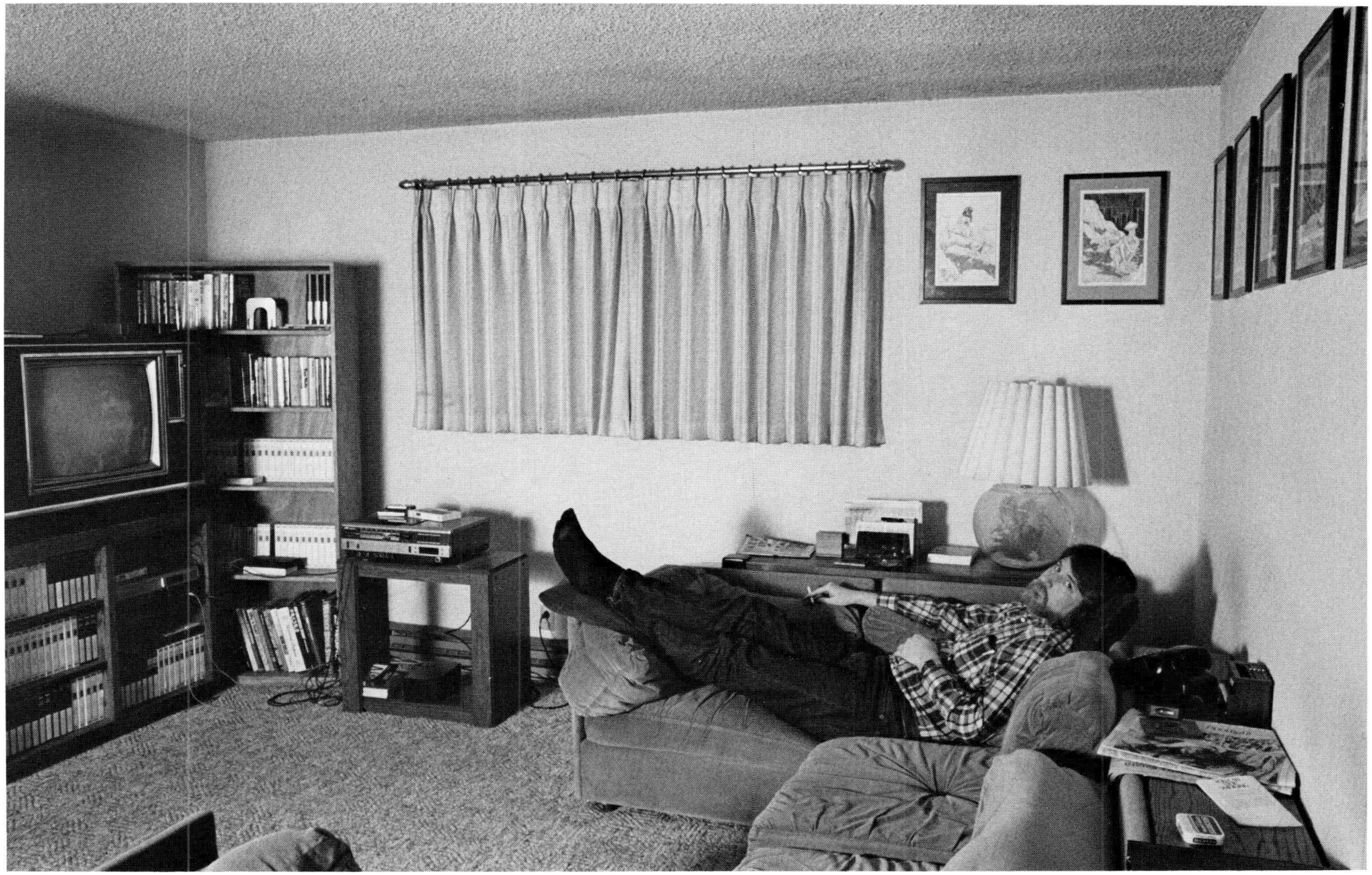

EDWARD BRYANT

At first I was planning to write a statement in the clever guise of an epitaph—just in case this book lasted longer than the subject of the photograph. That statement could never date.

A friend astutely pointed out that I would merely muddy the waters by convincing the vast group of readers who have never met me that I was in fact dead, and thus whatever fuzzy professional image of me was lurking in their bookstore-browsing frontal lobes would be further obscured. Not good for name recognition. Even worse for convincing folks to read my stories and books.

So I'll admit it. I'm not dead yet. I'm a dedicated writer who was born three weeks to the day after the first nuclear attack, who can't get the vast open spaces of the American West out of his soul (and who doesn't want to), and who loves rock 'n' roll, dinosaurs, and movies.

As long as I live, I'll probably confuse people, since I'm an essentially serious person whose profoundly silly streak seems to throw some observers off. Do I sound unhappy about that? I'm not complaining.

Writing is an intrinsically risky business, a wearing, draining task. Admittedly I sometimes feel the nagging suspicion that I won't be able to keep up the storyteller's trade forever. My consolation is the knowledge that I do what I do because it's precisely what I want. If there were something I'd rather attempt than write, then I'd do it.

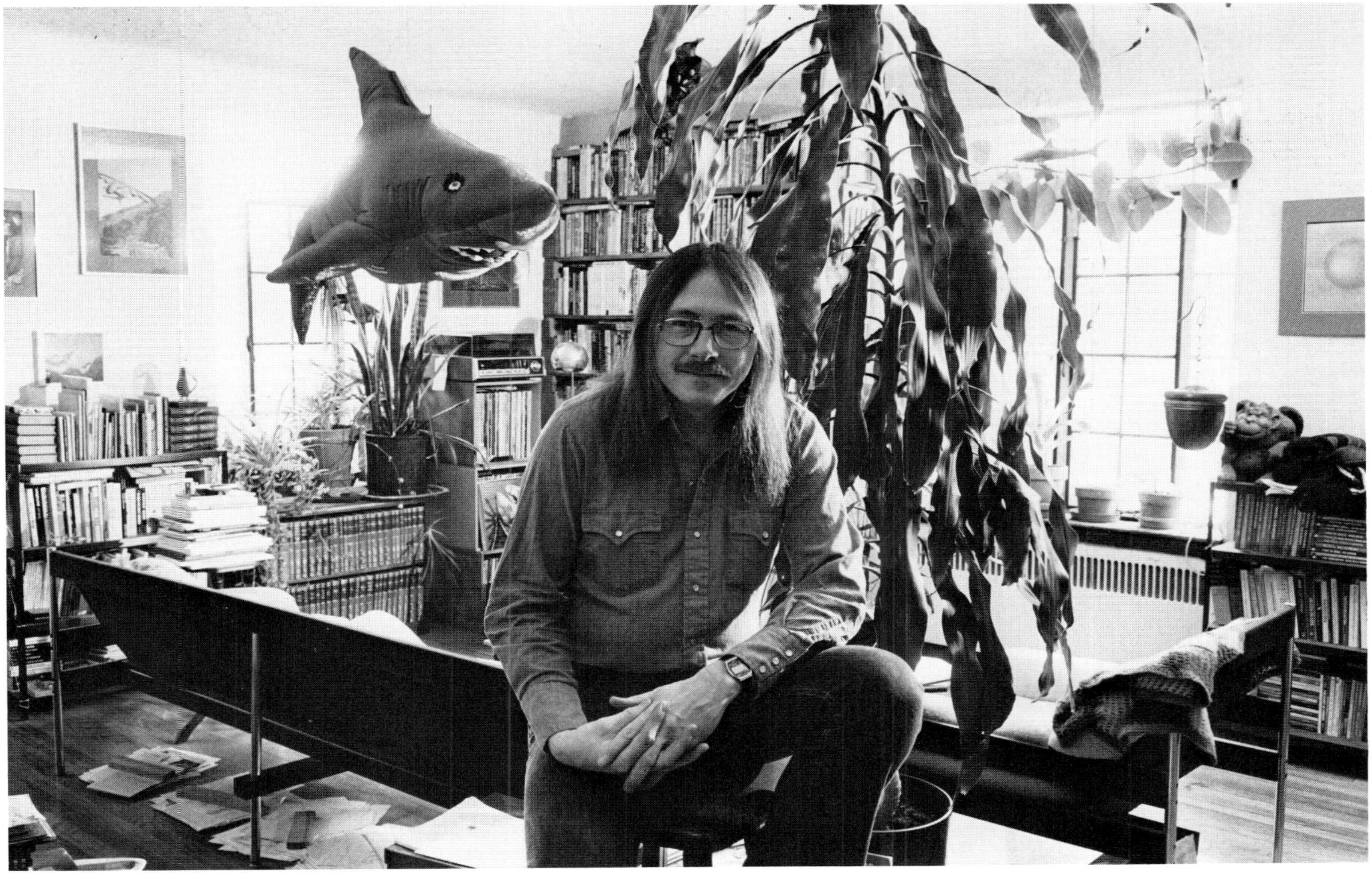

ALAN DEAN FOSTER

Talkin' 'bout what it's all about: perspective.

One person standing tall on a tiny insignificant world circling a minor grade star drifting aimlessly among a hundred million others that together comprise only one of a billion galaxies. Science fiction brings that whole grand, gallumphing universe home to you. The end result is that you know your place in the Cosmos, which means it's hard to take anything too seriously. You laugh a lot.

Talkin' 'bout what it's all about: immortality.

Mayflies live a life in a day. Sequoias squat in one spot and watch the world pass them by for fifty centuries. Stars live lives in the billions of years. Science fiction holds within its pages all time and lets you know you're not going to be around long enough to do anything the universe is going to take note of anyway. The end result is that you don't worry about death. You love a lot.

Talkin' 'bout what it's all about: freedom.

Why write about what's going on in a Connecticut bedroom when you have the whole Cosmos to explore? When you can meet folks who don't exist, visit worlds that might, and exchange political views within something that sees over into the infrared? Science fiction lets you extrapolate on everything now, past and forever. You live a lot.

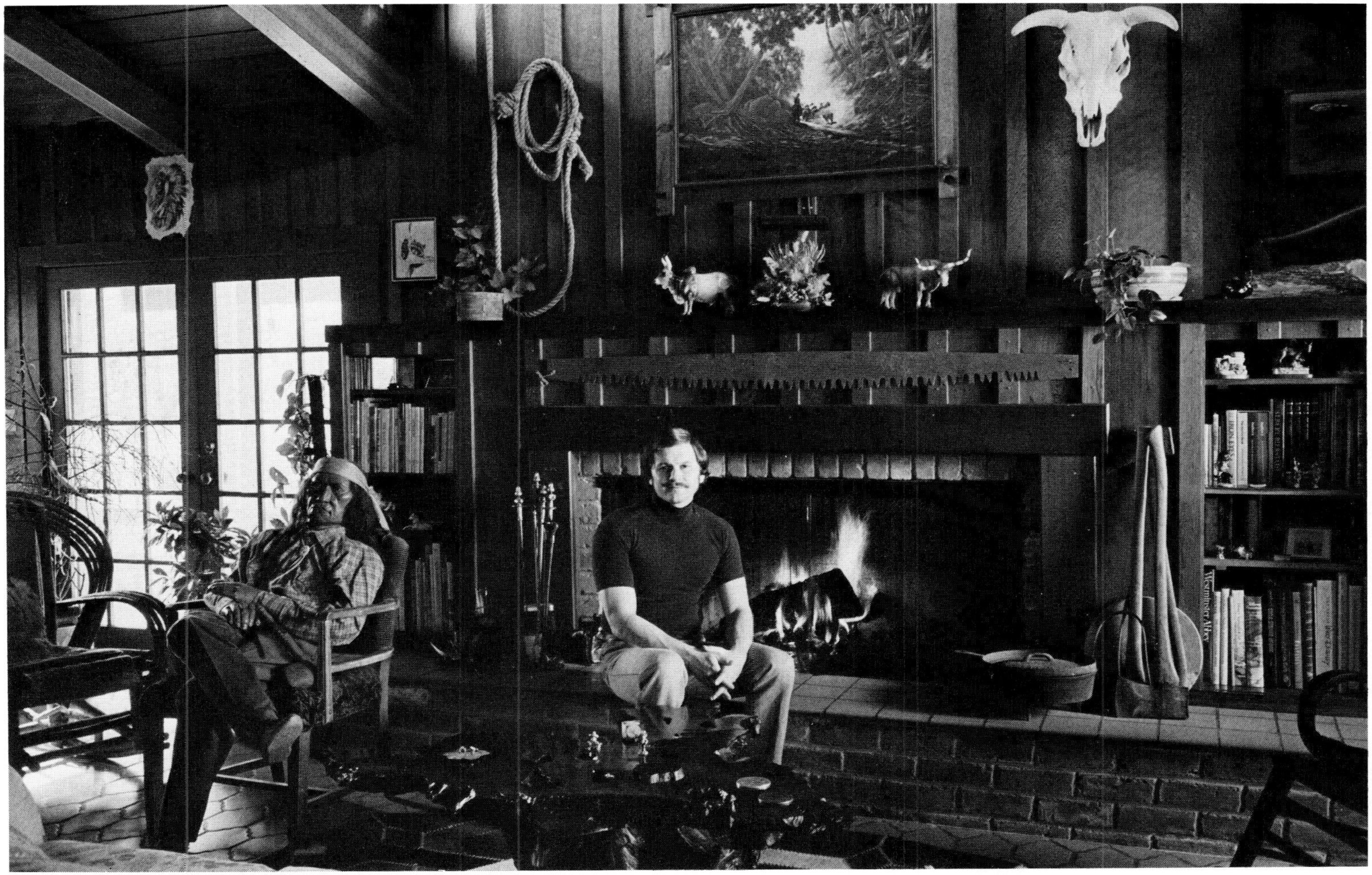

JULIAN MAY

First and foremost I'm an entertainer, a teller of tall and grotesque and marvelous tales. My stuff is melodrama; Puccini could have set it to music. What you get from my books is bizarre futurism, violence, sneaky mythic analogs, sex, humor, teleology, and thundering action. I love that kind of science fiction. I wish there was more of it around today.

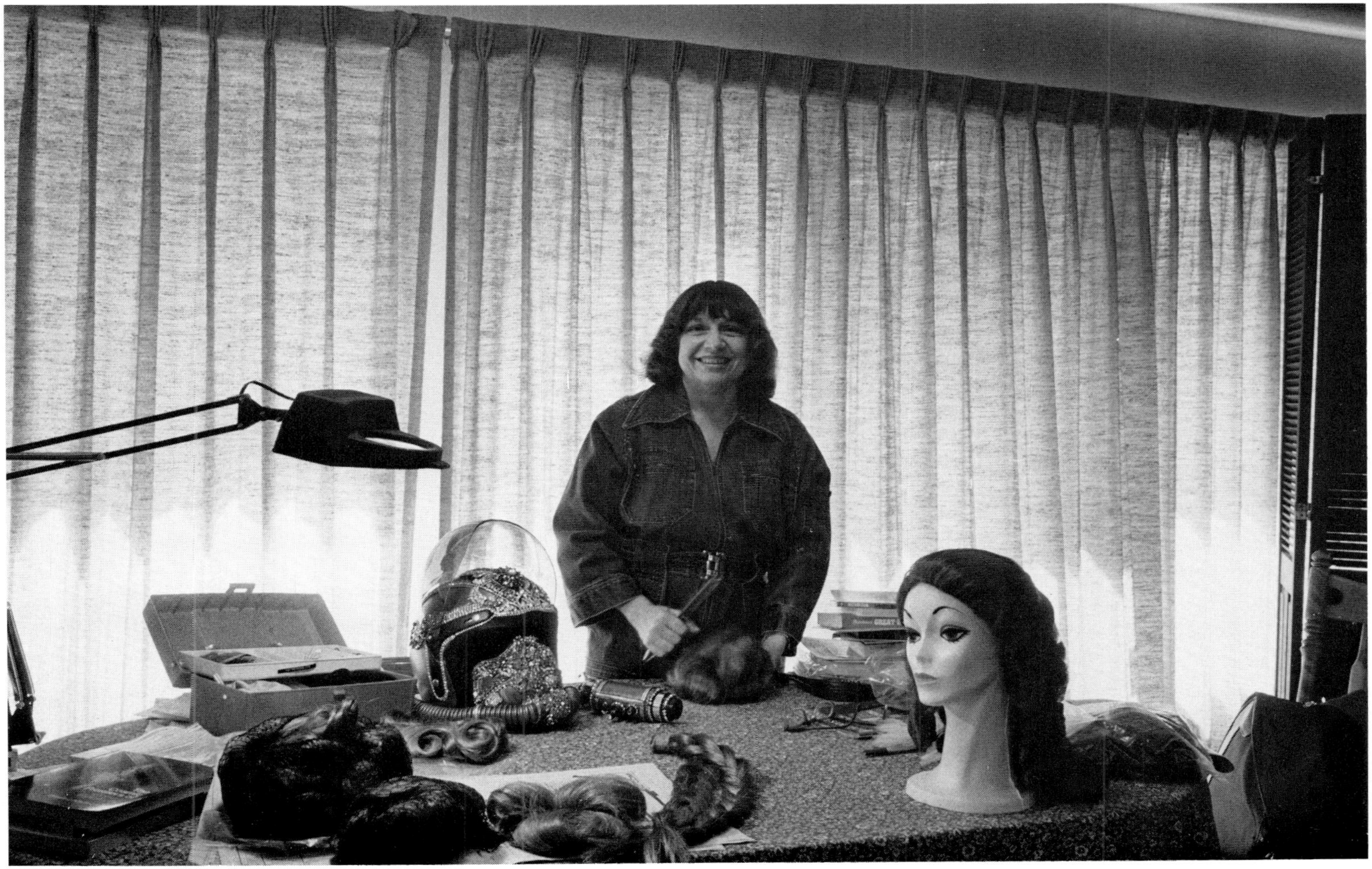

JERRY POURNELLE

The late Richard McKenna once described meetings of science fiction writers as trapper's conventions: those who have never been out in the great alone, can't possibly understand why those odd people act so strangely when they get together. The truth is that writing is the solitary vice *par excellence.* Writers spend so much of their time alone in a room with no company but characters of their own creation. This is enough to render many normal writers unfit for social intercourse; imagine the effect on writers whose creatures are often not even human.

McKenna believed that those who've been part of this craft have more similarities than differences.

I suppose there are exceptions, but he had hold of a truth. Perhaps it will show in your picture. Perhaps not. In any event, it's about time someone preserved the images of a generation of fantastic tale spinners—but the very fact that such a book can exist also shows just where this business has got to go.

We've become respectable again, after a long dry spell. If fame and fortune don't ruin us, I expect the embrace of academia will. Suffering is said to be good for art. It's odd how many artists agree to that proposition, and how few of us prefer deprivation.

We've had our ups and downs before. I feel fortunate to have been on an upswing.

Ours is an old profession. It certainly goes back at least as far as the times when bards would wander up to a warrior encampment and say, "If you'll fill my bowl with some of that stew, I'll tell you of a place where men can fly; and if you fill my cup with wine, I'll tell you a story about a virgin and a bull . . ."

Salud!

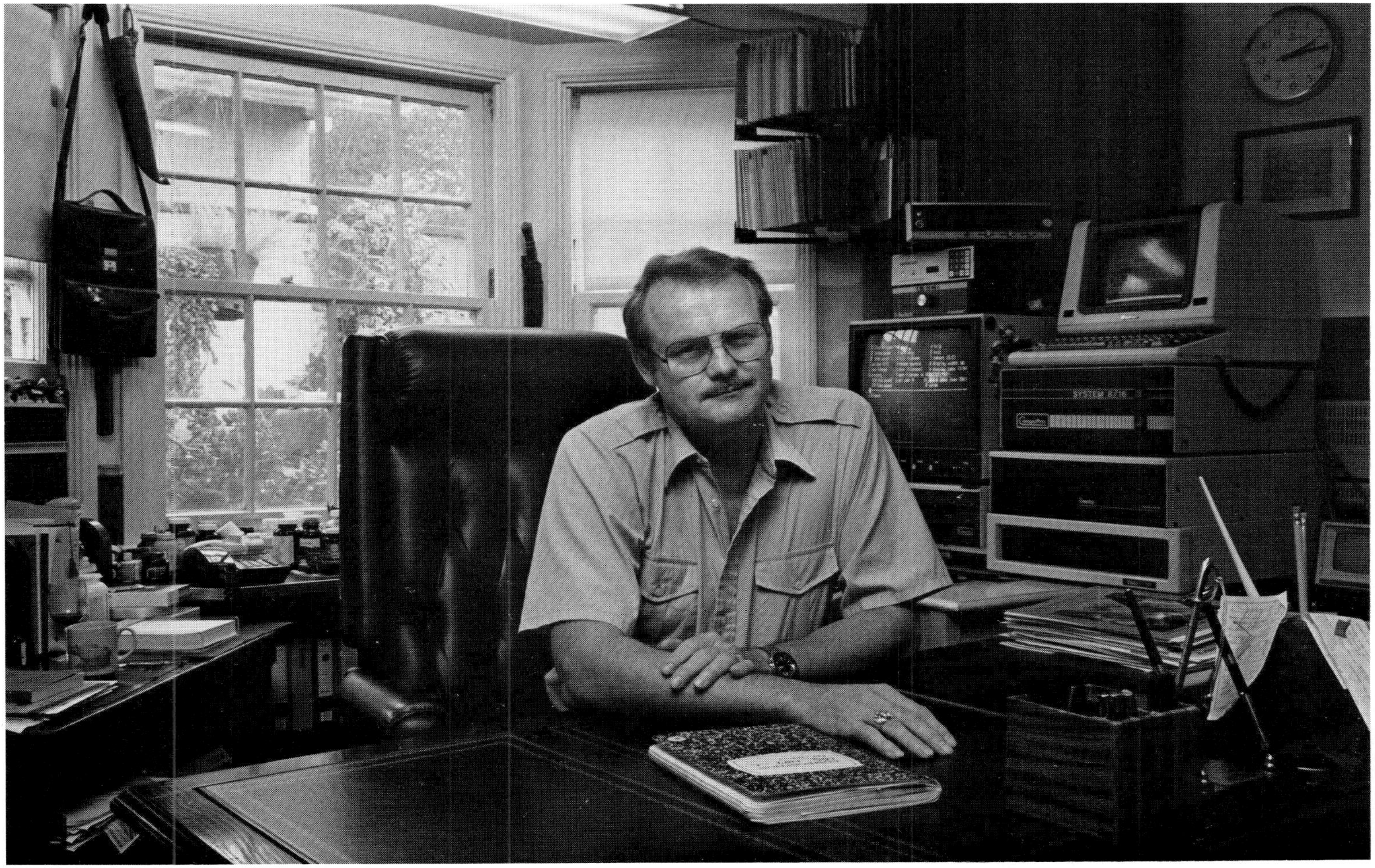
SYSTEM 8/16

KEITH LAUMER

Life is so inexhaustibly marvelous that no one could possibly learn to fully appreciate it in just one lifetime. For that reason I'm going to take at least two. You may check with me on June 9, 2065, my 140th birthday.

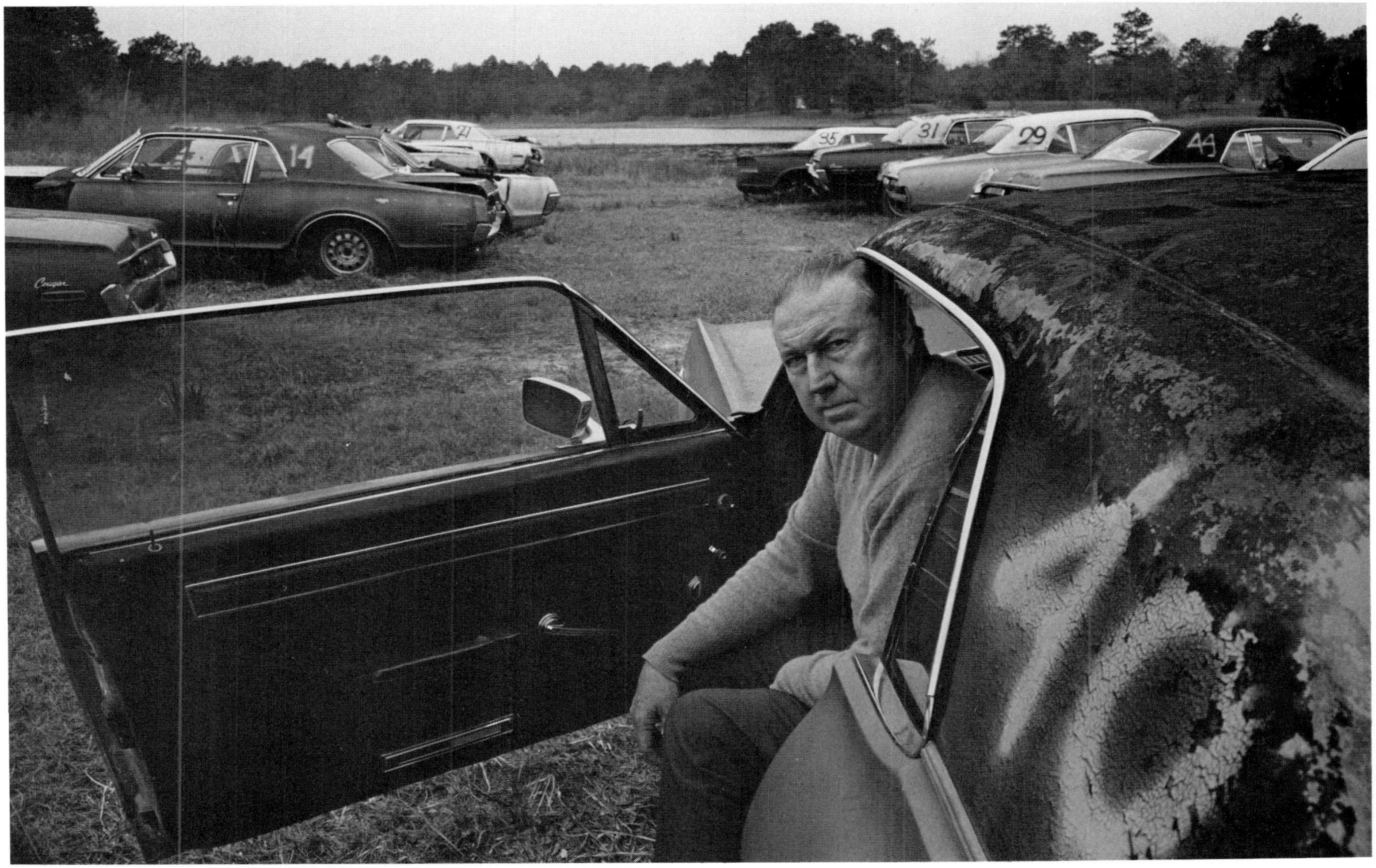
14
31
29

LARRY NIVEN

NIVEN'S LAWS

To the best I've been able to tell in forty-six years of observation, this is how the universe works. I hope I didn't leave anything out.

1) Never throw shit at an armed man.

Never stand next to someone who is throwing shit at an armed man.

You wouldn't think anyone would need to be told this. Does anyone remember the Democratic National Convention of 1968?

2) Never fire a laser at a mirror.

3) Mother Nature doesn't care if you're having fun.

4) FS = k. Freedom times Security = constant. If you expect more freedom of thought and/or action, you must give up some security, and vice versa. These remarks apply to individuals, nations, and civilizations. Notice that the constant is different for every civilization and different for any individual.

5) Psi powers, if real, are nearly useless. Over the lifetime of the human species we would otherwise have done something with them.

6) *Niven's Law for Musicians:* If the applause wasn't louder than the music, something's wrong. Play better or softer.

7) The immortal poets always understand the most active science of their day. Today's potential poets—the ones with a dilettante's grasp of today's sciences—are seduced into writing science fiction. In another age they would write both. Kipling did. Dante wrote the first hard science fiction novel, in verse!

8) Any damn fool can predict the past.

NIVEN'S LAWS FOR WRITERS

1) Never be embarrassed or ashamed by anything you choose to write.

2) Writers who write for other writers should write letters.

3) It is a sin to waste the reader's time.

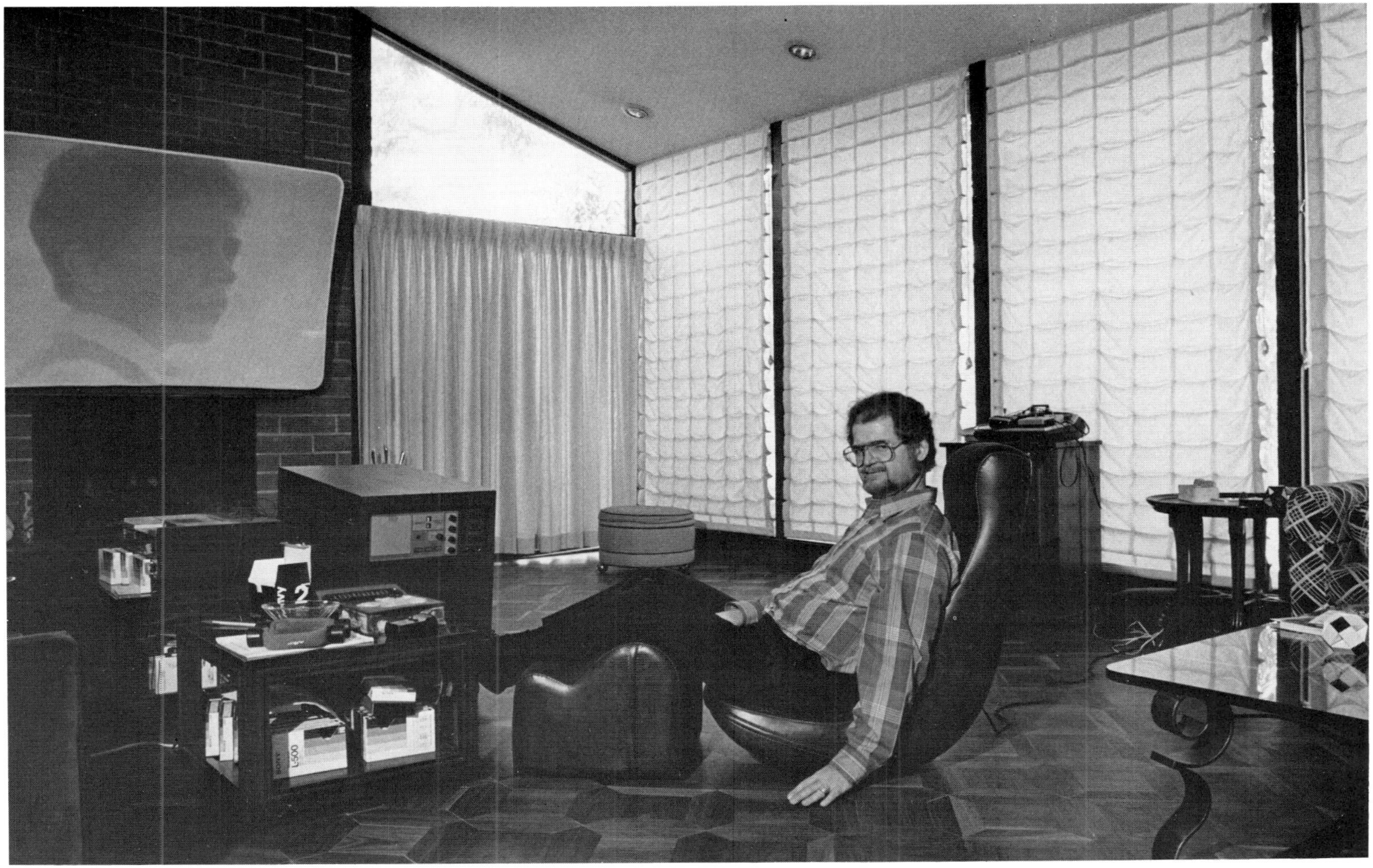

DEAN ING

I sold a few pieces in the 1950s and then quit for twenty years to try things that proved lovely grist for more writing: engineering; development and test of sports-racing cars and survival gear; behavioral sciences; the professorial life; solo backpacking; parenting; model aircraft. Sometimes I enjoy writing more than these other things, but other times I waver . . .

From all this, I collected biases toward "hard" science fiction, adventure, and research to bolster plots and settings. I used to tell undergrads, "If you can talk knowledgeably for ten hours on a topic, you might risk doing it in public for *one* hour." To me, that goes for writing fiction, too.

Much of my work reveals a cheerful outlook toward those who learn to take risks intelligently. I believe that spacefaring is the smartest gamble this nation can ever take; and speculation is the way we copper our bets. It's time that all academicians recognized that *mere* and *speculation* are not irrevocably joined at the spine.

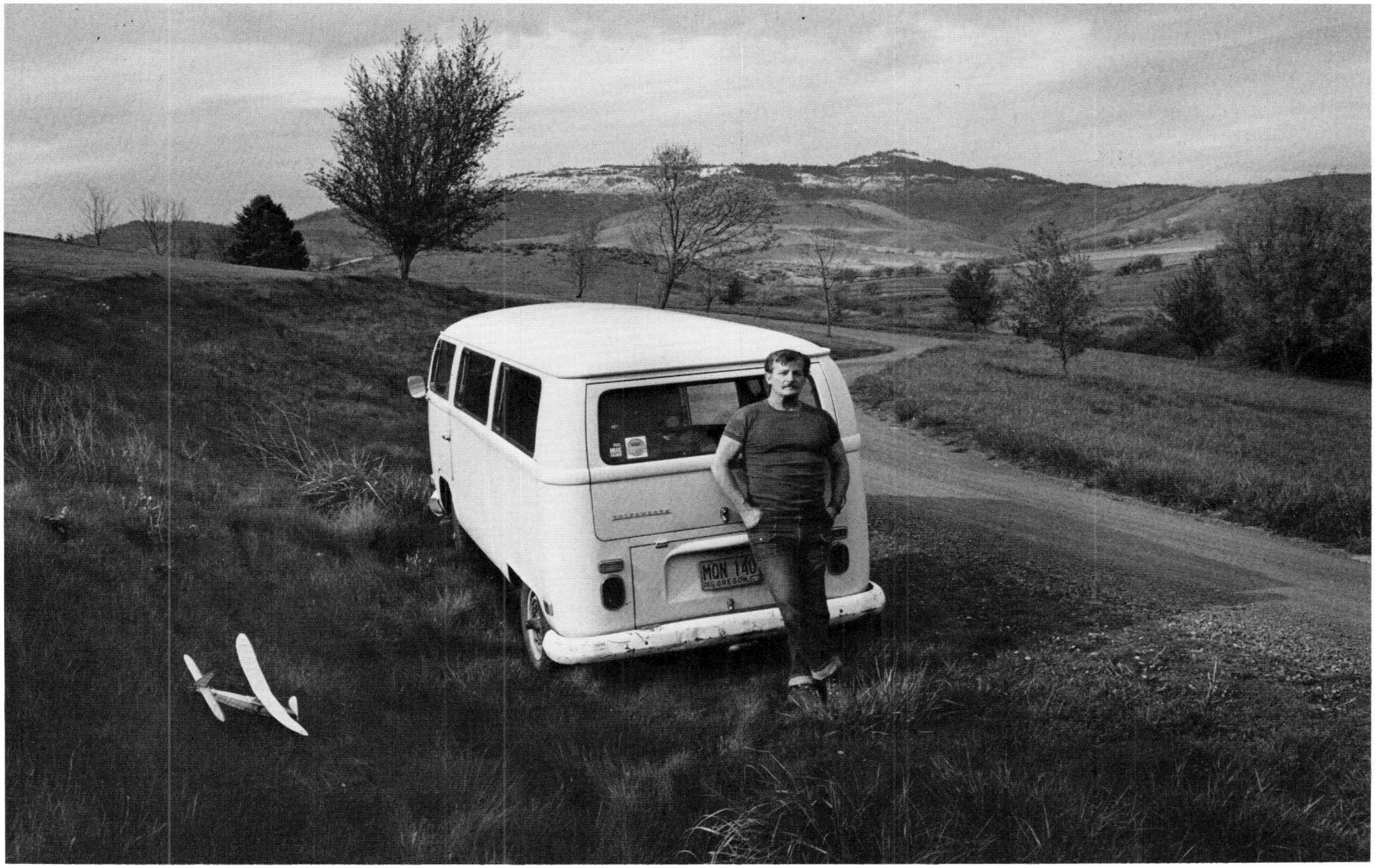
MON 140

JACK L. CHALKER

Getting a professional novelist to say anything in just two hundred words is a real problem, but I'll try it.

I consider myself one of the really fortunate people, able to make a very good living by doing just what I enjoy doing most, which is story telling. I write the kind of books I liked to read as a fan, and because I tend to write quite fast and have a lot of stories to tell I try to get as much variety in my writing as possible, doing serious political and social books one time, satire another, sheer fun comedy, and fast adventure. Story and characterization come first, but I dislike being pigeonholed into any thematic categories—light, heavy, serious, and tongue-in-cheek keep variety in my own work and keep it from becoming boring and repetitious either to me or, I hope, to my readers. My degrees and teaching background are in the social sciences, so that tends to come out strongly in my work.

At any rate, it's been very successful and allowed me to sleep late, choose my own vacations, and support my primary editor, my wife Eva Whitley, a son, a temperamental Pekingese and a 17 pound tomcat who eats his weight every day in a comfortable manner, and it's a fun way of life.

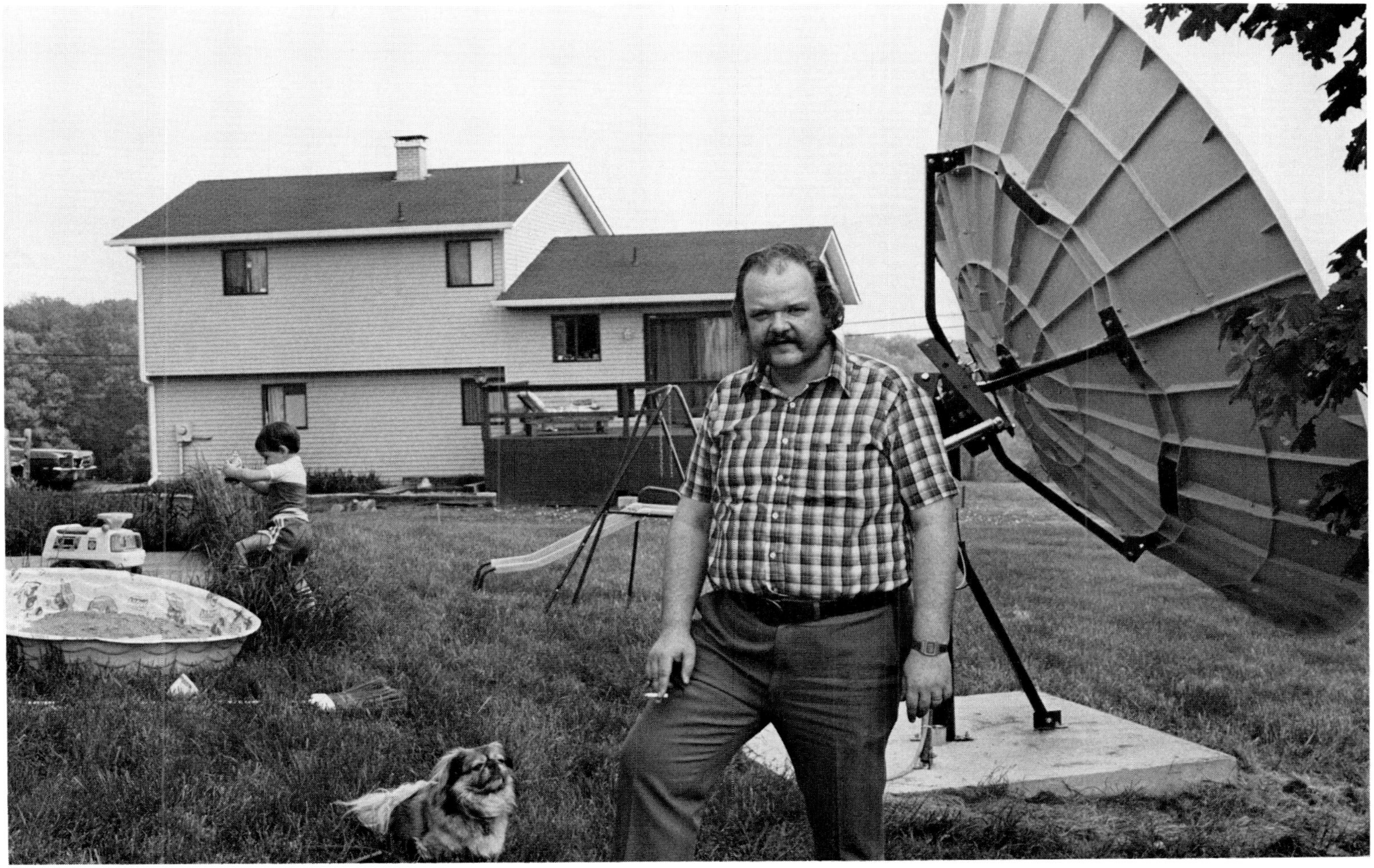

ROBERT BLOCH

What am I doing in this book?

True, I've written science fiction. That is to say perhaps a hundred or so of my stories have first appeared in science fiction magazines, then seen reprint in anthologies under the science fiction label.

But several hundred other stories have been published as dark fantasy or supernatural horror, and a sizeable number—including many books—deal with mystery and psychological suspense. Aside from a few *Star Trek* episodes the same holds true for my radio work, television scripts and screenplays. And my Hugo Award was bestowed on a deal-with-the-devil fantasy which had nothing more to do with science fiction than my new Jack the Ripper novel.

So what am I doing in this book—surrounded by portraits of authentic science fiction writers with genuine credentials and real beards?

Maybe it's because for the past 50 years I've been a science fiction fan, writing for fanzines, attending and offending science fiction conventions. Possibly these activities serve as qualifications; there's apt to be a wild card in every deck.

Science fiction writers are frequently described as members of one big family. If so, then I'm an illegitimate son.

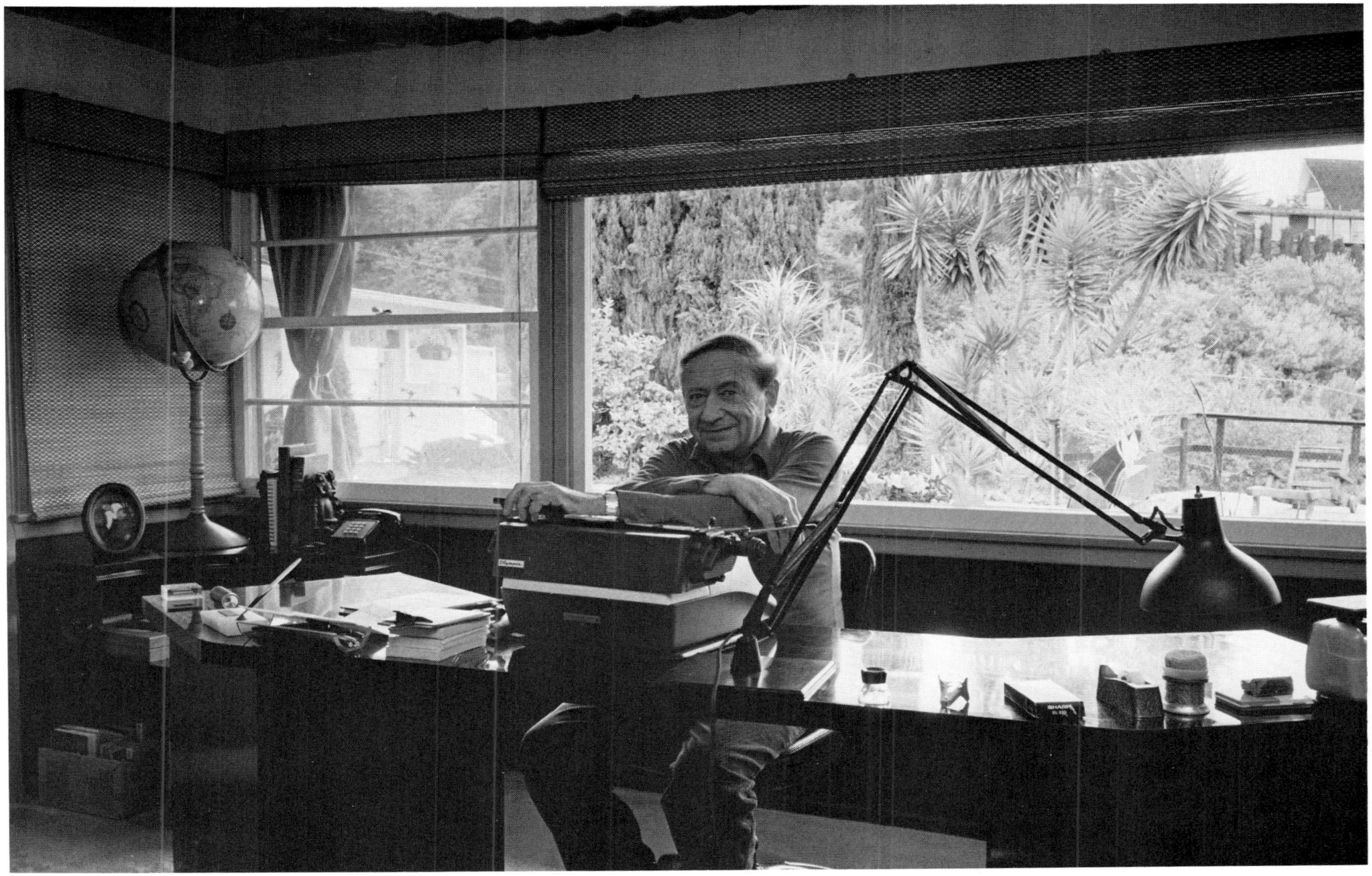

FREDERIK POHL

Science fiction is the name given to a lot of old pulp magazines, some thousands of books, a handful of blockbuster movies and television programs and scores of trashy ones—and a way of life. When I was ten years old, I began to read science fiction, when I was twelve to write it. Ever since then it has been what I have done with my life, in one form or another: writer, editor, lecturer, occasionally teacher, always reader.

What science fiction is about is change, and change is the central fact of life for all of us inhabiting this planet now. The people who read science fiction are by and large the most alert and forethoughtful group of human beings in the world. There are clods among them, to be sure, and maybe even one or two villains. But if there is a hope for humanity, I think it lies among those who have contributed to or learned from science fiction. I've spent my life among them, and I wouldn't have it any other way.

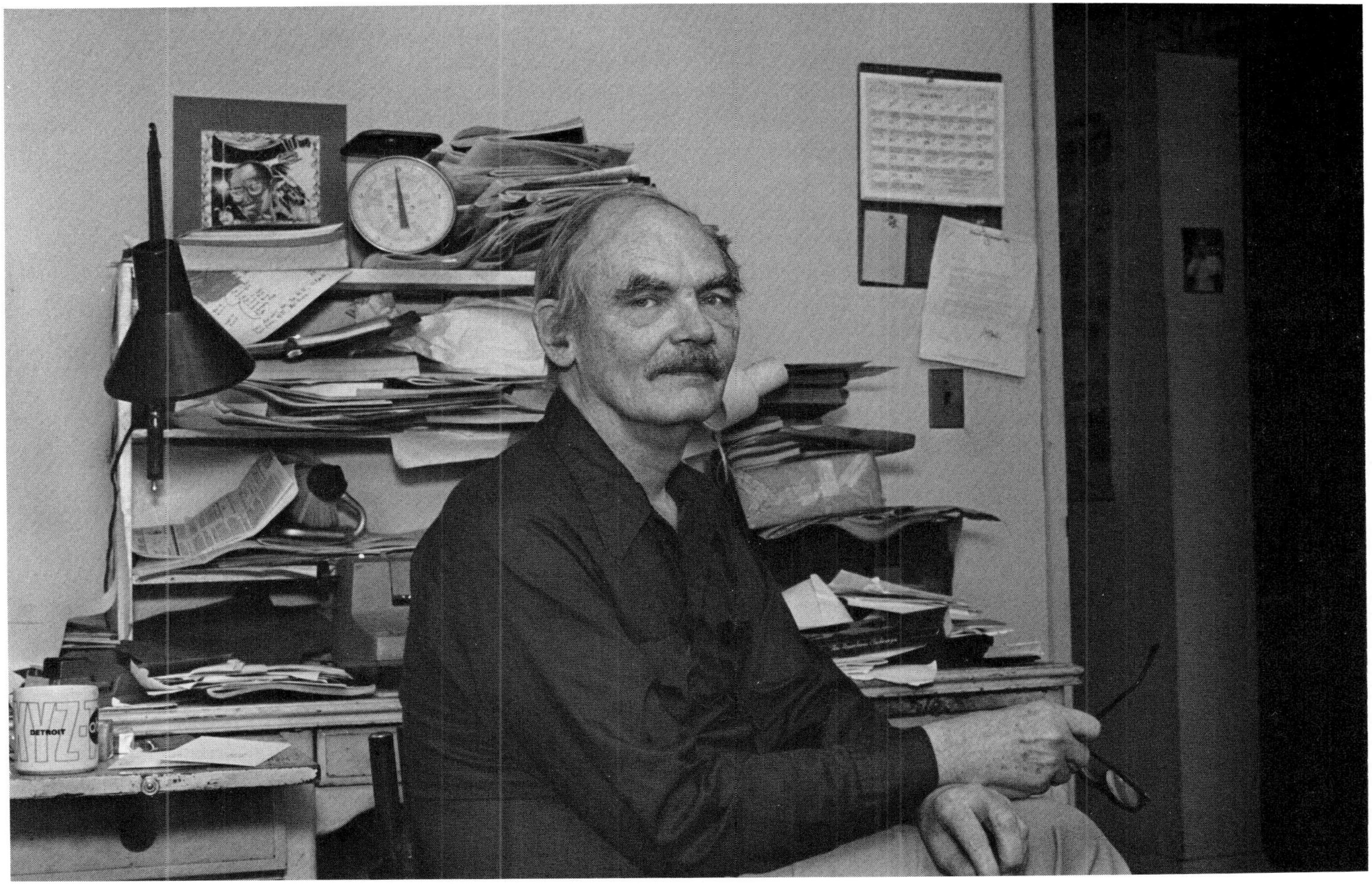
DETROIT

JAMES GUNN

Science fiction has a peculiar hold on its readers. It turns people into fans and fans into would-be writers; it changes people's lives. It did that for me.

I first encountered science fiction in my grandmother's closet. It was in the form of Edgar Rice Burroughs' *Tarzan* novels that one or another of my uncles had read and put away. They weren't quite science fiction, but they were enough like it to start me on a quest for more such reading experiences. I would discover the Burroughs Martian and Pellucidar books much later, because the Kansas City public library didn't think them respectable enough to add to its collections. Instead I went on to the hero-pulp magazines that were, along with library books by the dozens, the major form of entertainment for our family during the Depression years of the early 1930's. Some of them were like science fiction, but they were not quite the real stuff, and I discovered this when I found a used magazine shop in which I could trade two of my pulp magazines for one of those with the colorful covers from the dusty stacks at the back: *Amazing Stories, Wonder Stories, Astounding Stories of Super Science.* Later, at the end of the 1930's, I would become enthralled, all over again, by the adventure fantasies reprinted from the old Munsey pulp magazines in *Famous Fantastic Mysteries.*

My father's father was a printer and a country editor, who also taught primary school, read law, and wrote verse. My father and several uncles were associated with printing in one capacity or another. So I came to writing naturally, though not without detours, and when I had the opportunity to write, just as naturally, I wrote science fiction. I had written a great many other kinds of things before I sat down one day to write a science-fiction story. *Thrilling Wonder Stories* bought it, and I was a writer. I was never to be quite the same again. Since then I have sold eighty other stories and twenty-five books. I have done other things as well, edited paperback books and magazines, written speeches, directed public relations for a major state university, and taught fiction writing and science fiction, as I do now, at the University of Kansas. I keep writing because when I am writing I feel more like myself and the world is a happier place.

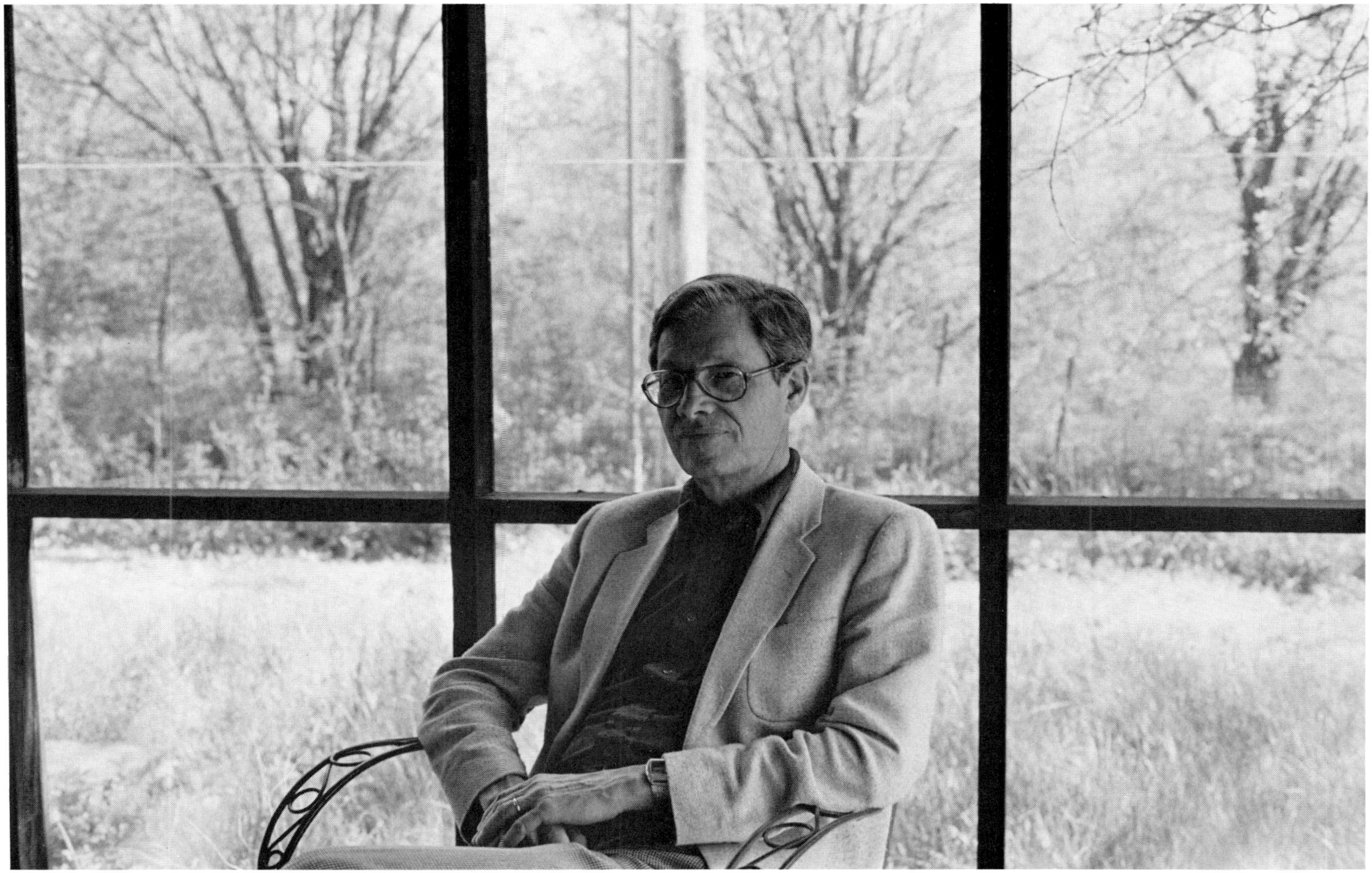

MANLY WADE WELLMAN

I wanted to write from when I began to read. At six, I scribbled little stories, fantasies, not very remarkable. Born in Angola of missionary parents, I heard strange tales from the people there, later in rural America I heard more. My relatives, teachers and schoolmates didn't see why I wrote such things, said I must be crazy, that I'd never succeed. I kept on anyway, began to sell when I was in college and, jobless at the bottom of the depression, got published in science fiction and adventure pulps. I've written ever since. In my eighty-first year, I write books and stories to speak of the wonder that is in mankind's deepest thought and soul. I've done more than seventy-five books, more than five hundred magazine and story articles, several highly realistic mainstream novels, a number of juveniles, but chiefly science fiction and fantasy. It's my way of life. It partakes, I think, of outlawry—anyway, it's living by your wits. I'll keep at it, in the lonesome valley where a writer must write, until I can't anymore. It's better than sitting with your feet up, waiting for nothing to happen.

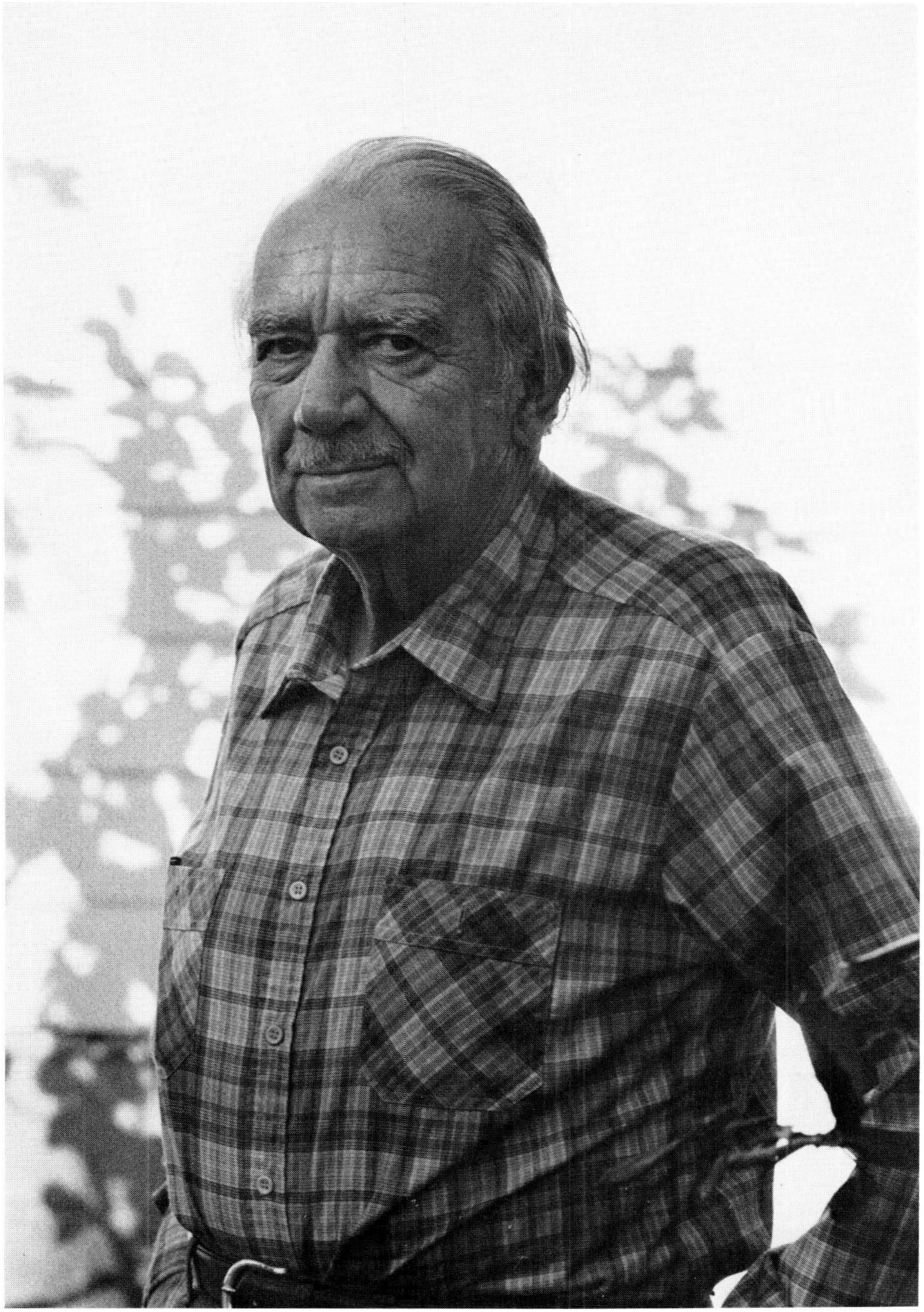

WILSON TUCKER

I live in a small town but despite the popular misconceptions about such places, it is probable that less than a hundred people know who I am or what I do. At home I live quietly, write slowly, publish infrequently.

My ego is content with all that.

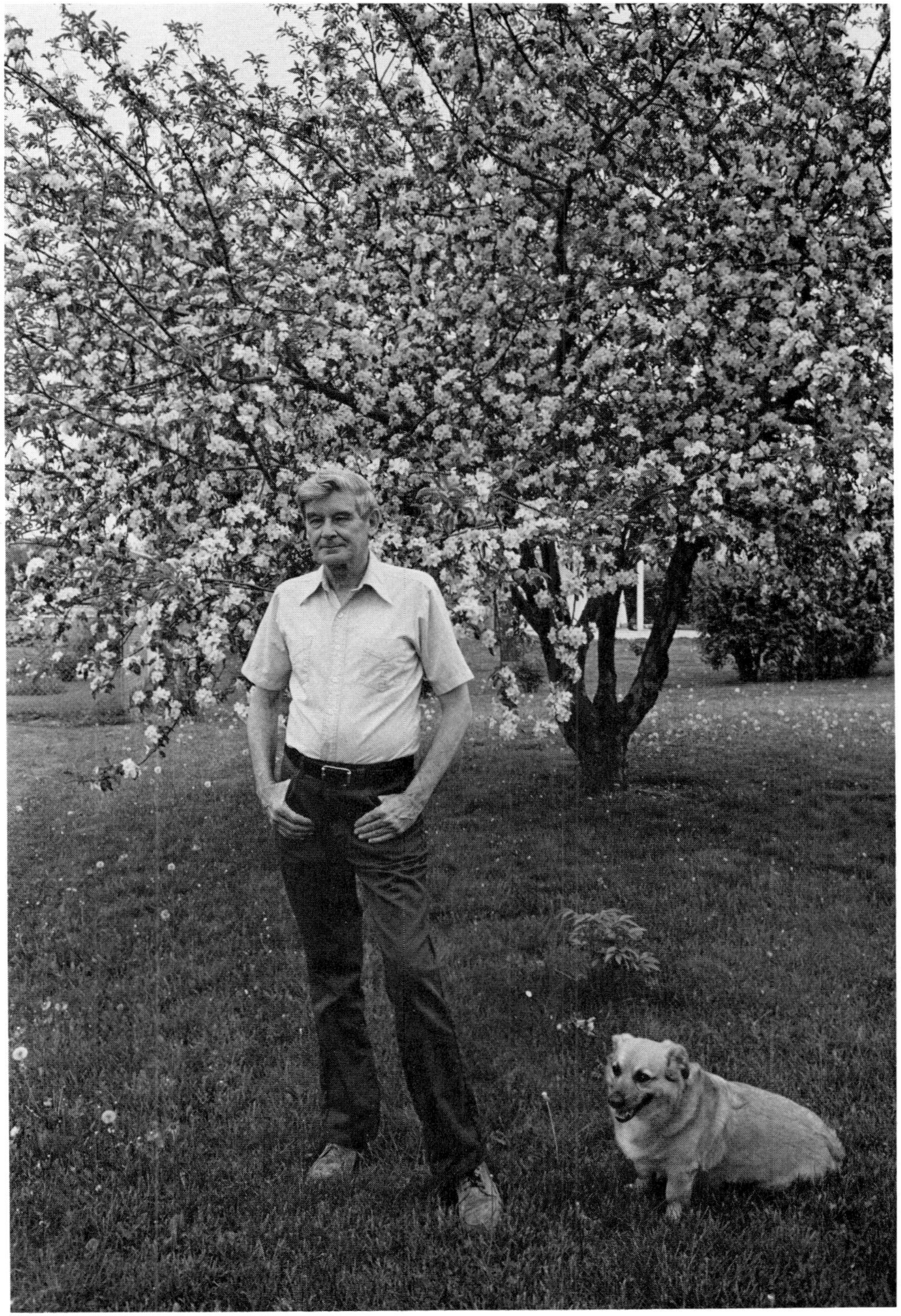

JEFFREY A. CARVER

If literature is a mirror to the human spirit, then science fiction is a funhouse mirror, reflecting the human endeavor with tricky illuminations and truths masquerading as shadows.

Writing science fiction is a curious process, being both a passion and an intellectual challenge, forever dealing with ambiguities and uncertainties, and yet constrained by the rules of logic. Characters and ideas spill from life, arising like ghosts out of the mysteries of science and humanity and creation, only to be tamed by the craft of the writer.

Once created, characters may move in strange ways, their paths and purposes guided by the laws of the world in which they are placed. It is in the nature of the brew that ideas and characters, bubbling together, often produce unexpected results. Picture the storyteller, peering at reality through a flask of glowing, effervescent liquids, ready at a blink to transmute or explode. In the instant of magic there may come glimpses of bewildering images, or illuminations as startling as the twists of a new romance or a friendship, and as rewarding.

It is the rewards of this sort that keep me writing, hoping always for another glimpse of those visions.

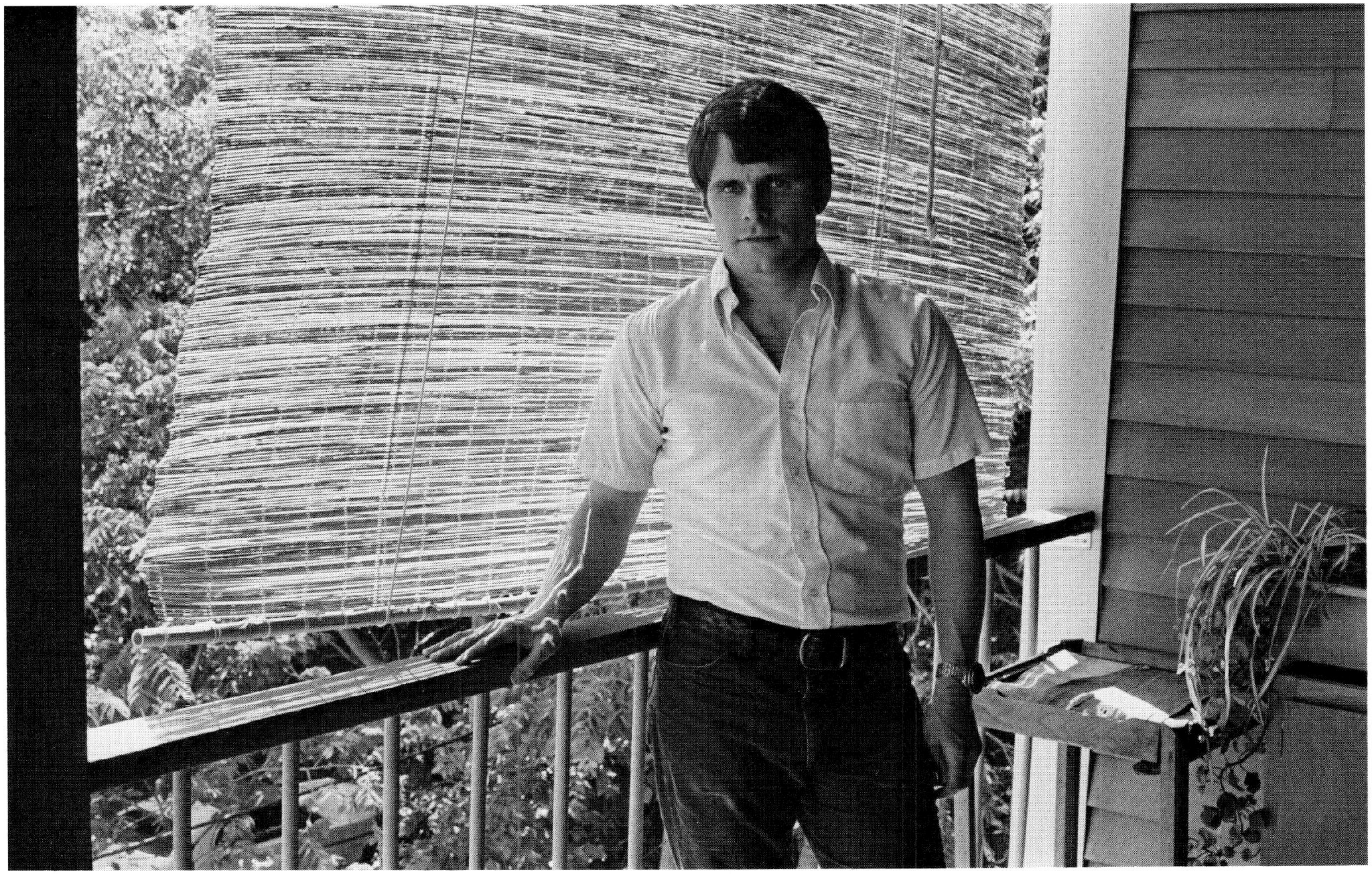

GORDON R. DICKSON

My mother not only read to me a great deal, when I was young; she recited endless stories and poems. And my learning to read began with my holding a book and pretending to read, while reciting from memory the words I had heard when it had been read to me. From this to actually associating the words on the page with the words I was speaking was a natural evolution. By the time I was six years old, I was making up my own stories and announcing that I intended to write books. No one told me at that time that this was anything but a good idea. The result was that by the accident of sheer luck, I was unconsciously starting to plan my life by the time I entered first grade. For fifty-four years I have not deviated from that plan.

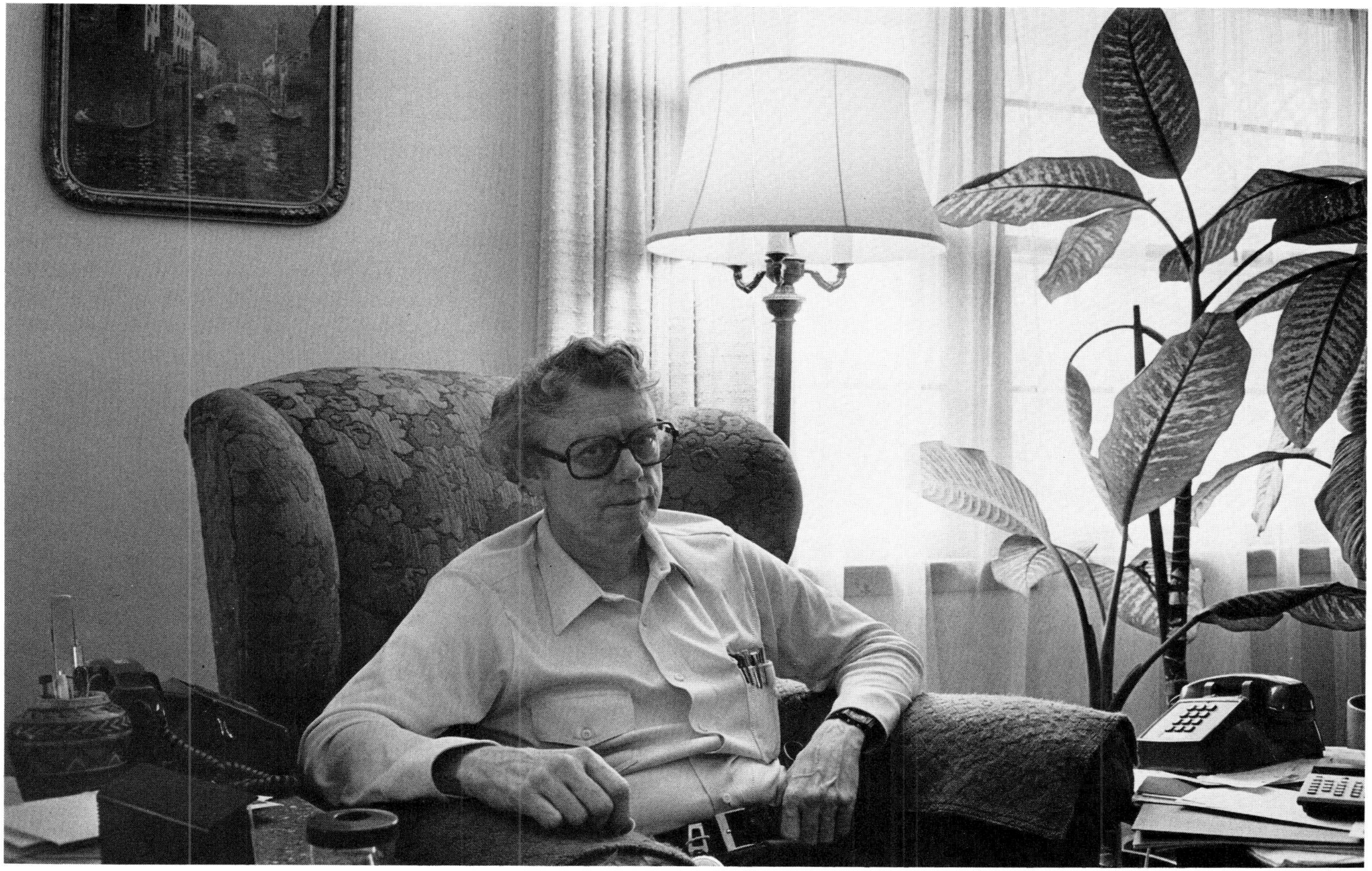

POUL ANDERSON

Camped high on a mountain, from my sleeping bag I look out at the stars. Out, not up; they are everywhere around this planet. Knowing their vastness and what immensities reach among them, knowing that they are nuclear furnaces and that older suns long gone have forged the stuff of our bodies, makes them infinitely wonderful and beautiful to me.

The eyesight of a friend is failing so badly that now he cannot read print. However, he is getting a scanner which will project text onto a large screen and so let him back into the world of books.

I was there when a ship departing for the moon filled night with radiance, thunder, and glory.

In the beasts of the field we see our kin; the very grass is of our own lineage.

Toil throughout our waking hours, in order to scrape out a bare and precarious living, has become unnecessary.

We are, at the most, only some hours' travel from anyone we love.

The left mastoid bone lies near the speech center of the brain. In a few years after a persistent infection had set in, death would have been the least unpleasant possibility before me. Surgery with precision instruments under a special microscope removed the danger.

Now that their writings have been deciphered, people dust these thousands of years are speaking to us.

We, who thought we understood the atom, are finding mystery within mystery—endless challenge.

The day is not so very far off when no child need ever again be born defective.

The greatest musicians play my beloved Bach for me in my living room.

Intellectuals assure us that modern science and technology are dehumanizing.

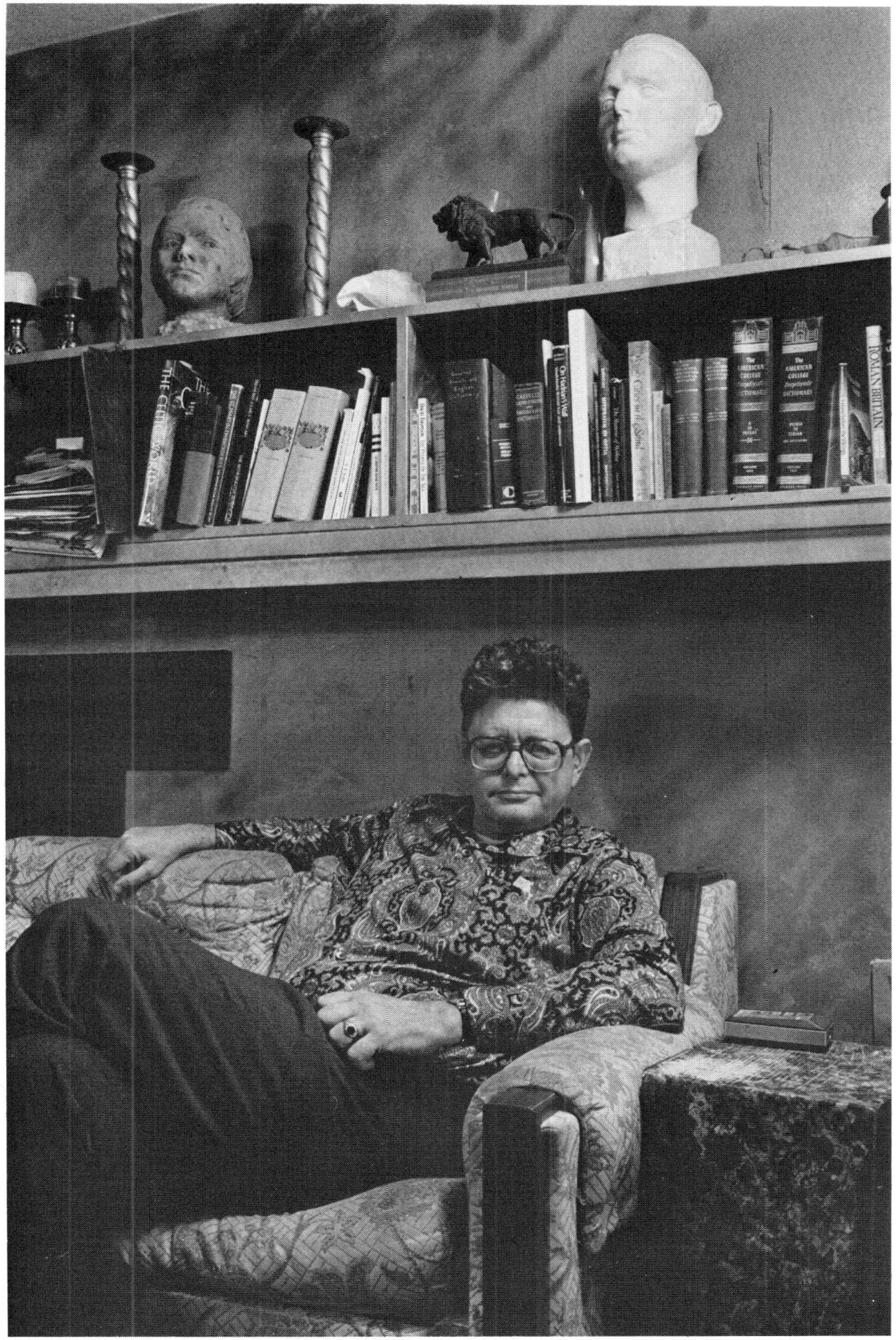

L. SPRAGUE DE CAMP

I began professional writing in the late 1930's; and I've had a most interesting time. I've been chased by a hippopotamus in Uganda, prospected for uranium by airplane, and spent an evening with the late Gypsy Rose Lee. I have entertained royalty and survived a train wreck on the way home.

My accomplishments are varied; I can ride a camel, shoot a bow, dance an Irish jig, and recite *Jabberwocky* in German. In addition, I have written a fair number of books. I find, however, that the course of my life has been determined less by my own faults and virtues than by sheer, dumb luck.

The best luck that ever befell me was when Catherine said "yes," and the smartest thing I ever did was to ask her, for she is my best friend, most faithful collaborator, severest editor, and favorite sex object.

CATHERINE CROOK DE CAMP

The day I graduated from college, I vowed I'd never do research again or read a learned tome. Then I got a job teaching English and scurried endlessly through library stacks to keep ahead of my classes.

At least, I thought, in summer I'll read only novels and fashion magazines. The next New Year's Eve I met Sprague. He was darkly handsome with a pensive air, a mind like a Roman candle, and the astonished disbelief of a brand-new writer.

Now, forty-five years later, we share our home with thousands of books. I toil at a high-piled desk all winter and summers too. I slip into any old thing each morning and rarely read novels except those on which I am working. And Sprague? Well, he's even more fascinating and fun to be with than he was that first New Year's Eve.

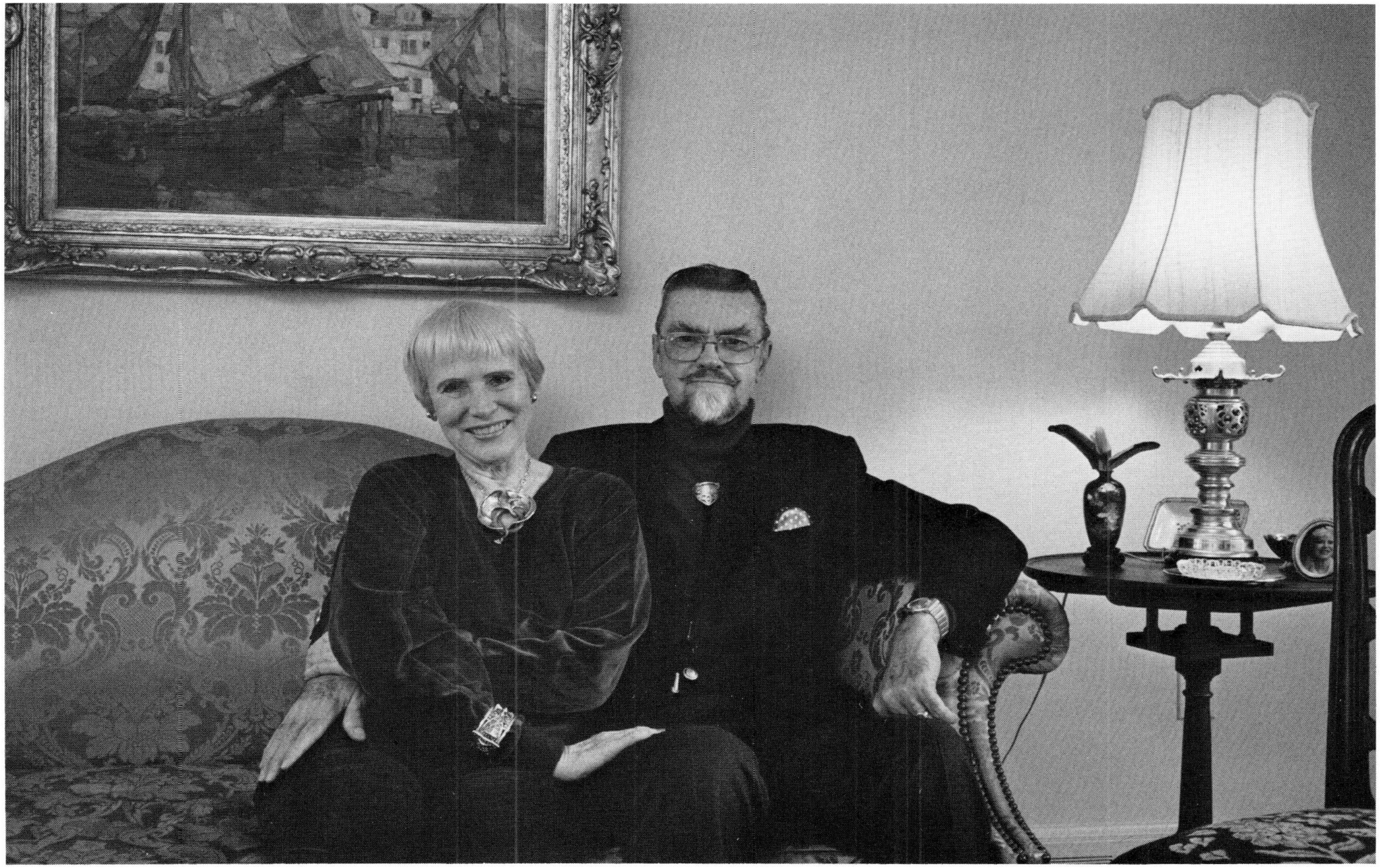

GREGORY BENFORD

There is a pervasive notion that nobody can write about The Human Condition—that marvelous, empty phrase—and simultaneously understand how his own refrigerator works.

But fidelity to the facts of the world is the central tenet of literary realism, and the best sf simply tries to enlist the techniques of realism in the cause of the fantastic. Wedding such seeming opposites turns us on the fulcrum of paradox—a lovely place to be; it focuses the mind wonderfully.

Of course, we must struggle against our class origins. American sf was born in that dear lost age of pulp fiction, when the great demand for wordage to fill the gaps between the ads led inevitably, through Darwinian evolutionary pressure, to the electric typewriter—the first machine which allowed you to write faster than you could think, with results now regrettably obvious.

Having transcended that age, sf now stands as a disheveled rude immigrant, begrudgingly allowed into the parlor but served only tea, no crumpets; *certainly* not asked to stay for dinner.

Despite this, we do (as C. P. Snow said of scientists) have the future in our bones. Our central tenet is that the future will be driven strongly by science, its worldview and side effects.

I have chosen, as my cranny in the field, depicting how scientists—an unstudied group in world literature—actually think and interact. The scientific habits of mind may be the most important legacy of the western nations, and perhaps explains why sf is so international a literature.

For me, confronting scientists with a new problem, and thus entering the realm of the fantastic, is the best way to see them, warts and all.

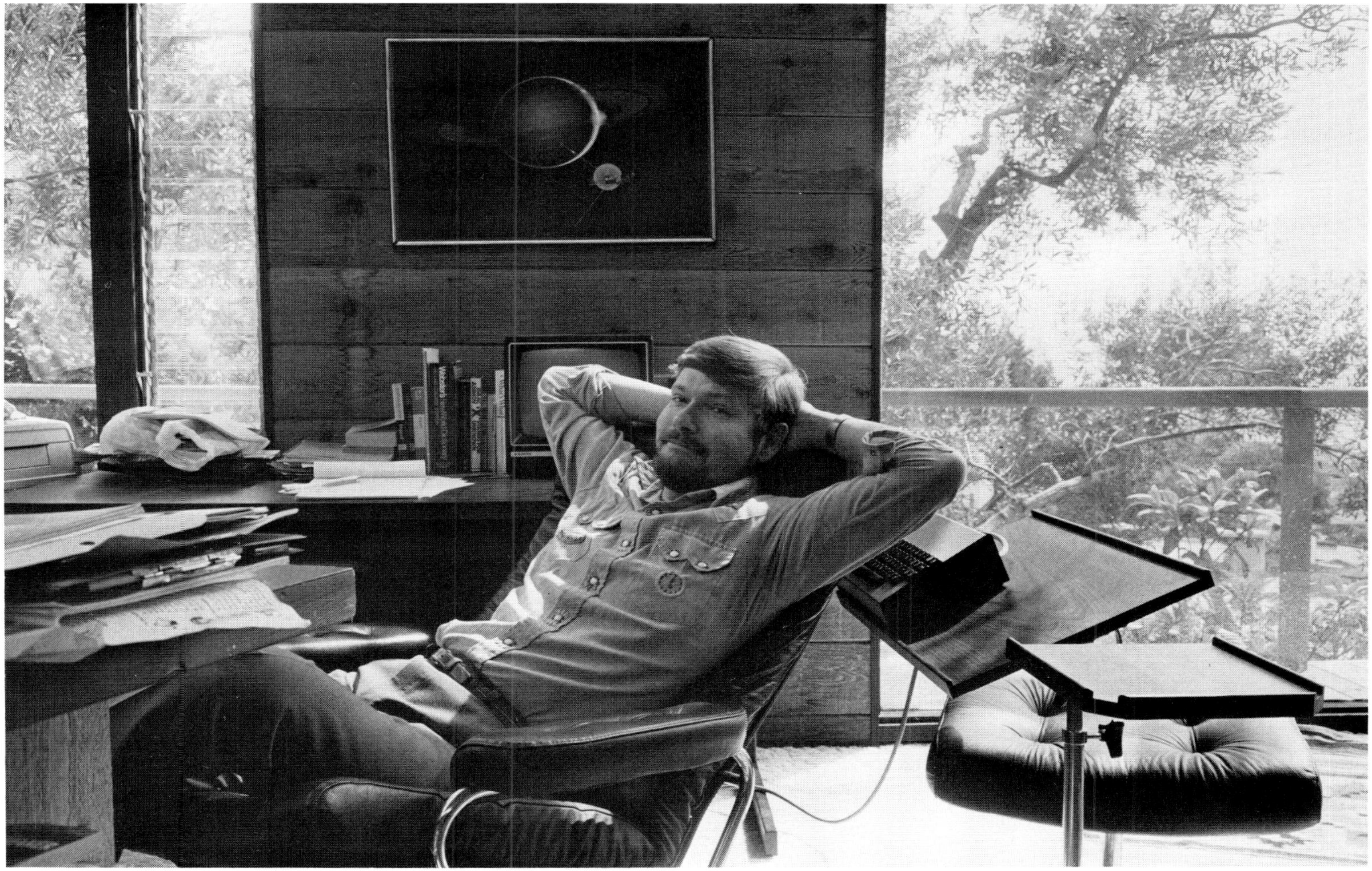

DIANE DUANE

I guess the chief delight for me, as regards the business of writing science fiction and fantasy, is the sheer joy of being able to *play* for my living. I simply sit at home, stare out the window, and have crazy ideas, which I write down . . . and for these flights of ideas, my publishers *pay* me. If this isn't precisely an illegal lifestyle, it sometimes *feels* as if it should be one. It's almost too much fun.

If I believed in luck, I'd say I've been incredibly lucky in doing, over the last thirty years, the things that have led to here and now—to this challenging, frightening, marvelous career, filled with opportunities to talk, in prose and elsewhere, about the things that matter most to me. And probably the least expected aspect of this line of work, and the best, has been the friendship of many fiercely intelligent, independent, committed people—other fantasists and science fiction writers—and the cordiality of the many, many reader-acquaintances who follow their work, and mine, in both genres. That friendship—the mere existence of these people—has made my world vastly richer than it would have been without them.

Writing for them—the friends, and the many unseen acqaintances—is a privilege, a joy. I intend to do it until I drop.

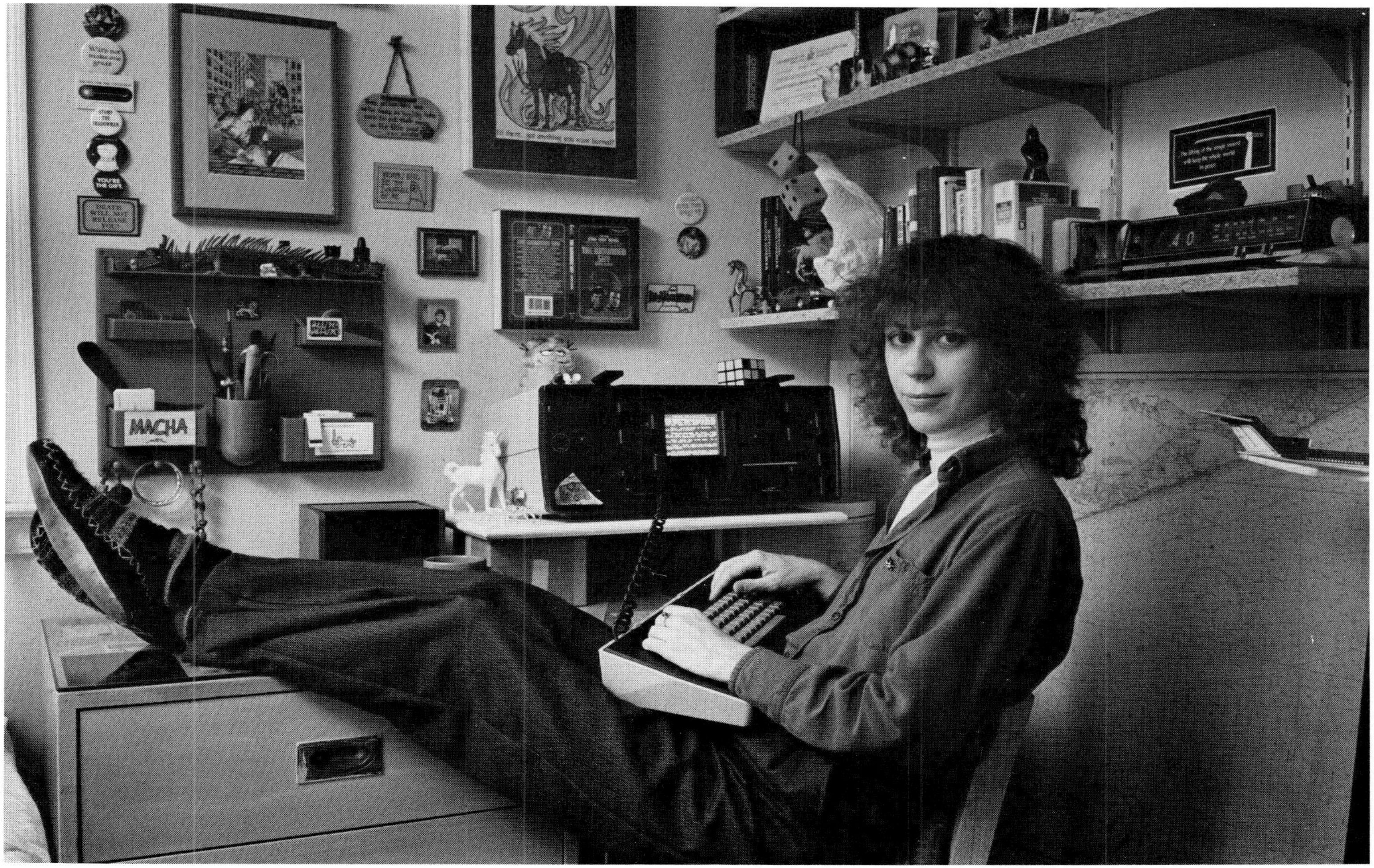
DEATH WILL NOT RELEASE YOU
MACHA

"Then I leaped out and caught a support rod with both hands. The plant personnel gasped. When I began a long slide inward, my feet dangling like window sash weights, they cried, 'Be careful, Mr. Kampa! Please be careful, sir!' Their shouts were reassuring hosannas. I slid the rod to an intersection beneath the tank, then hung there in the arid breeze gazing westward after Monicah. For the duration of my stunt, at least, I was a very happy man."

—*No Enemy But Time*

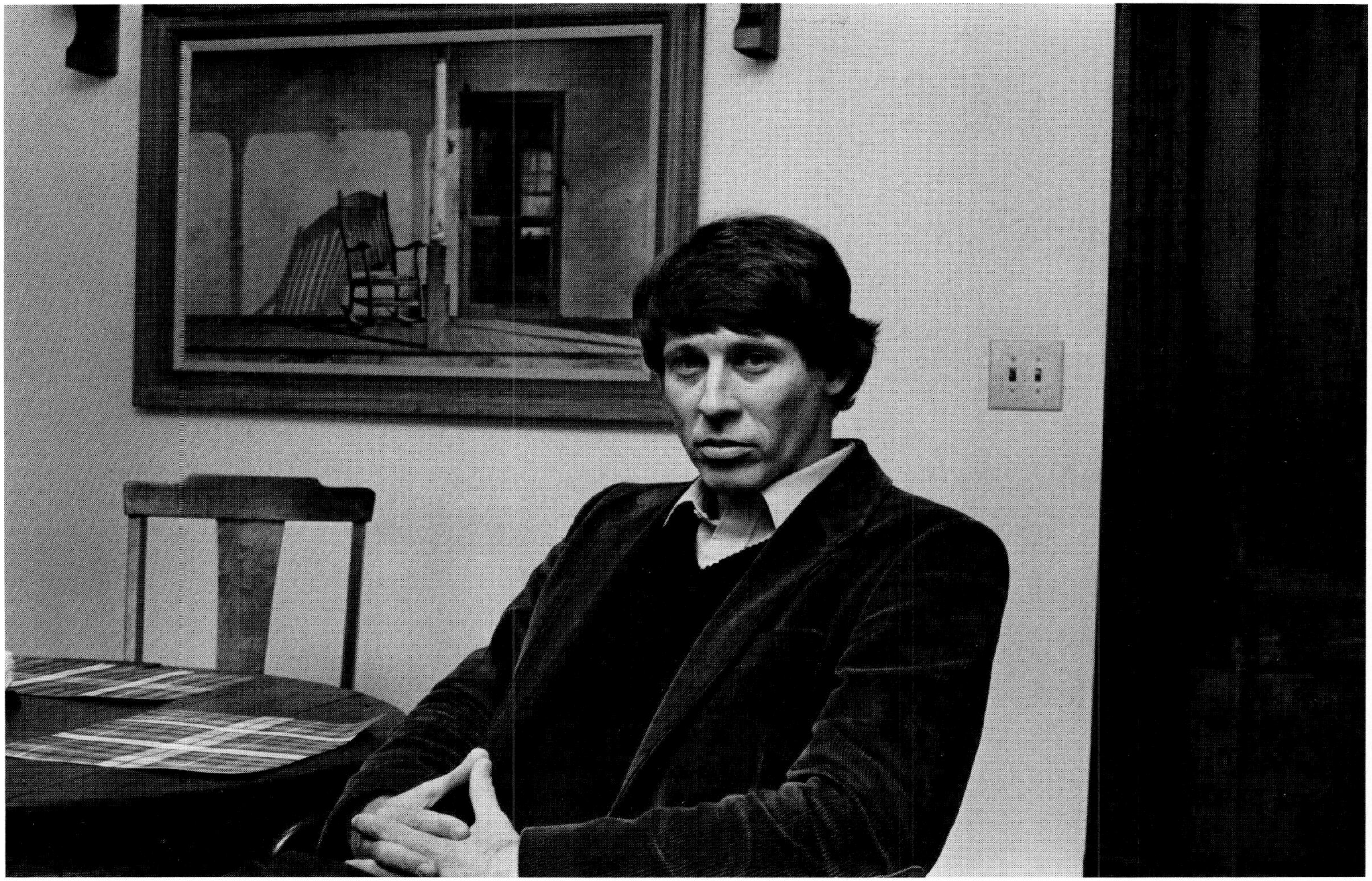

Why does Life always turn green in the wash?

Who has the warranty? Is there one?

Life is . . . like this and like that and like that and like this and like, you know, reading about Life is part of life.

Never mind.

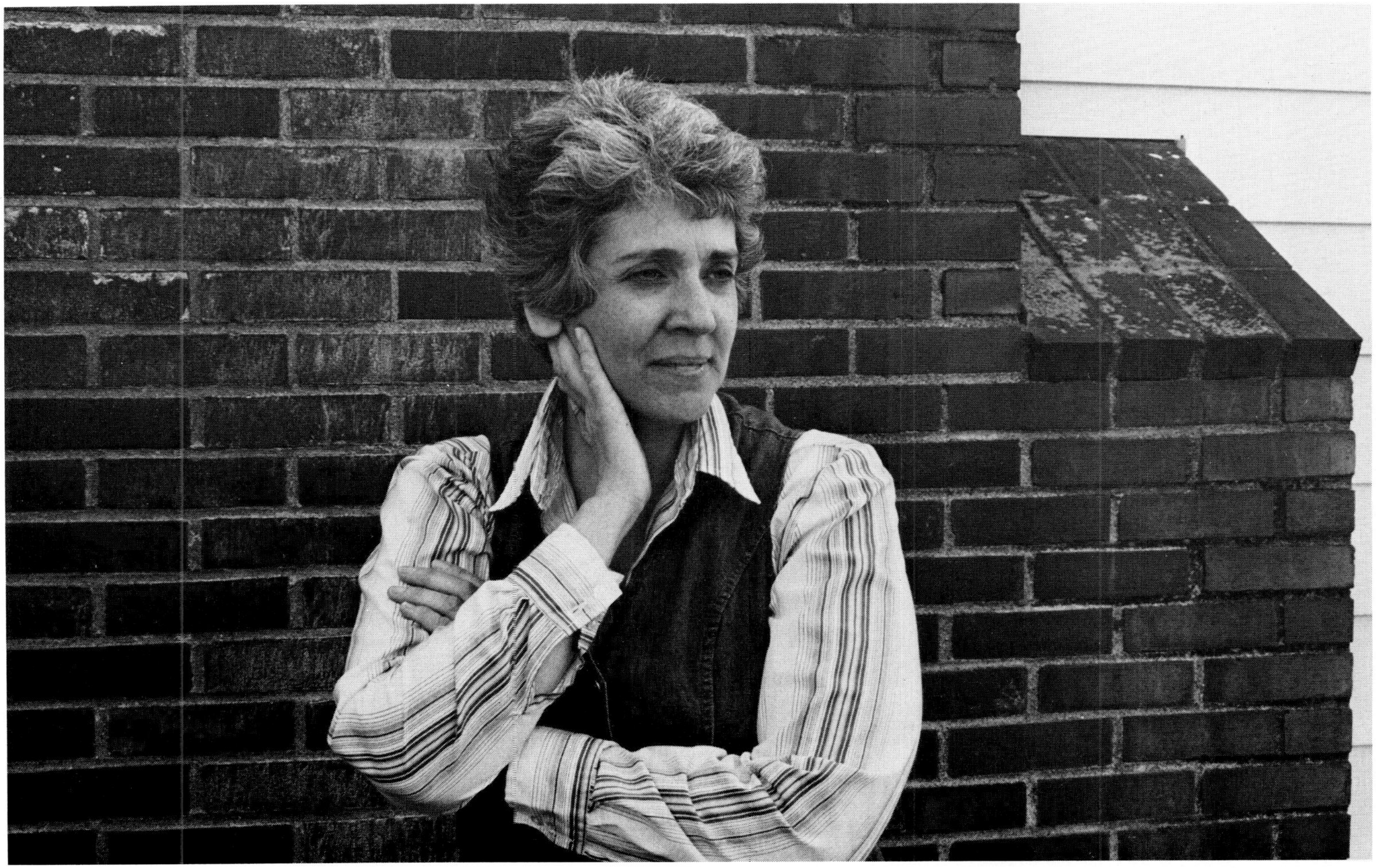

LEE KILLOUGH

Story telling has always been part of my life. Bedtime stories, magic tales like *King of the Golden River, The Water Babies* and *Black Beauty.* Saturday morning at the library, the librarian reading fairy tales in the hush of a study room warm and golden from sunlight pouring through the glass brick wall. I never wanted those stories to end. I relived them on the way home, and with lights out at bedtime, I used to make up new chapters or whole new adventures, whispering them to my sister in the darkness. Finishing a comic book or a favorite radio or TV show, I continued it in my head. Maybe it was a refuge. I might be shy, awkwardly tall, and short of friends, but I had my stories, my own private episodes of *Wild Bill Hickock, Straight Arrow, Dragnet, Perry Mason,* and *Have Gun, Will Travel.* So of course when I discovered science fiction, and had read through all of it in both the school and public libraries, I made up my own. But unlike before, giving up Bill Hickock for Joe Friday, then Joe for Perry Mason and Paladin, sf held me. Perhaps because I discovered it as body of literature, I never felt limited to a single set of characters. My own personal universe was inexhaustible.

Story telling has absorbed me, often possessed me, sometimes to the exclusion of other activity and even friends. But then, it has given me much, too. The pleasure of solitude. Sharper awareness of my own world and time as I study them to build better alien/future worlds. Immortality. Even if the greed or paranoia of governments should destroy the future, I shall have lived a thousand lives everywhere and everywhen.

But most of all, story telling gives me the pleasure of giving pleasure, of entertaining, of sharing with others my visions of alien societies and worlds and times. And isn't that what story telling is all about?

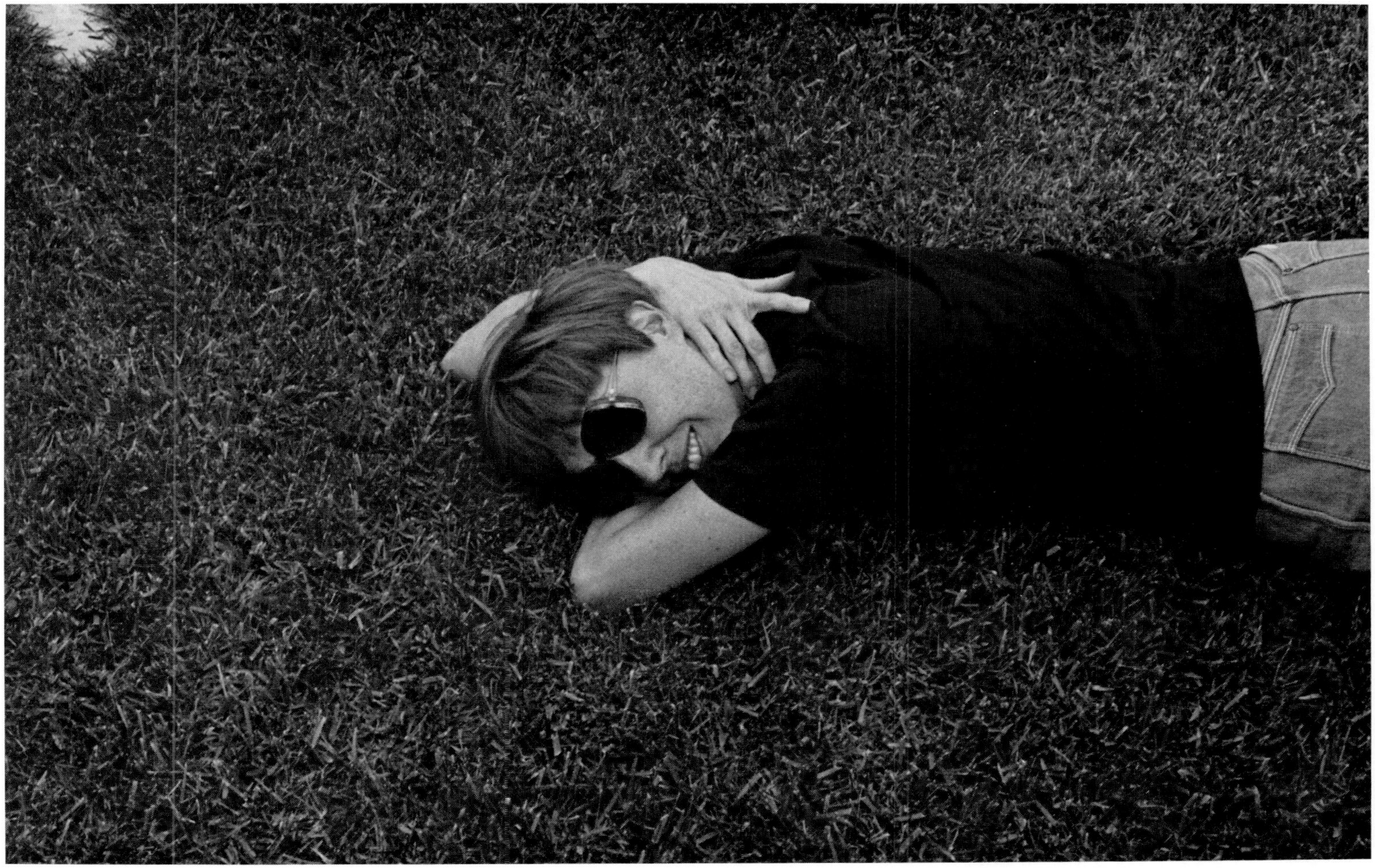

BEN BOVA

Writers are all schizophrenics.

Writing itself is hard, lonely work. You sit in a solitary chamber with some implement—a pen, a typewriter, a word processor—and try to make marks on a page that accurately transcribe the thoughts in your head. At the same time, you try to arrange those thoughts so that they say something interesting enough for someone else to read and care about.

Yet, in order to have something to say, a writer must go out into the world and sample life, meet people, learn their innermost fears and deepest desires, observe how they interact with one another.

Most non-writers firmly believe that writers all lead wonderful lives. That is because the general public only sees writers when they are having fun, at parties or interviews or autograph sessions. No one sees a writer at work (except possibly for Harlan Ellison, who seems to enjoy writing in the midst of an ogling crowd).

All the time a writer is out in the "real" world, gathering material, a voice within is insisting that he get back to that lonely room and put words on paper. All the time he is at the laborious task of writing, another voice whispers that he should be outside in the sunshine, learning more about life. Hence the schizophrenia. Divine Madness.

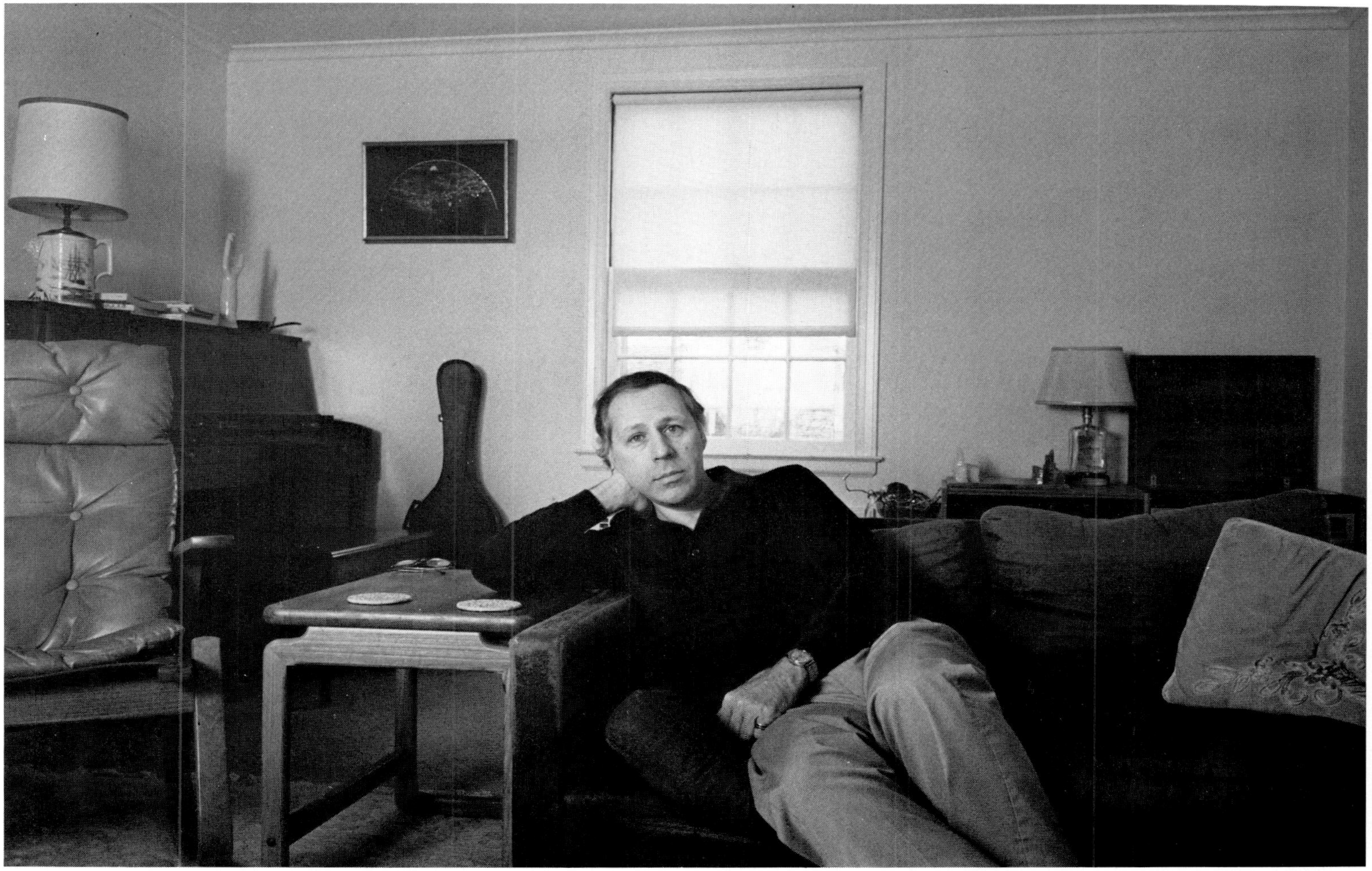

JAMES TIPTREE, JR. AKA ALICE B. SHELDON

When James Tiptree Jr., after over a decade of being accepted as a volubly corresponding man, turned suddenly into a friendly, voluble old woman in Virginia, some curious reactions were seen. One of the more curious was that several male acquaintances of Tip's were simultaneously struck by the need to speak in a condescending tone, and emit other covertly, overtly hostile noises. The curious part wasn't the misogyny, it was that some of these men were genuine friends and supporters of other women writers. Why was I different?

One of my friends explains it as the effect of being "fooled," and for so long. (Though I had no intent to play tricks.) There are, it seems, people—perhaps of both genders—to whom the ability automatically to distinguish male from female is Very Important. Such people may lack the useful category of "General Human Being." At any rate, it may have been the *confusion* of gender rather than the gender itself which distressed those men.

But there may have been some misogyny there too; after all, what happens to the value of being Number One in a class of two—if people can't tell the difference?

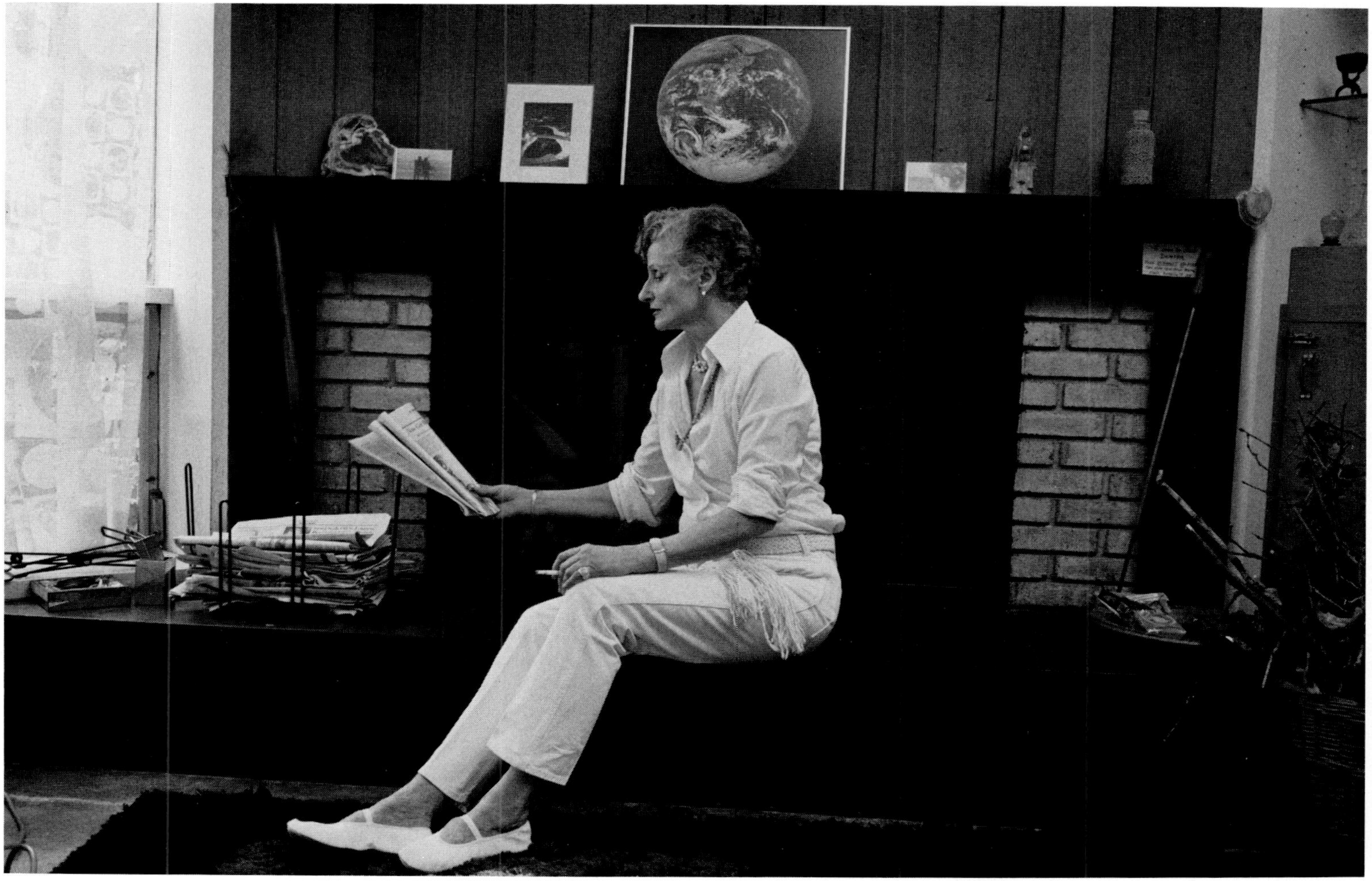

F. M. BUSBY

I did not begin reading until shortly before my fifth birthday; approx four years later I first encountered real live science fiction, as distinct from the usual grade of children's fantasy. Wrote my first story, having rehearsed stories verbally to my tolerant parents, at age seven: one handscribbled page of text, and the title character was a rosebush. No plot at all.

I write sf because it gives me room to breathe—to put my character into predicaments that cannot happen in Mainstream. The trouble with Mainstream is that it is stuck with the present and the agreed upon past, which may or may not relate to any truth whatsoever. Whereas sf can deal with things that may well have happened but who knows, and Right Now isn't all that solid either. Put on balance, the future is where we can find the handles to grab ourselves by the imagination and swing like Tarzan.

Ninety-eight percent of the time I write stories centered on people (characters) I like. Because I'm not interested, much, in doing people I do not like. Such as losers, or folks who do not care whether they win or lose: Futilitarians. Because that way lies a batch of readers who don't care, either.

What I'm saying, of course, is that I write the kind of fiction I like to read. Which is the only way to fly.

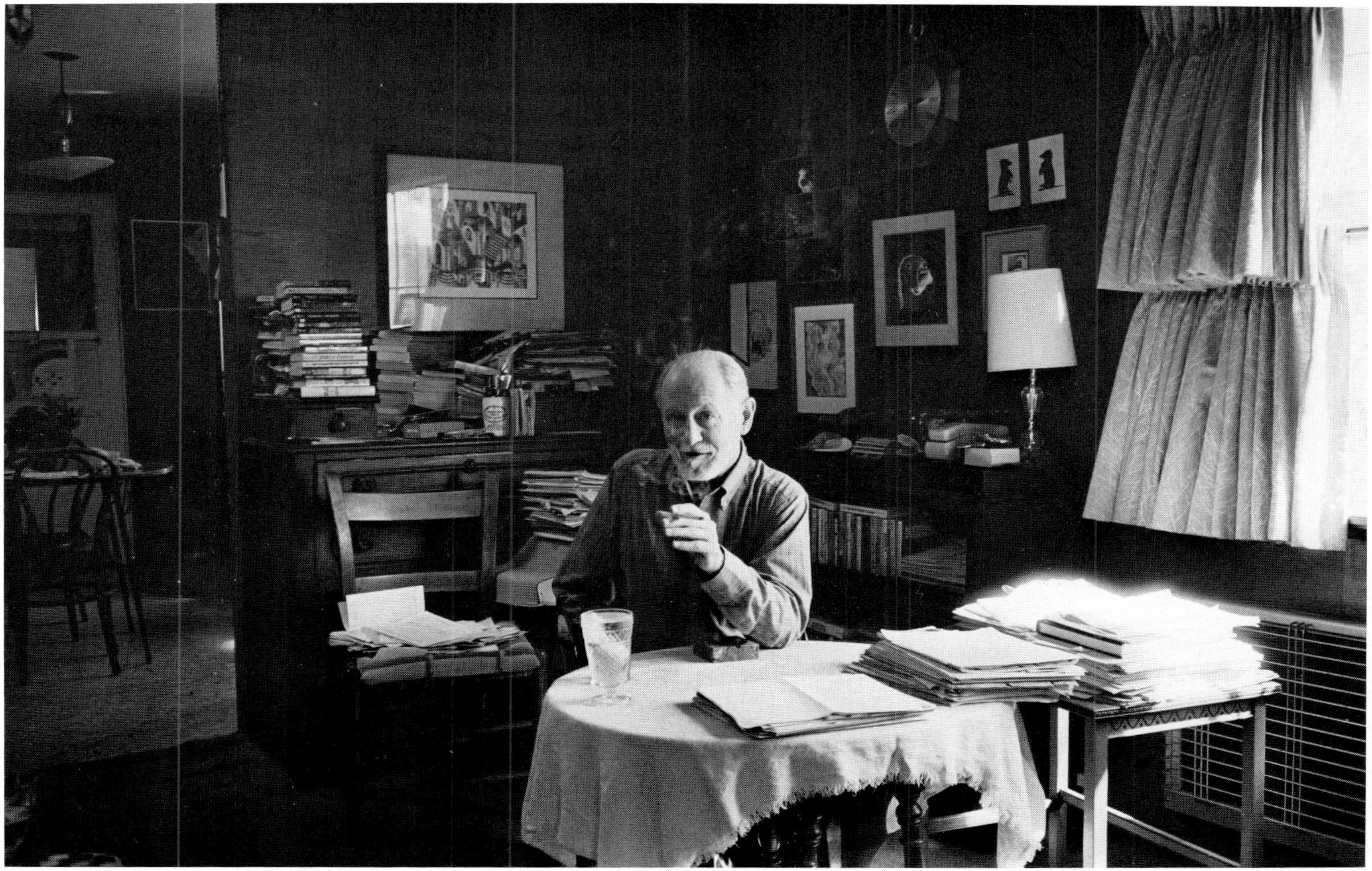

IAN WALLACE

Four bogus quotations, which I put into the front or back matter of my first two novels, express concisely the philosophical underpinning of all my writing. I will re-quote two in context.

In *Dr. Orpheus.*—Having defined *human* in a mode not restrictive to Homo sapiens, the Code of the Interplanetary Union stipulates:

> *Minimum Human Value System:* No human shall, by force or by guile, be deprived of his ability to resist volitionally the will of another creature—except under due process of law, and even then, not by guile.

In *Croyd,* Nike Pan, 24th-century humanist, sees matter as cosmically primeval pre-soul enslaving itself into compulsive systems of mutual attraction-and-repulsion; sees structured and conscious pre-human mind as an evolving extrusion out of evolving material systems and mostly matter-directing, ultimate reality. Here is his consequent aesthetic-ethical contexture:

> Reason is sterile without feeling. But the insidious enemy of rational action is irrational passion. The delight of a dance of bodies is heightened and enriched to the extent that it is also a dance of minds—the more so, the higher and richer—tending toward, although of course unable ever to quite attain, an impossible bodiless interfusing *flight of mind.*

Conflicts and resolutions in my stories generally arise between protagonists who tend to embrace this code in this contexture, and antagonists who aggressively reject or ignore this code in any contexture.

Background portrait by Martin Kallman

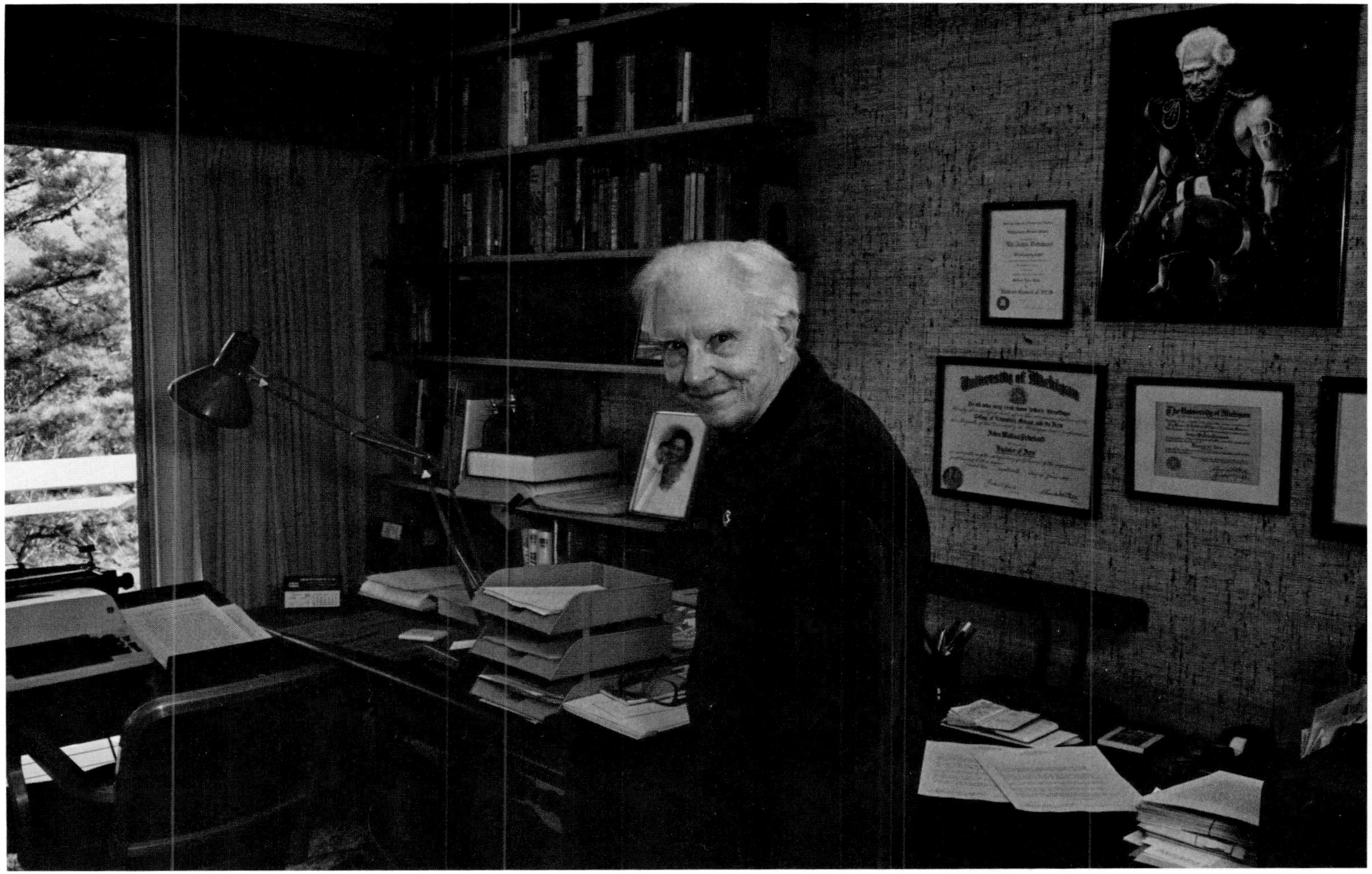
University of Michigan
The University of Michigan

MARTA RANDALL

My great-great-grandfather and his wife left Independence, Missouri for the California gold fields. On the way she gave birth to twin daughters, and died. One child died, too. The wagon train had to move on before winter hit the Sierras; my great-great-grandfather stayed on the Great Plains with one daughter, a goat, and the graves of his wife and child.

He named the baby Elizabeth, after his wife. When the child was old enough to travel, he strapped her on his back and walked to Independence, worked his way to New Orleans, took ship to Panama, strapped Elizabeth on his back again, and walked across the Ithmus. It was a vicious crossing. On the Pacific shore, he took ship to California, left Elizabeth in a convent, and disappeared into the Motherlode. He was never heard from again.

She married Modesto Baleme, originally of Switzerland, and their child John married Jenny Randall, whose last name I bear, and whose people came West in 1852 over the Oregon trail. John and Jenny had three sons, one my father Richard.

I like having my roots in this state.

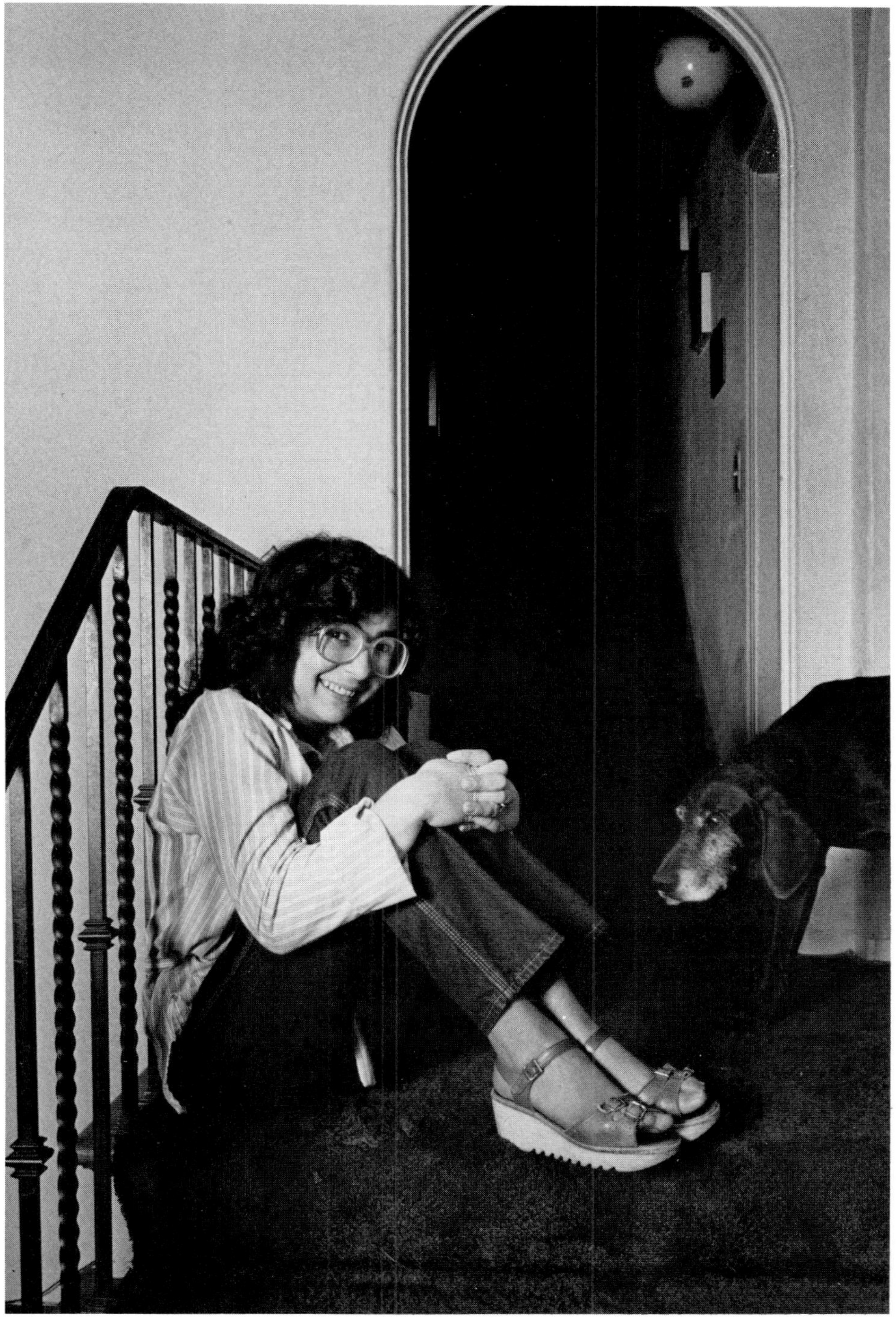

JACK C. HALDEMAN II

CASTROVILLE MEMORIES

Acres of artichokes,
miles of delicious vegetables
nestled between ocean and road.

I want to take off all my clothes
and run naked through your spiny beauty
carrying a bucket of lemon-butter.

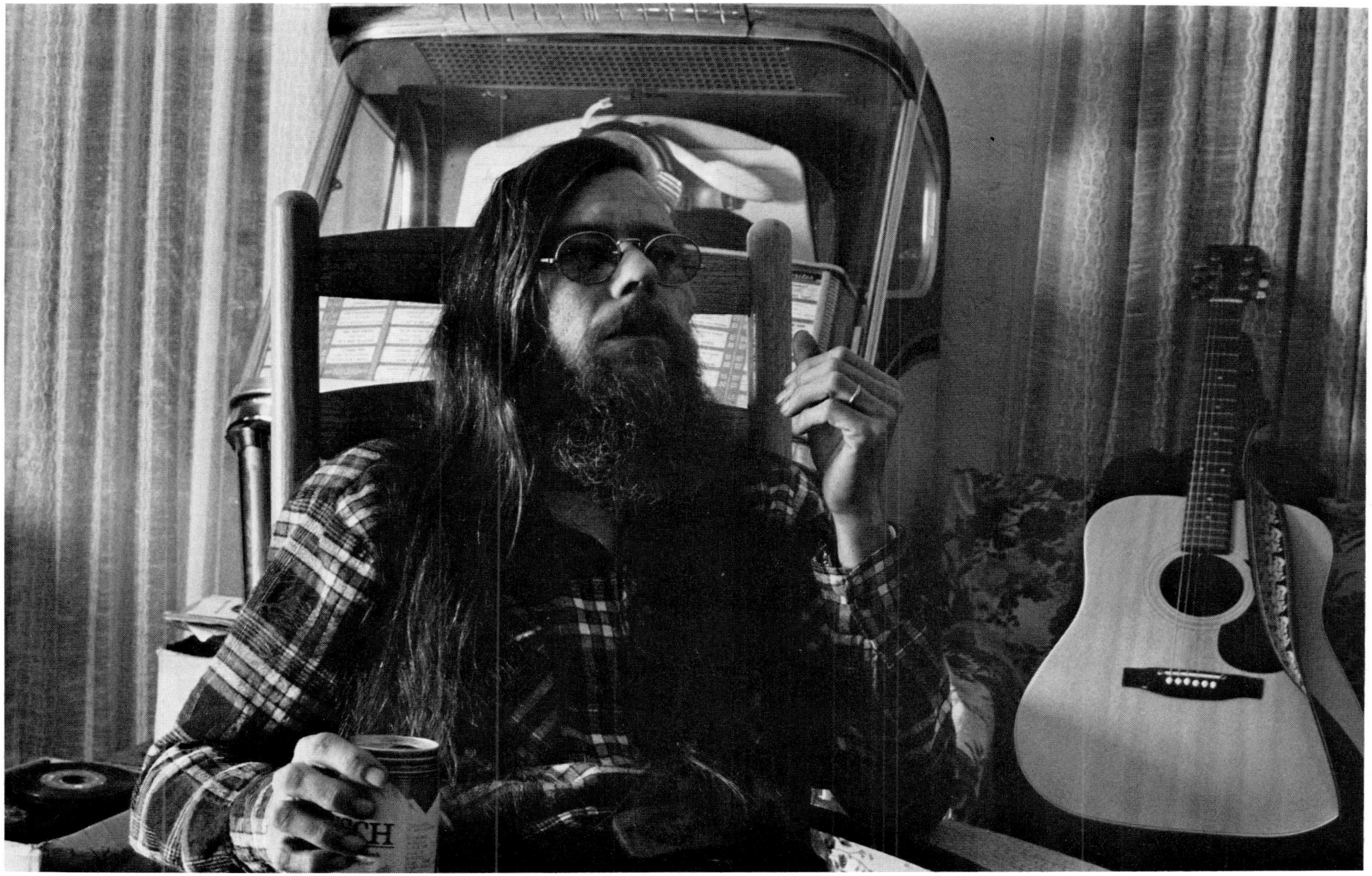

ROBERT ADAMS

Question: "Mr. Adams, why did you start writing science fiction?"
Answer: "Well, you see, I'm too lazy to work for a living and too nervous to steal, so what else could I do?"

That's my stock answer to that often repeated question. It's not true, of course, but like most natural storytellers, I never have allowed mere truth to interfere with a good tale. I started out writing the kind of story I would like to read and apparently my tastes are those of a large number of other readers.

Done properly, writing is very hard, very demanding work. When I am nearing a deadline for a novel and putting in sixteen to twenty hour days at the typewriter, I curse and bitch and complain, but I love it, withal, and will likely keep it up until the day I die.

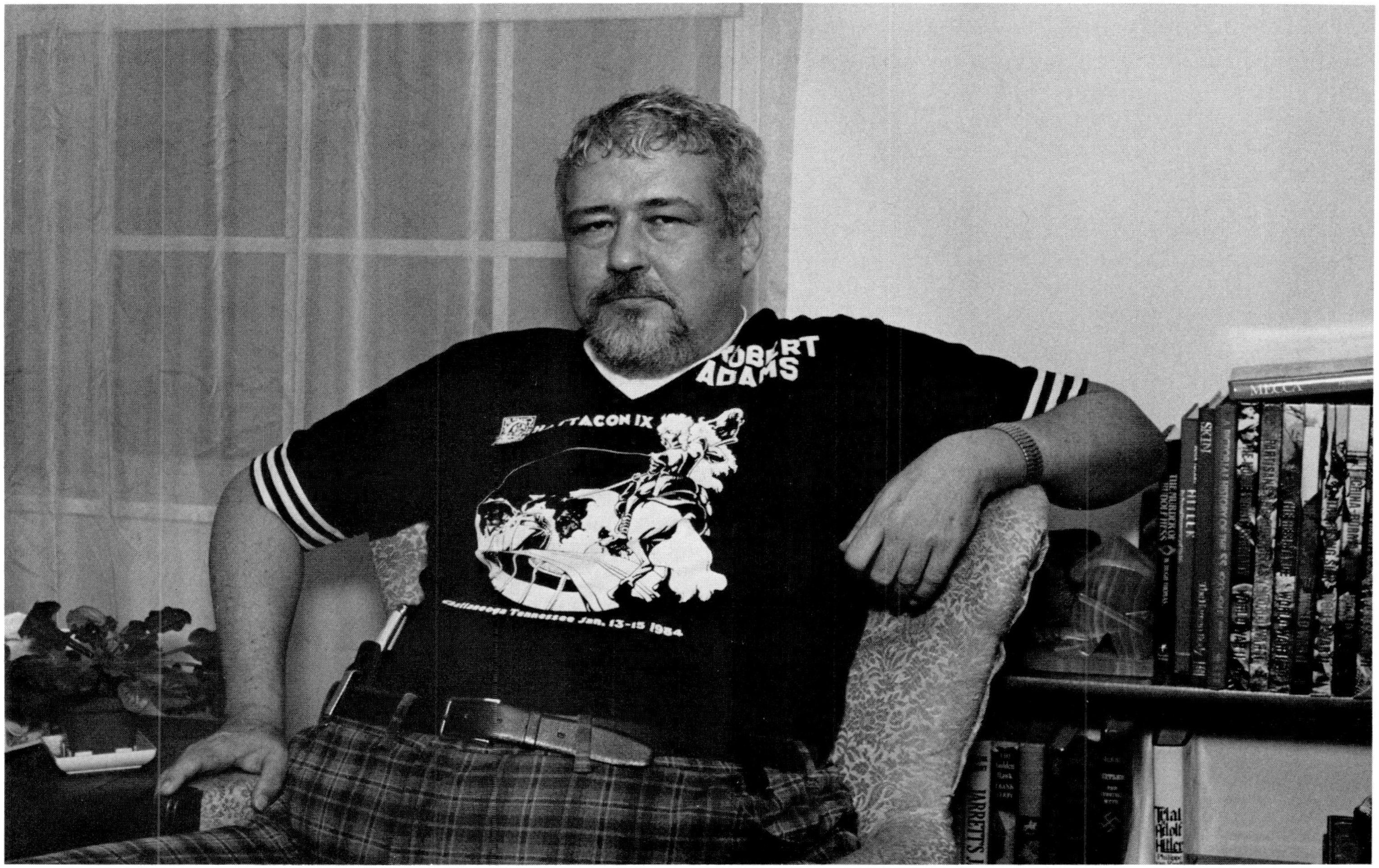
ADAMS
Tennessee Jan. 13-15 1984
MECCA
SKIN

THOMAS M. DISCH

Lives there a man with soul so dead
He's never to his toaster said:
"You are my friend; I see in you
an object sturdy, staunch and true;
A fellow mettlesome and trim;
A brightness that the years can't dim."?
Then let us praise the brave appliance
In which we place this just reliance
And offer it with each fresh slice
such words of friendship and advice
As "How are things with you tonight?"
Or "Not too dark but not too light."

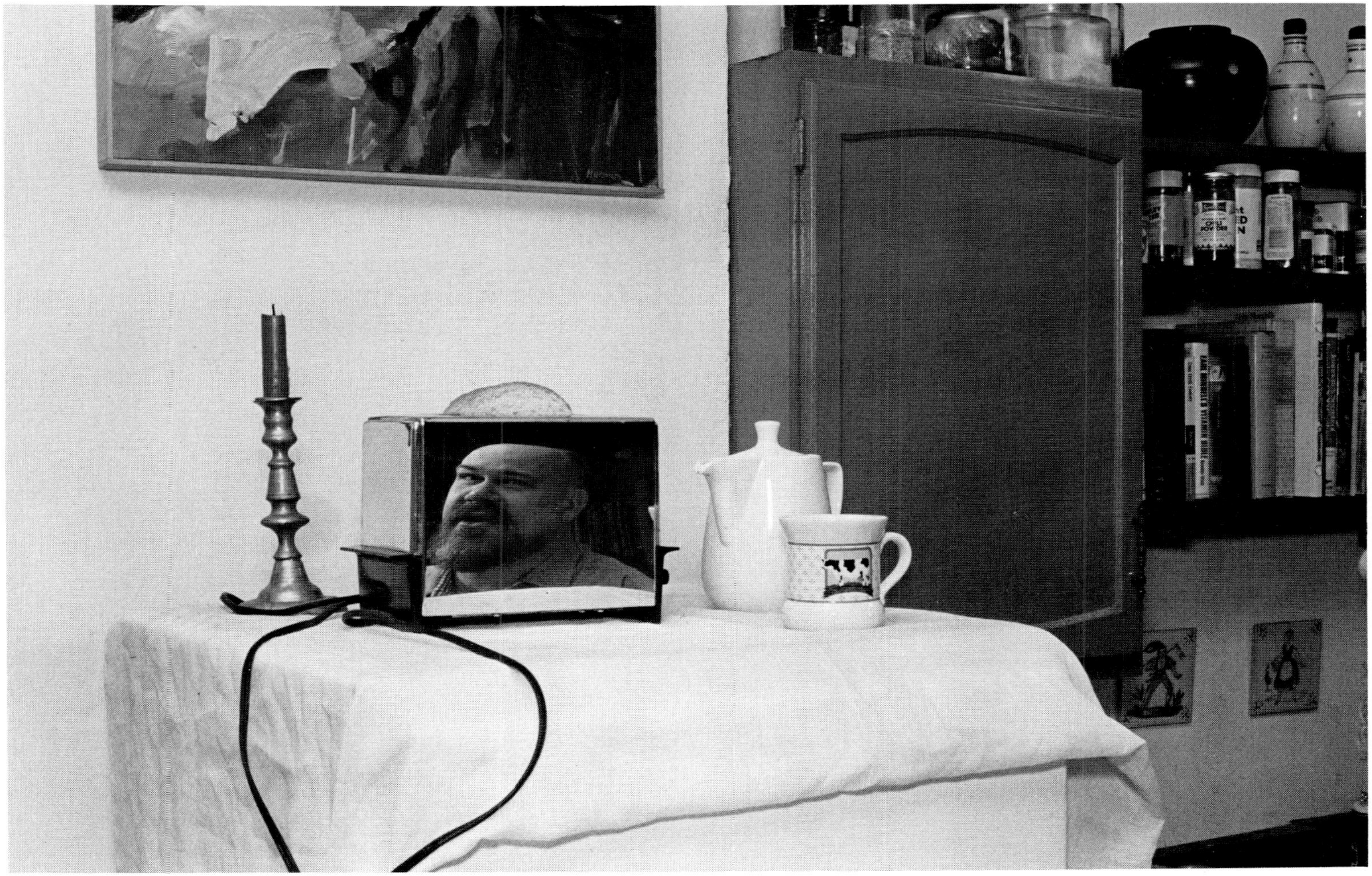
CHILI POWDER

JACQUELINE LICHTENBERG

It's hard for writers to be colorful or dramatic about their own lives, because one of the reasons we become writers is that far away places with strange sounding names are much more interesting than our own drab daily existences.

The only real "color" in my life is the things I dream and do, and the things that happen to me because of them, not what I am. So I don't feel there's anything "personal" about me that's at all interesting.

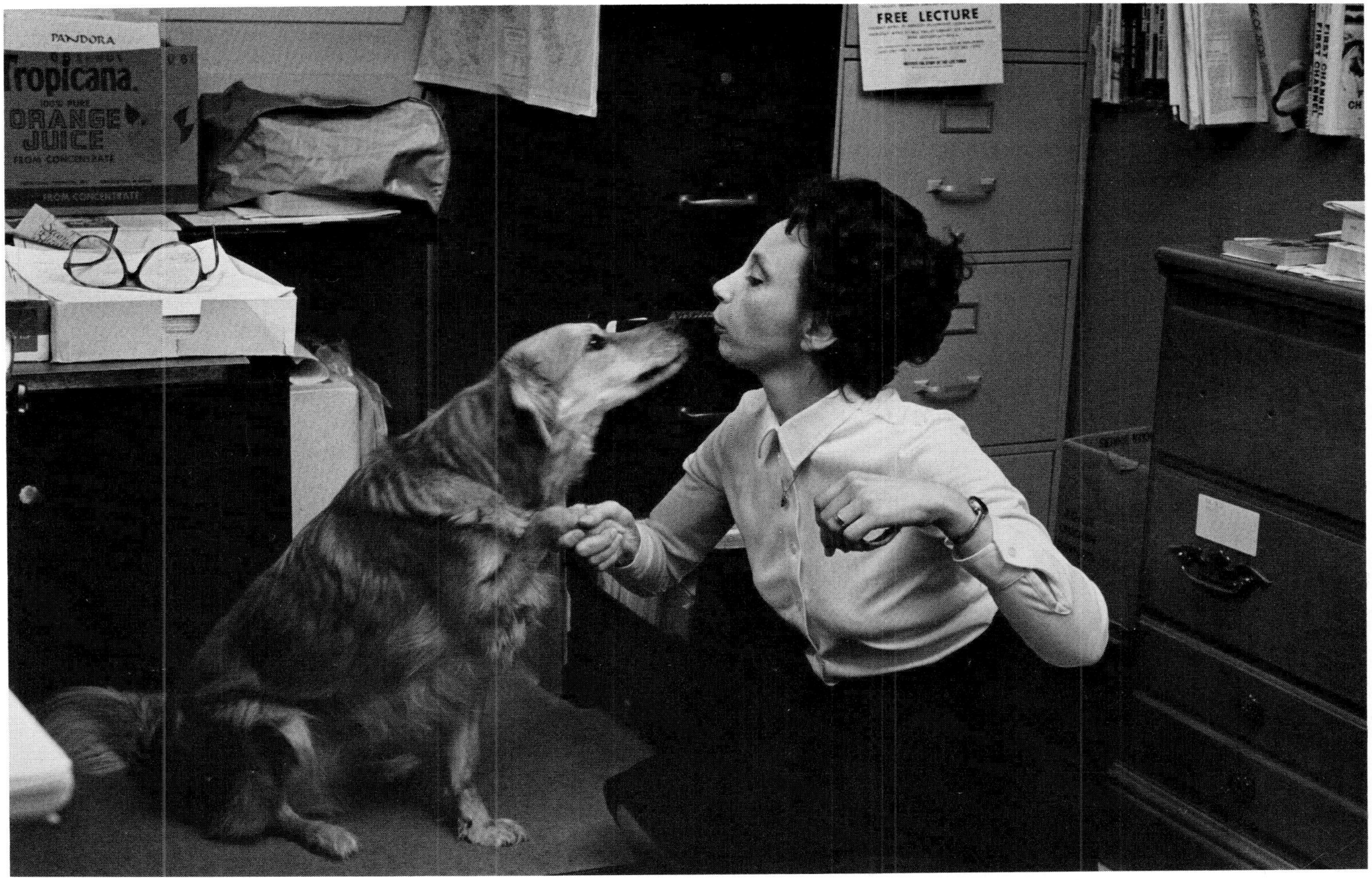
PANDORA
Tropicana
ORANGE
JUICE
FROM CONCENTRATE
FREE LECTURE

GENE WOLFE

The artist Turner said that painters were the slaves of light. He might with much more truth have said it of photographers, who let us see in fact how the shadows fell once upon the faces of Marilyn Monroe and U.S. Grant.

Lewis Carroll was a photographer, like you and (much more humbly) me, and because he was, we can see that Alice Liddell wore the cropped black bangs of Colleen Moore and not the flowing locks that Tenniel gave her. One awaits the eventual development of a print of the White Rabbit.

It is to the White Rabbit who found the path underground that we owe our desire to see Alice Liddell, and not to the Rev. Charles L. Dodgson, mathematics teacher and Fellow of Christ Church. I recently got a copy of *The Man Whose Teeth Were All Exactly Alike,* by Philip K. Dick, published by my friend Mark Zeising. On the back of the jacket is a photograph of Dick feeding a white chicken; on the front is a skull painted by Dell Harris. Perhaps it should remind us that artists and photographers can see into the skull only when there is nothing more there to see—that the light comes in only when the light goes out.

And yet how good it would be to see the faces of Aesop and Herodotos, and how the future will bless you for Lafferty and Tiptree. How late—how very late—it's getting, and how fast the light fades. My paws and whiskers!

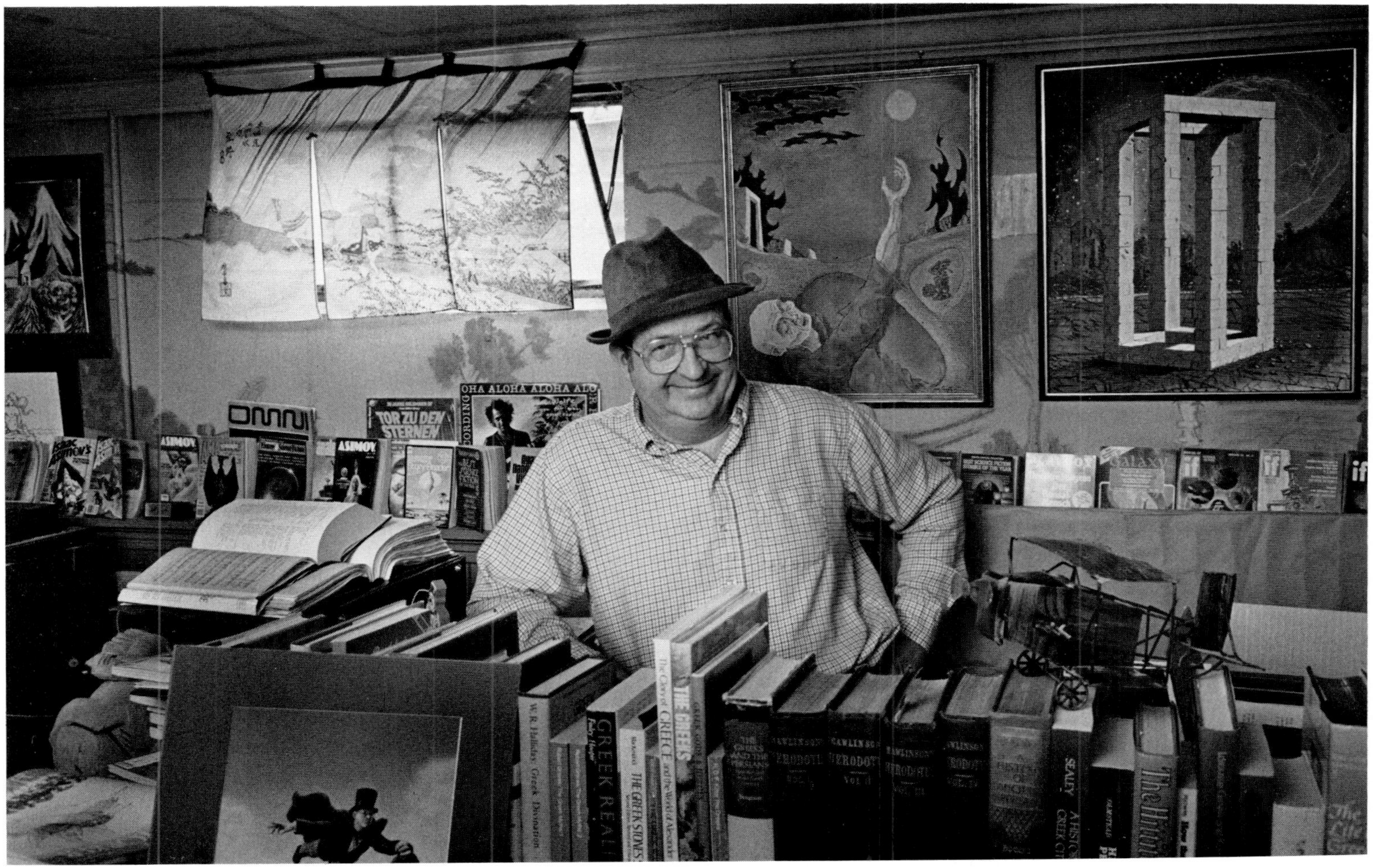
OMNI
OHA ALOHA ALOHA ALO
TOR ZU DEN STERNEN
ASIMOV
ASIMOV
THE GREEKS
GREEK REAL
SEALEY

JOAN D. VINGE

It was very difficult for me to choose what I wanted to say here; which is ironic, because I think the most important ability human beings have is their ability to communicate. I only wish we could all put it to better use. One of the main reasons I write is because I need to communicate—especially to communicate the importance of really trying to understand another person's point of view. Communication (or the problems caused by a lack of it) is a subject that I seem to write about over and over. For me that seems to be the most universal theme of all.

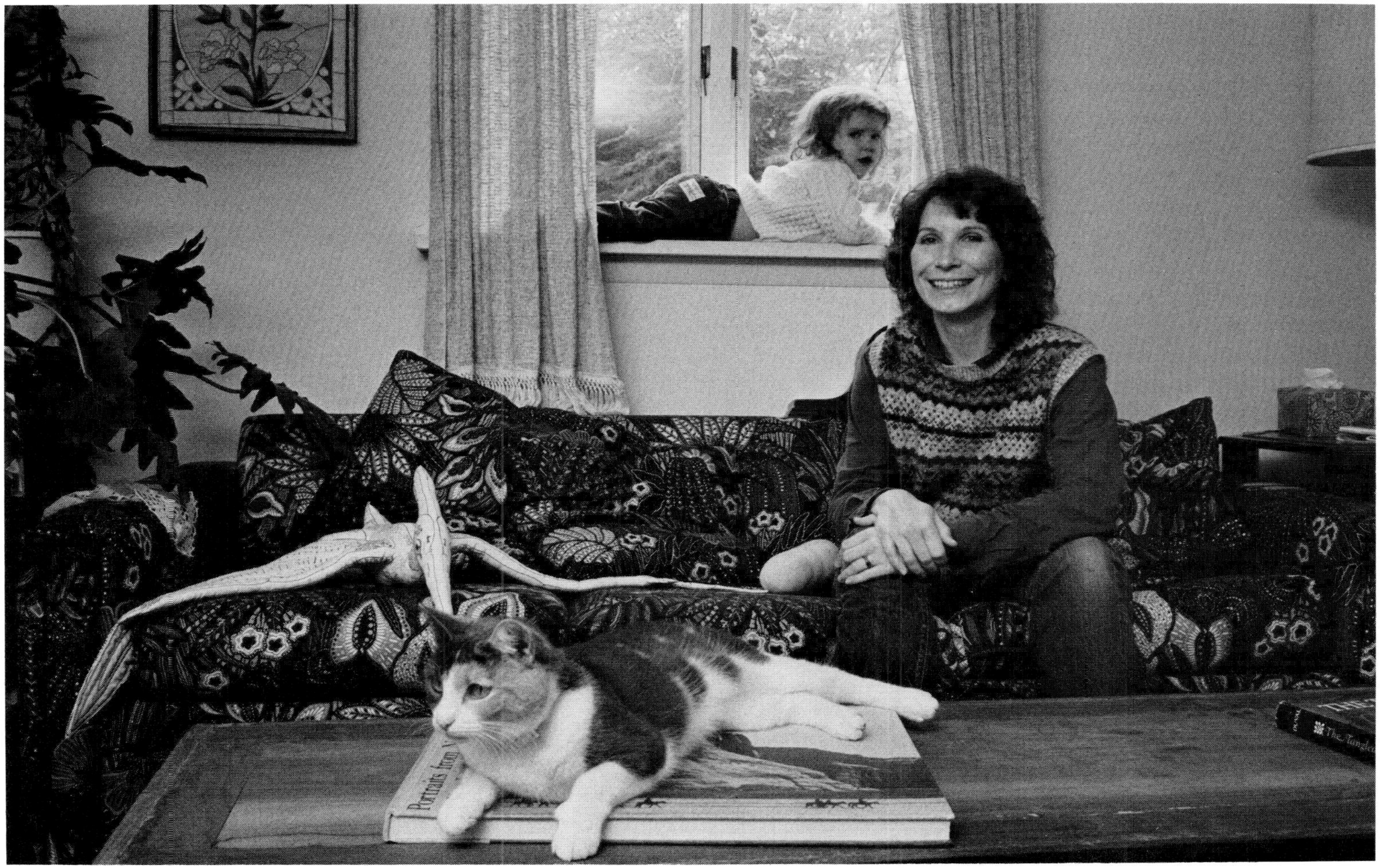

GARDNER DOZOIS

You have to be a little crazy to try to do good work in SF, a field where indifferent, run-of-the-mill, lowest-common-denominator work is often not only tolerated but actively rewarded—and where good work is often not only ignored but in many cases greeted with outright hostility. About the only thing that has saved sf, kept it evolving, is the constant influx of new young writers, writers young and enthusiastic enough to actually work *harder* than they need to work for the same kind of money they'd have gotten for producing a formula space opera. Eventually, many of them burn out, wear themselves smooth, get tired and cynical, and opt for the easier way. But sf has so far been lucky in always having a new generation of writers waiting to snatch up the torch (with naive enthusiasm, of course) as the previous generation lets it slip from numbed hands. As long as this remains true, as long as there are good new writers coming along—and there is more exciting new talent entering the genre here at the beginning of the '80s than at any time since the middle '60s—then SF as a genre will probably endure, and quite possibly prosper.

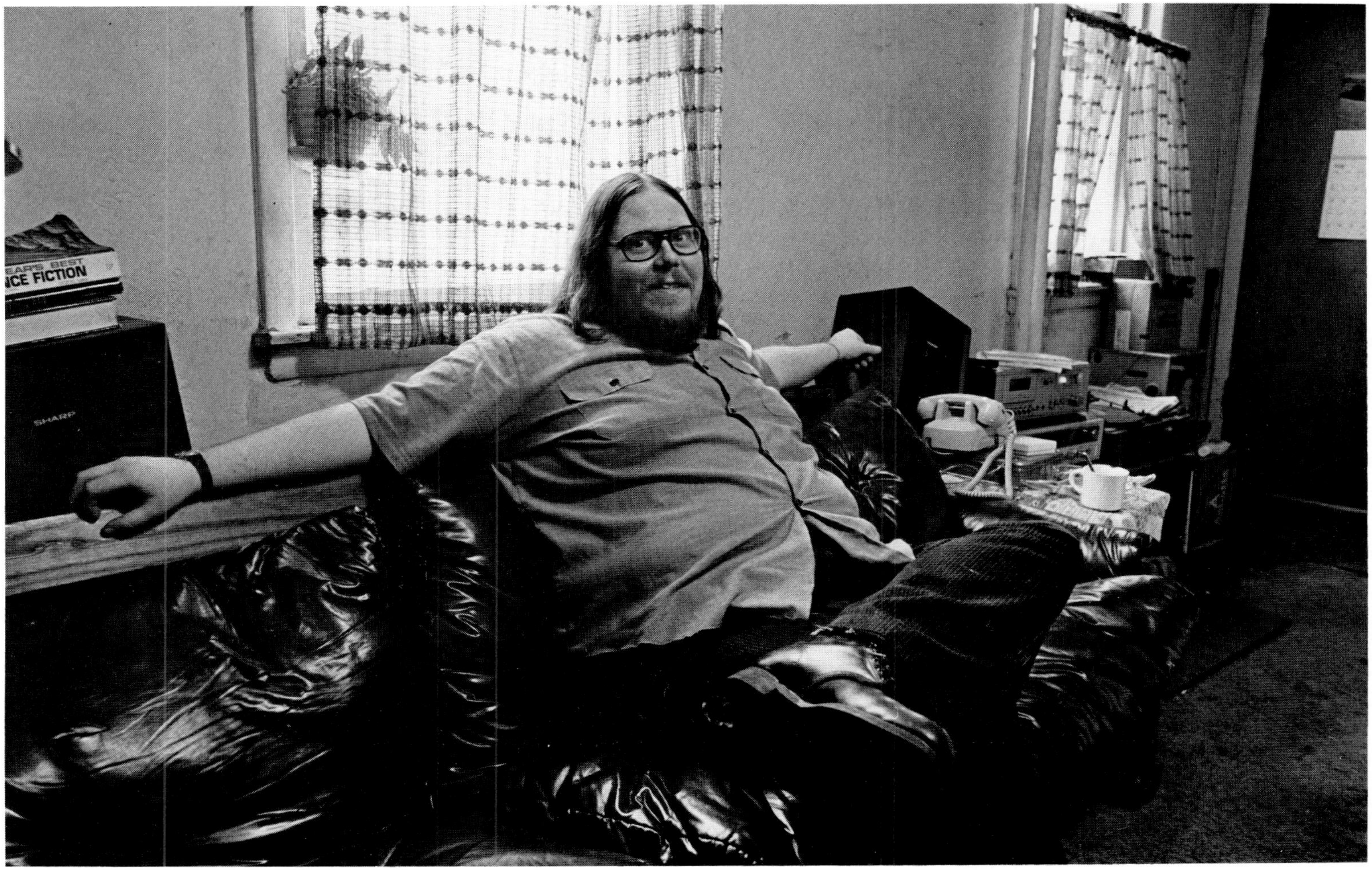
EAR'S BEST
NCE FICTION
SHARP

ANDRE NORTON

Through the years there have been many learned and unlearned disparaging remarks made about the writing of "escape" fiction, under which heading are classed a number of different types of novels—the romantic, the historical, the mystery-detective-spy, the western and the science-fiction-fantasy.

Since the primary purpose of all fiction is, and always has been (in spite of the cries of critics) to entertain, to open doors on imaginative action and other worlds, I see no reason for making "escape" a term of opprobrium. If any writer can free for a period of time, lasting from minutes to hours, a reader from care, burdens of daily living, unhappiness of one type or another—then that spinner of tales is justifying his or her purpose in working at all.

Of all the fields, fiction science-fiction-fantasy has developed the most devoted readers. Which other genre can support, or does, conventions around the year, and the world, for the meeting of avid readers whose imaginations have been opened to future possibilities and speculations about the past?

It is my contention that I have made a worthwhile contribution if I lead a single reader to explore some idea I have advanced.

Many a "why can't this happen?" has been fruitful in our own time. Thirty years ago a character or two walked in space—today this has happened. Forty years ago characters landed on a barren moon—we have lived to see such a voyage portrayed on a screen in our homes (also a science-fiction dream suggested generations back).

Our "escapes" become real; in spite of scoffing comments, as we open doors for mankind in our own way. This may be pretentious but it is true.

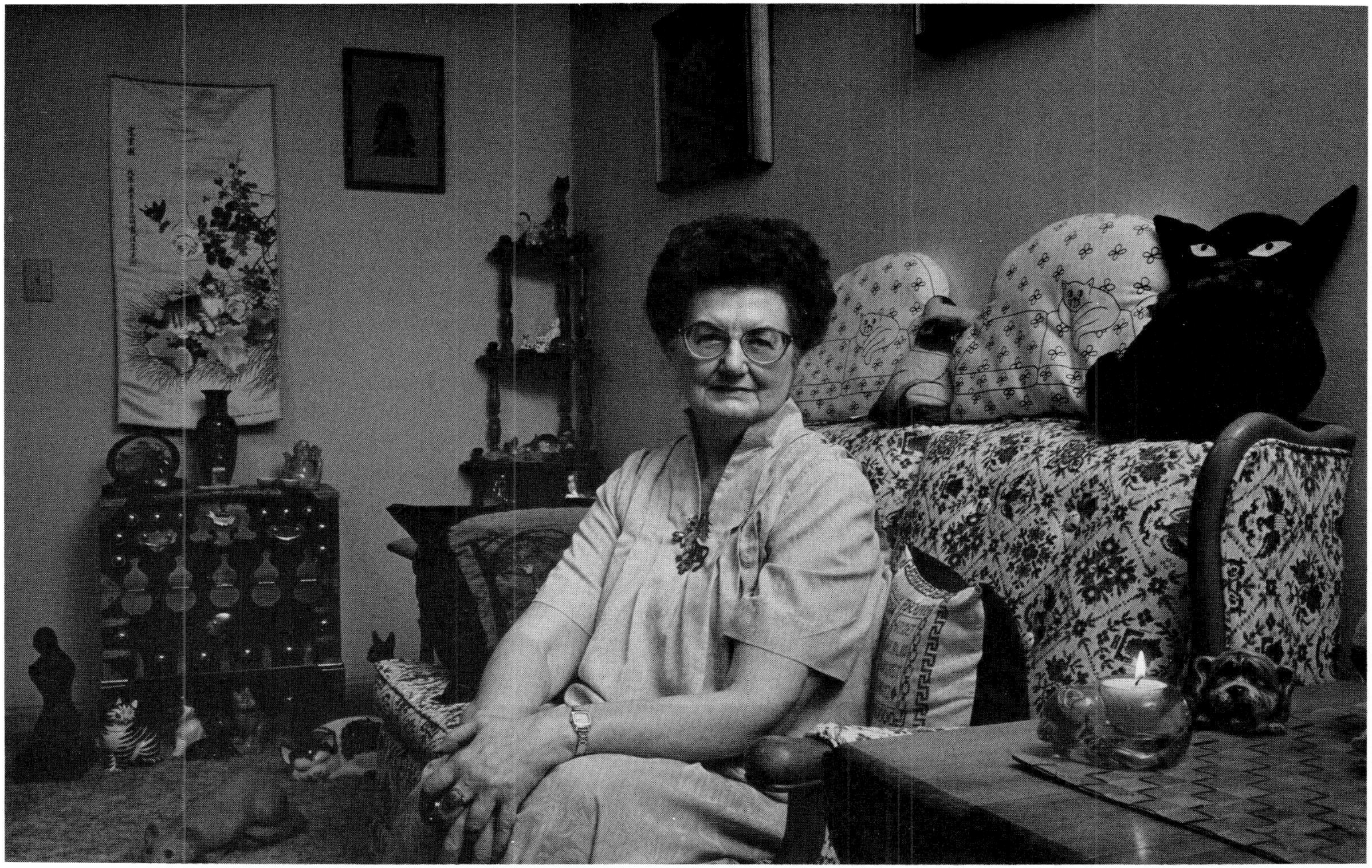

STEVEN BARNES

For the sake of argument, I would like to divide art into "Pure Art" and "Commercial Art," neither term denoting any particular level of skill or intrinsic worth.

Pure Art is a spontaneous expression of aliveness or "Is-ness". Therefore, books, sculptures, symphonies etc. are not in themselves Art, but "objects of art", signposts along the Path, or sparks flung out of the furnace of creation. In a bizarre way, the finished product is irrelevant to the question of Pure Art, it being neither validated by acceptance, nor invalidated by rejection.

Where Pure Art is Self-expression, *Commercial Art* involves communication. Generally, it is the proper work of a Commercial artist to cause a change in the emotional state of the largest possible number of viewers, readers or participants. Factors such as critical acceptance and sales become valuable, because they reveal how many, and what kind of, people have been touched by your message.

Needless to say, by this philosophy, the happiest of artists is the one who has found a balance between these two states. I don't know if I've found that, but I can say that I don't write for money—I make money so that I can spend more of my time writing.

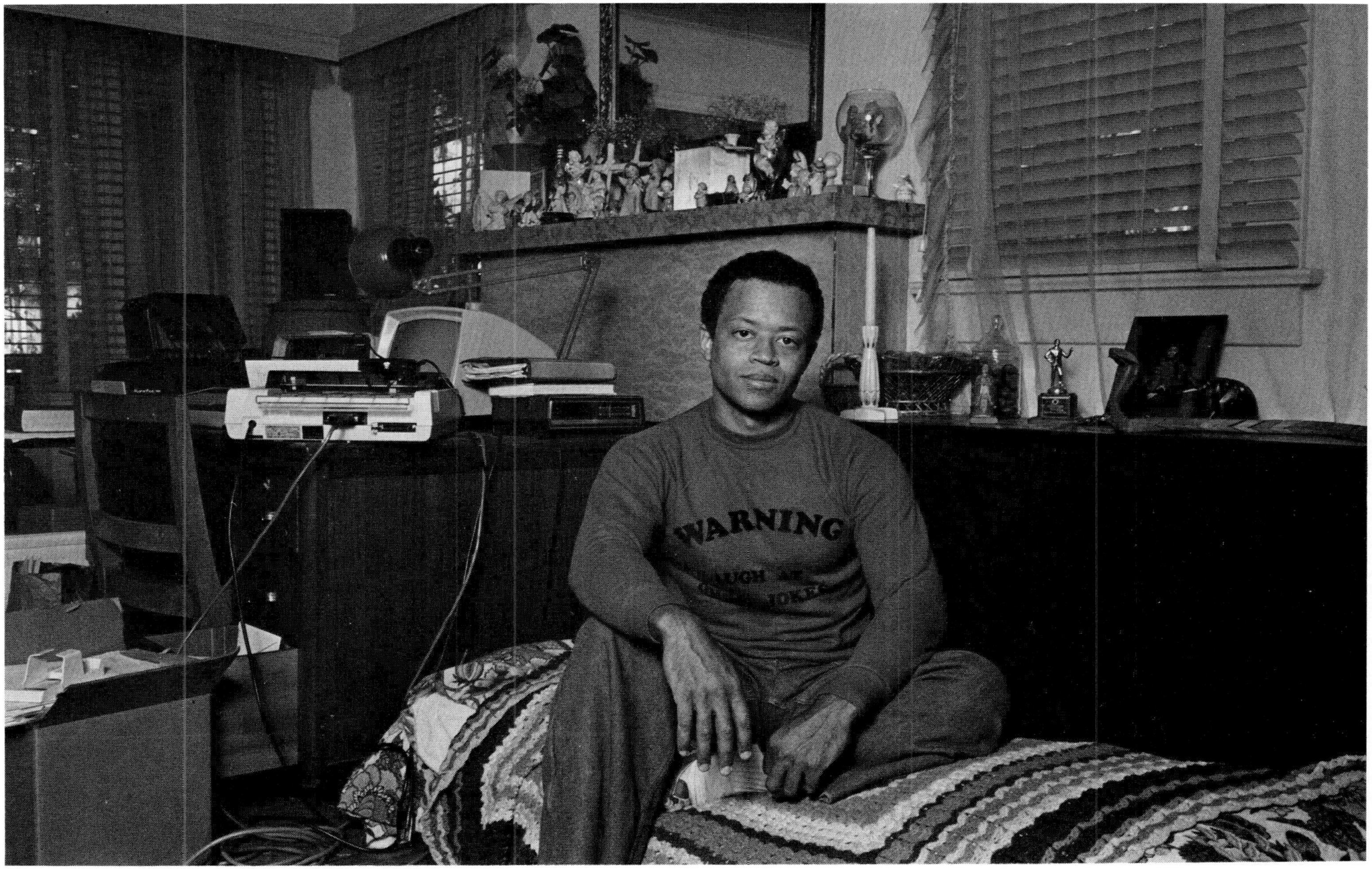
WARNING

GEORGE ALEC EFFINGER

I am more comfortable in science fiction because it embraces more diverse styles and points-of-view and attitudes than any other genre. The kind of material that entertains me has been called anti-realist or absurdist. There is room in our field for this sort of storytelling. I would have a much tougher time of it if I tried to sell my particular brand of story as a western or a nurse novel. The science fiction world is especially open to bizarre innovations in plotting, characterization, and style. I can mix 'n' match elements as wildly as I like, limited only by my ability to make sense of the result. The mystery readers are stuck with their locked rooms and police procedurals; the romances have a short menu of people and situations to choose from; but I have the liberty to set up my tales as outlandishly as I like. If I want to mix an Edgar Rice Burroughs setting with a J. D. Salinger heroine, I can—and will. Or I can invent a whole new world that obeys my natural laws, instead of those of the known universe. I don't see why everyone doesn't write sf. I mean, if you're going to play God, why not start from scratch and do it right?

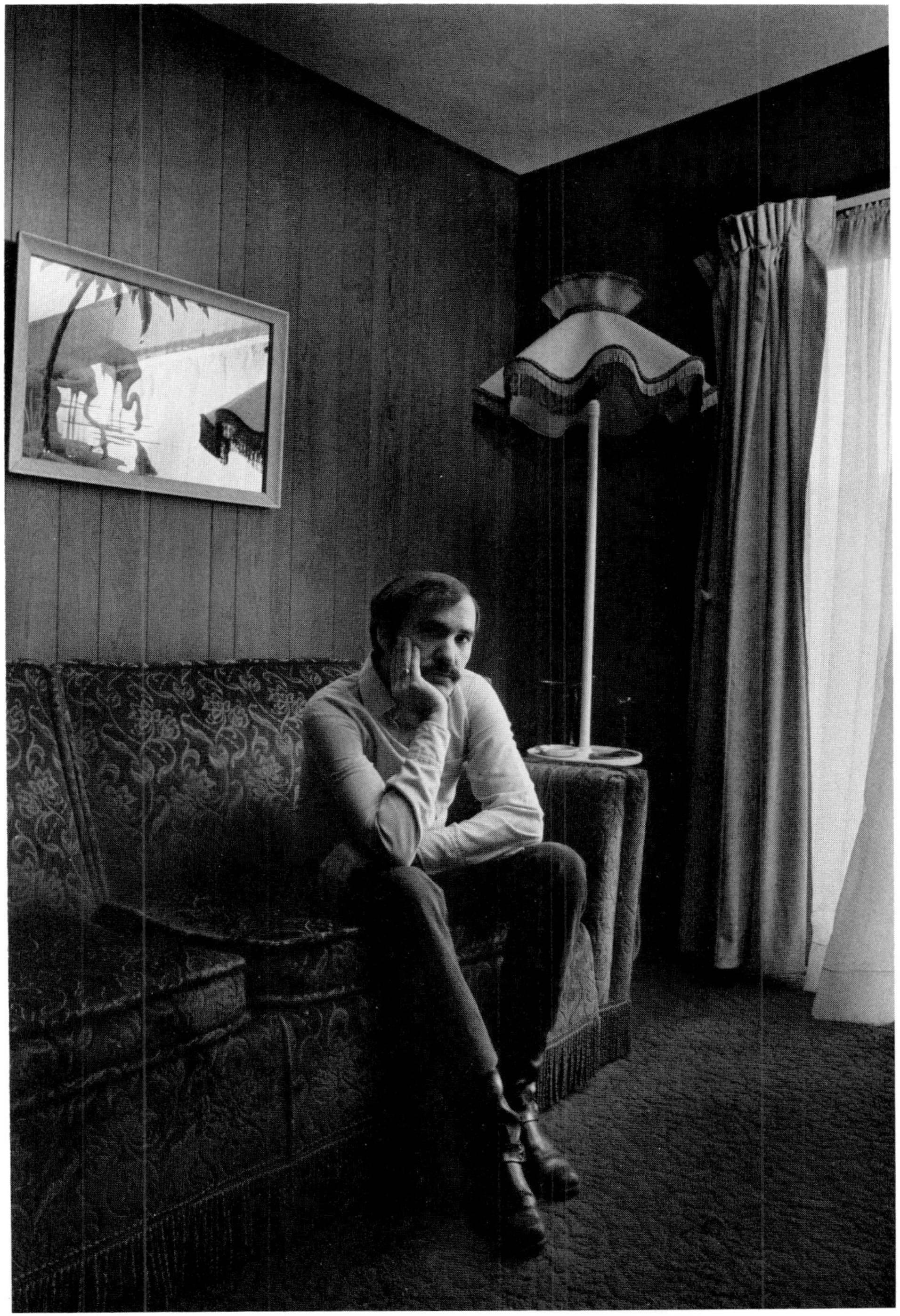

A. E. VAN VOGT

I early became a system person, and I observed—early—that, in a sense, everything one does is a study of some aspect of life. Among other truths—to me—it is no exaggeration that all individuals, everywhere, are constantly, automatically, taking future possibilities into account in their daily activities.

For me, on the system level, science fiction became a study of the future; but it also turned out to be a dependable way for me to earn a living.

I'm looking forward to the science fictional future when whatever exercise does for us—it has to be bio-chemical—is available in pill form in the local drug store. But back in 1968 I did an exercise experiment that, eventually—because exercise is boring—included the learning of languages while striding. For that I had to invent a new system of language teaching; and, as one result, the languages I started recording at that time are now promoted nationally. Second result: I met and married Lydia, a Superior Court interpreter for five languages.

Meanwhile, by reading and writing science fiction, I understand immediately just about every development in science itself.

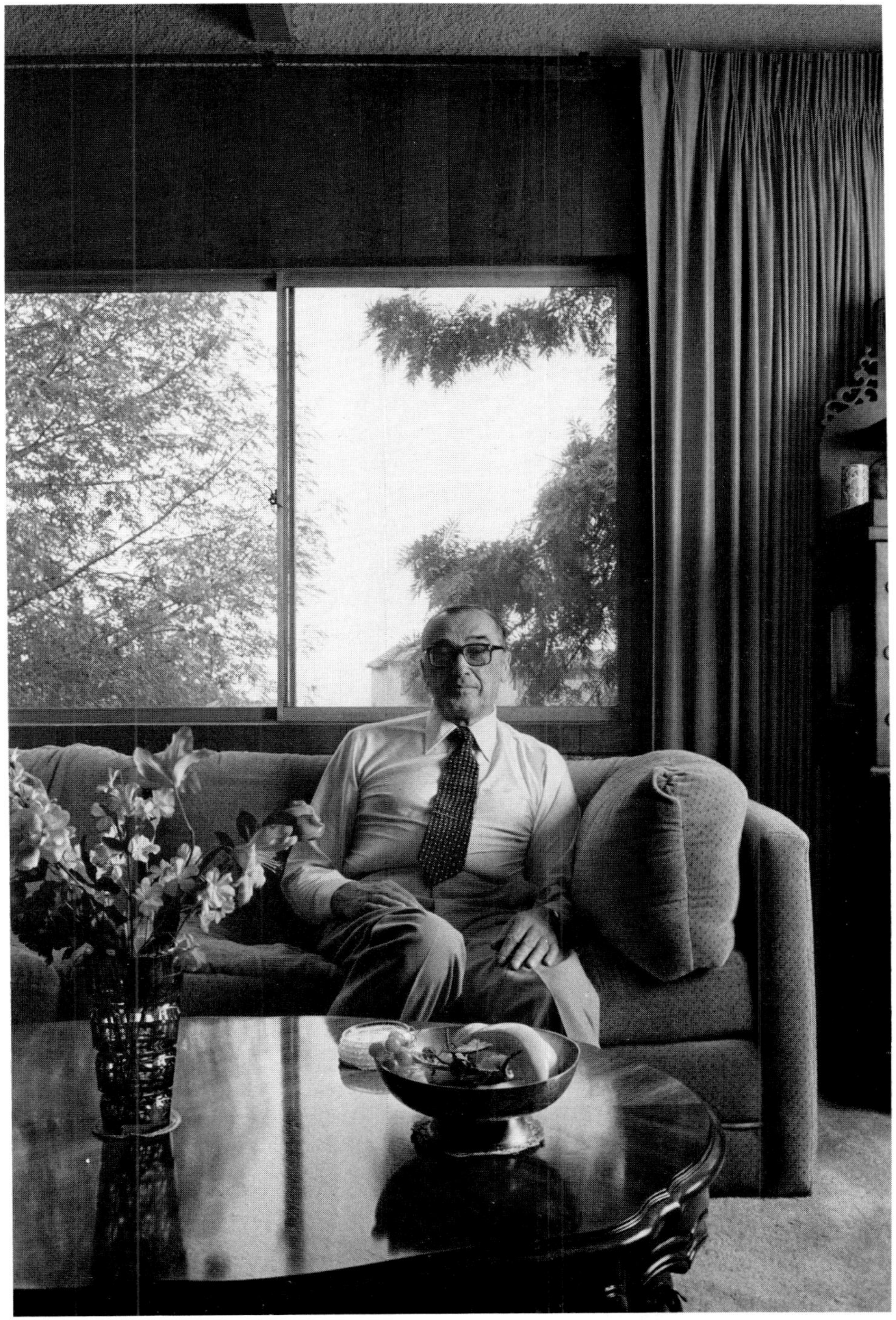

ROBERT SILVERBERG

Captured on film . . . frozen in time. In my own lair, no less. There was a time when I was uneasy about letting my photograph be used on my books—when I was twenty-five or so, precociously professional. I was thinking ahead to the time when I would be old—say, forty—and when I happened to take one of my early books down from the shelf there I would be, forever youthful, mocking my older self with uncorroded visage.

Well, forty has come and gone. The face is not quite what it was when I was twenty-five, but not all that different, and those changes that have occurred are, by and large, okay with me. I am just as happy that I didn't use bookjacket photos a couple of decades ago, but for a reason I could not have understood back then. It isn't that the youthfulness of my former face would upset me now. Far from it: it's the callowness that would bother me, that bland unformed look. What is that *kid* doing on my bookjacket, I would say? Who is he, anyway? What made him think he knew how to write a book?

So be it. I am less troubled about the business of published photographs these days. My face is my face; I change (a little) from year to year, and so does the face. This is the face I was wearing on a sunny spring day in 1984 in California. What, I wonder, will I think of it when I take Patti Perret's book down from the shelves some drizzly winter afternoon in 2003?

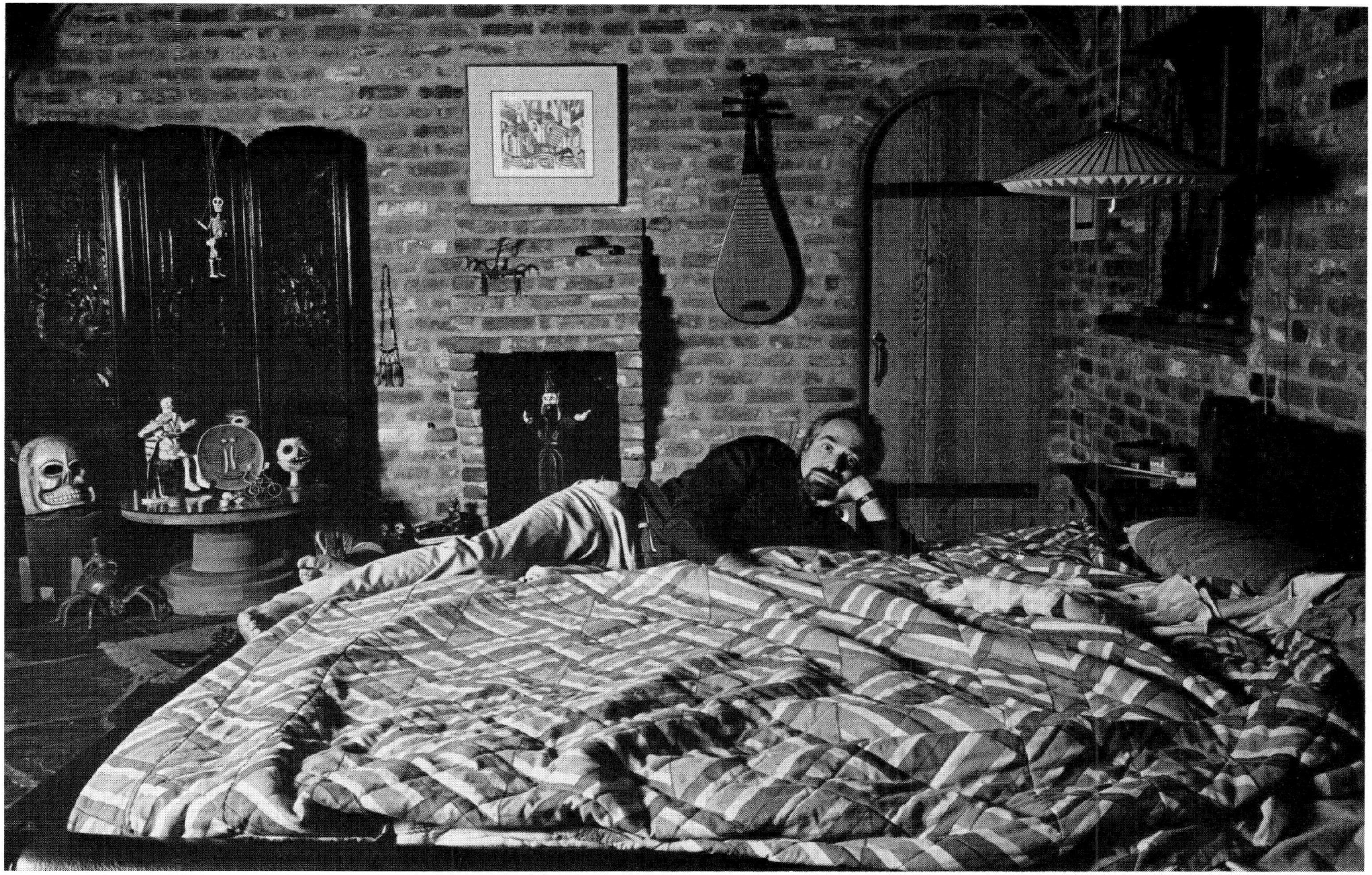

SAMUEL R. DELANY

For me science fiction is a way of reading, a way of making texts labeled "SF" not only make sense, but make the richest sort of sense. It starts with knowing how to read the sentences—knowing, say, that "Papa remarried, a man this time and somewhat more happily," from Disch's SF story "Angouleme," not only tells me about Papa's sexual predilections but also about the changes in the laws of the future world. Then it goes on to include the history and the tradition of our very lively practice of writing: knowing who did what, when, and under what circumstances. For that's the best way to hear, clearly and richly, all the resonances in the dialogue each new SF text sets up with the texts of the past, as well as the best way to see most sharply, etched against imagination's sky, the riches of its future vision.

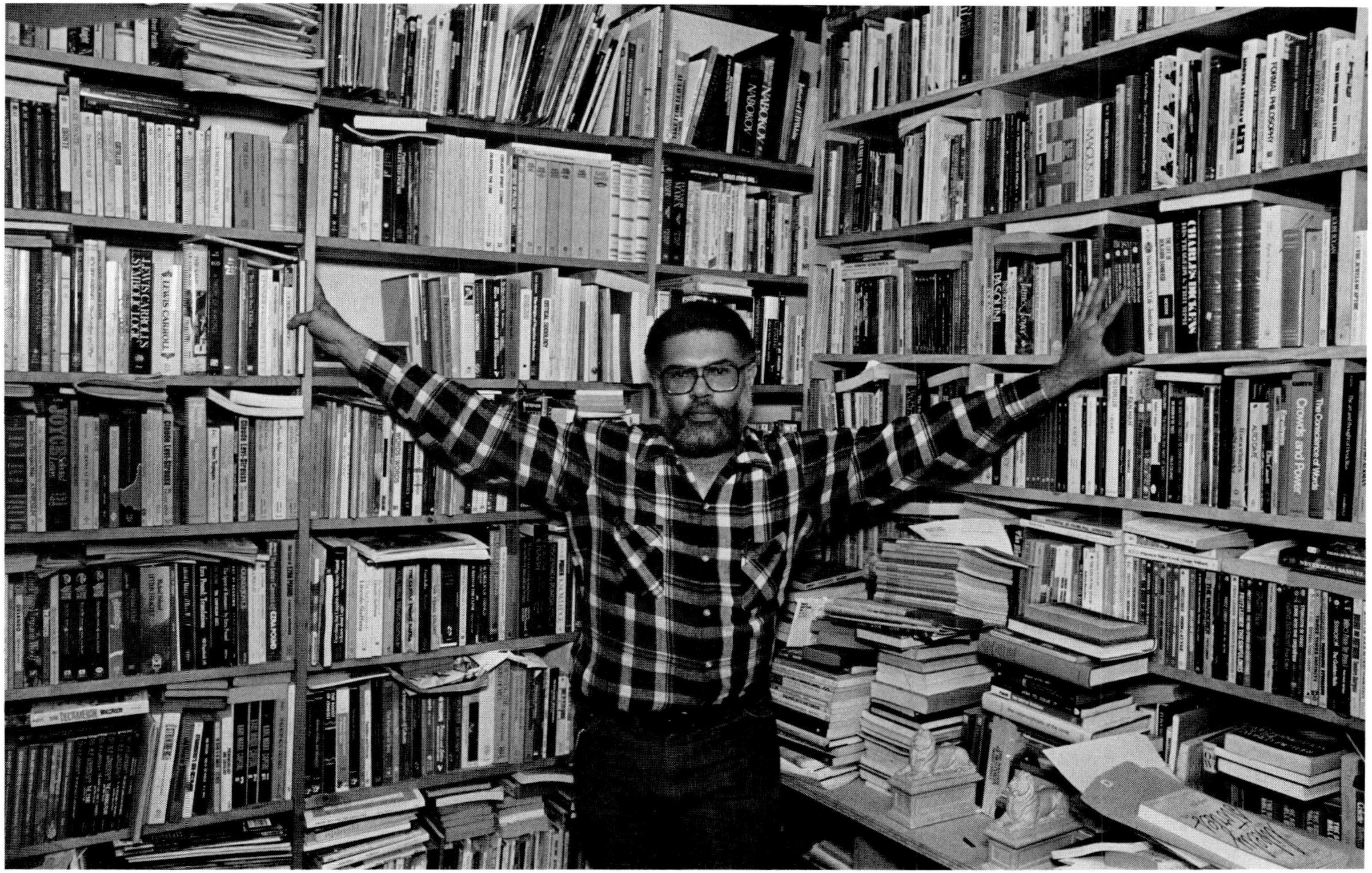
NABOKOV
LEWIS CARROLL
FORMAL PHILOSOPHY
Crowds and Power

KARL EDWARD WAGNER

Shortly after 1970 our world ended and with it died any hope for intelligent life on Earth. Let there always be some small refuge from time where it is eternally the autumn of the 1960s.

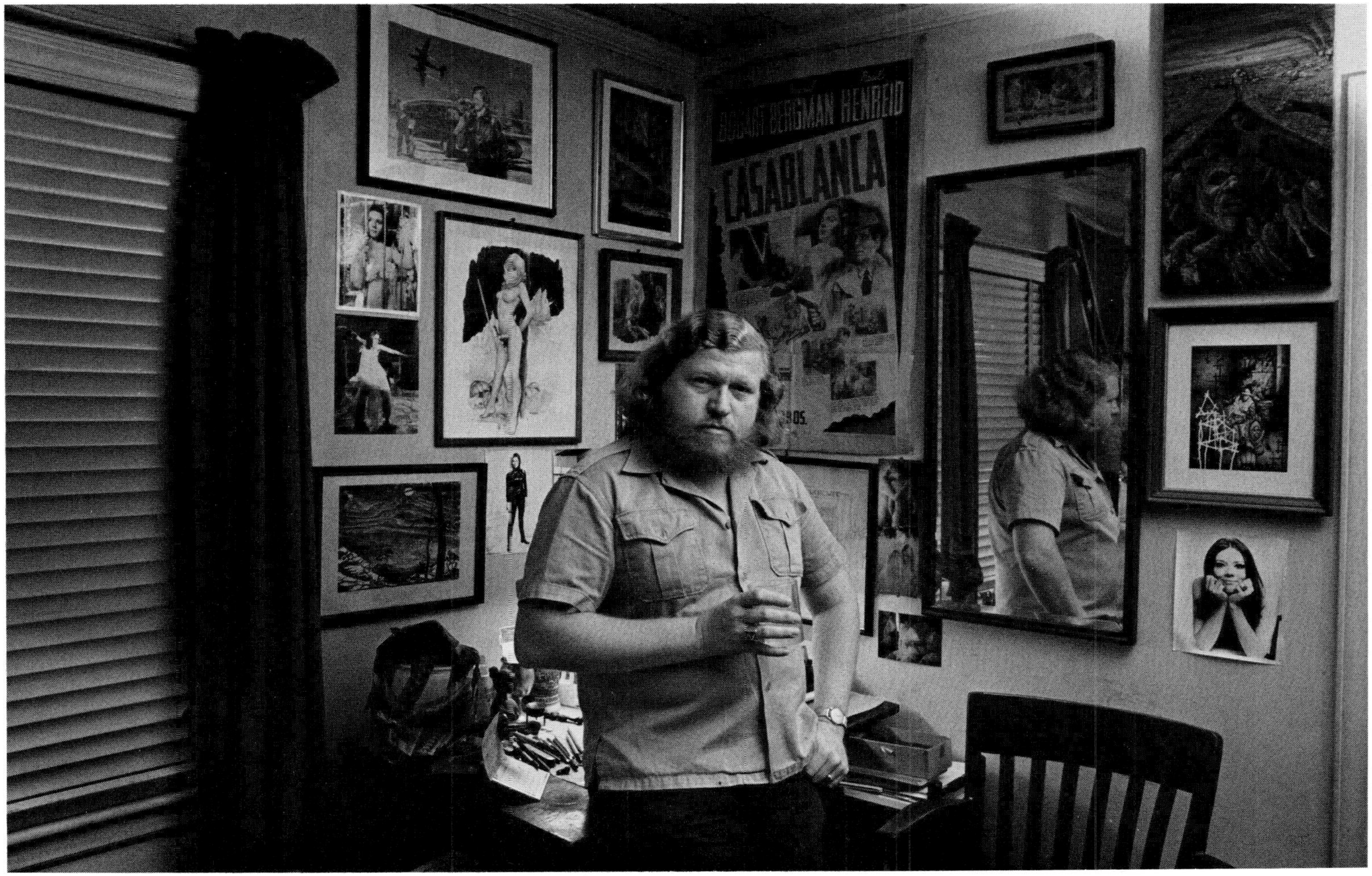
BOGART BERGMAN HENREID
CASABLANCA

DONALD A. WOLLHEIM

Science fiction is intimately and always involved with the future and the infinite possibilities of time and things to come. Having been involved deeply and personally with science fiction, I am always concerned with the future as the events of the present twist and turn and change the aspects of it. The past, for me, is done and unchangeable, so I prefer not to brood over it. I never look back—and that is probably the key to my life. Don't panic, don't look back, and keep on travelling into the future without flinching.

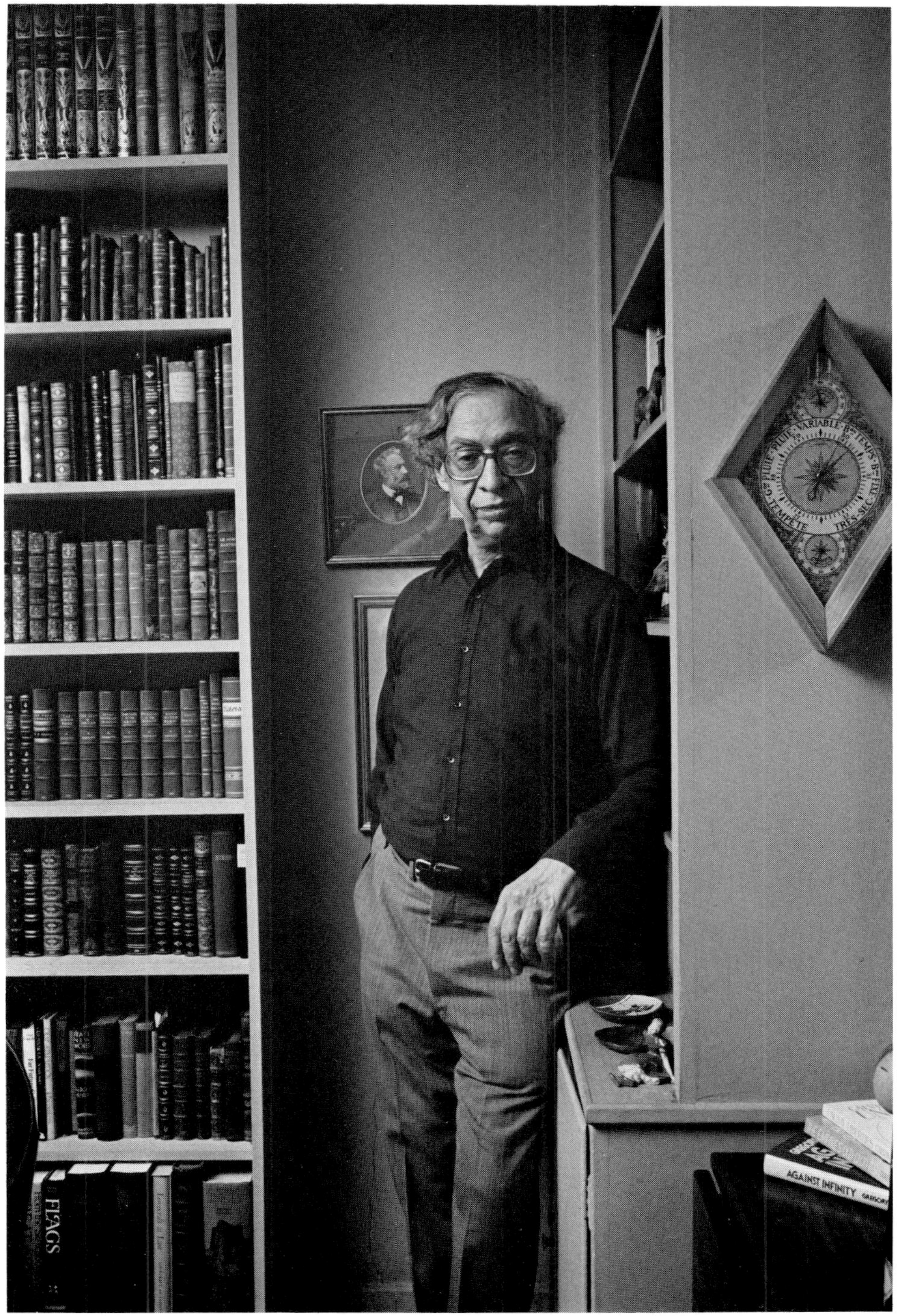

FLAGS
AGAINST INFINITY

ABOUT THE PHOTOGRAPHER

PATTI PERRET was born in Baton Rouge, Louisiana in 1955. She grew up in New Orleans, attending Ursuline Academy where she was the tallest and skinniest girl in her class from grades 6 through 12. After graduating from Indiana University in 1977, she moved to New York City. There she found work as a photographer in a variety of situations, including the 1980–81 season of *Saturday Night Live* for which she received the Art Director's Club Merit Award for the show's opening montage. In 1982 she returned to New Orleans where she presently resides.